The Evil 100

ALSO AVAILABLE IN THE "100" SERIES

The Evil 100

Martin Gilman Wolcott

CITADEL PRESS
Kensington Publishing Corp.
www.kensingtonbooks.com

CITADEL PRESS BOOKS are published by

Kensington Publishing Corp.
850 Third Avenue
New York, NY 10022

All Kensington titles, imprints, and distributed lines are available at special quantity discounts for bulk purchases for sales promotions, premiums, fund-raising, educational, or institutional use. Special book excerpts or customized printings can also be created to fit specific needs. For details, write or phone the office of the Kensington special sales manager: Kensington Publishing Corp., 850 Third Avenue, New York, NY 10022, attn: Special Sales Department, phone 1-800-221-2647.

First printing: June 2002
First paperback printing: January 2004

10   9   8   7   6   5   4   3   2   1

Printed in the United States of America

Library of Congress Control Number: 2001099103

ISBN: 0-8065-2555-X

Dedication

To all the innocent victims
of *The Evil 100*, especially the victims of the
September 11, 2001, terrorist attacks

WARNING!

This book is about evil people, and it is an unavoidable reality that evil people do truly terrible things. In chronicling the stories of the people in this book, it was necessary to be explicit in the reporting of their deeds.

There are graphic descriptions in this book of physical and sexual torture, rape, serial and mass murder, necrophilia, cannibalism, pedophilia, mutilation, coprophilia, incest, and other abominable and disgusting acts that some readers may find extremely disturbing. Some of the things these evil people did are unspeakably horrific; therefore, senstitive readers should be wary.

Although it should go without saying, we will say it anyway: This book is absolutely NOT FOR CHILDREN.

Reader discretion is advised.

MGW

CONTENTS

PREFACE

A universe of death, which God by curse
Created evil . . .

John Milton, *Paradise Lost*

What is evil?

This question has haunted mankind since we first achieved consciousness and became able to conceive of ourselves in the abstract.

The question that follows; the corollary to "What is evil?" is, then, "Is man intrinsically good or evil?"

Man has often turned to religion for answers to these questions.

From *The Catholic Encyclopedia*:

Evil, in a large sense, may be described as the sum of the opposition, which experience shows to exist in the universe, to the desires and needs of individuals; whence arises, among humans beings at least, the sufferings in which life abounds. Thus evil, from the point of view of human welfare, is *what ought not to exist*. [emphasis added]

And yet evil does exist.

We see it in the faces of the Nazis who herded Jews into the gas chambers; we see it in the smoke rising from the tarred-and-burned-alive bodies of Roman slaves lining the road to Rome in Nero's time; we see it in the colorful face paint of John Wayne Gacy; we see it in the insane eyes of those who raped and tortured children as part of heartless and deliberate ethnic cleansing.

The Evil 100 was, frankly, an almost impossible-to-write book. It required an evaluation of people based on their perceived-to-be evil deeds. Was the prime determinant the number of people who died as a result of the person's actions? Partly. Using "evil does damage" as a jumping-off point, we also factored in sadistic glee—pleasure in the hurting and killing of innocent people—as a facet of the person's behavior to qualify him or her for the ranking.

Another of the factors that greatly influenced this ranking was the element of helplessness; that is, if someone took vile advantage of and heinously exploited the innocent, the helpless, the defenseless for purposes of doing harm, they were given extra consideration, for it could be argued that there is nothing more evil than someone with strength and power deliberately hurting someone weaker.

Evil can manifest itself in many forms. And this compilation is numbing in its recitation of the manifestations of evil.

The Evil 100 are human blights; destructive toxins to the living body of humanity.

Their stories can serve as a warning.

Martin Gilman Wolcott
New York City
2002

The Evil 100

Adolf Hitler

(1889–1945)

The passions which ruled Hitler's mind were ignoble: hatred, resentment, the lust to dominate, and, where he could not dominate, to destroy.

>—from *Adolf Hitler: A Study in Tyranny* by Alan Bullock

I suddenly encountered a phenomenon in a long caftan and wearing black side-locks. My first thought was: Is this a Jew? I watched the man stealthily and cautiously, but the longer I gazed at this strange countenance and examined it section by section, the more the question shaped itself in my brain: Is this a German? For the first time in my life I bought myself some anti-Semitic pamphlets for a few pence.

Was there any shady undertaking, any form of foulness, especially in cultural life, in which at least one Jew did not participate? On putting the probing knife carefully to that kind of abscess one immediately discovered, like a maggot in a putrescent body, a little Jew who was often blinded by the sudden light.

>—from *Mein Kampf* by Adolf Hitler

Humanity has been blessed with the likes of Mother Teresa and Gandhi and Jesus and Mohammed.

By conrast, it has been cursed with the likes of Adolf Hitler, the man with the ignominy of being ranked in this book as the most evil human being ever to live.

Others in this book have been responsible for more deaths than Hitler, but body count is not the overriding criteria for placement.

In *Panorama of Evil*, Yale University's Leonard Doob's (1978) sage analysis of the nature of evil and evildoers, Doob writes:

> No nation, no group, no one of us is guiltless, yet the generations of Germans in the period from 1930 to 1945, in my opinion, reached the abysmal depths of all conceivable evils. . . . I am neither asking that present-day Germans be persecuted for what their elders once did nor that those elders be forgiven. The Nazis are simply a horrifying, horrible case history to serve as a warning to all mankind.

The Germans Doob refers to were inspired, encouraged, and led by Adolf Hitler, who had as his life's goal—what he christened the Final Solution—the complete annihilation of the peoples he deemed inferior, a group which included Jews, Gypsies, blacks, homosexuals, the mentally retarded, and the handicapped, in his perverse pursuit of creating the perfect Aryan German race.

Hitler called his regime the Third Reich—the third empire—believing that he was creating a successor to the Holy Roman Empire and the nineteenth-century German Empire formed by Chancellor Otto Von Bismarck.

As part of his plan, Hitler's Nazi Party abolished all freedoms in Germany and deliberately began a calculated pogrom of persecution, targeting first the Jews, but soon expanding to encompass the others Hitler considered inferior.

The evil that emanated from Adolf Hitler and the evil nature of his deeds seem surreal today when rendered in plain words and simple declarations. The Holocaust is now iconic and the gruesome details of the atrocities and horrors committed from 1939 through 1945 need not be revisited here. Countless images, vivid and visceral, spring into our consciousness from a simple recitation:

Final solution. Auschwitz. Ovens. Zyklon-B gas. Treblinka. Six million. Swastikas. Ghettoes. Master Race. Mass graves. Buchenwald. Lampshades made from human skin. Medical experiments. Mass genocide. "We knew when the people were dead because their screaming stopped" (Rudolph Hess, commandant of Auschwitz). Making real the unimaginable. Himmler. "Another improvement that we made over Treblinka was that we built our gas chambers to accommodate two thousand people at one time . . ." (Rudolph Hess). Mengele. Never again.

Adolf Hitler was born in 1889 in Austria, the son of Klara and Alois Hitler, a customs officer. Hitler's siblings all died in childhood except for a sister, Paula, who outlived him. Paula changed her name to Wolff, never married or had children, and died in 1960. Adolf Hitler currently has relatives living in anonymity in Long Island, New York.

Hitler's sister Paula once told a journalist that their father was a violent and abusive man: "[Adolf] challenged my father to extreme harshness and he got his sound thrashings every day."

Hitler was a poor student and twice failed an entrance exam to the Academy of Fine Arts. He wanted to be an artist and for a time supported himself by selling some of his drawings and sketches.

In 1907, Hitler was living in Vienna when his mother died. He decided to remain in Austria, where he soon began to hate anyone who wasn't German, and to hold great contempt for the Austrian government for treating all ethnic groups equally. This was the beginning.

In 1913, Hitler moved to Germany and fought in the German Army during World War I. He was twice decorated, and the regimental commander who recommended that Hitler receive the Iron Cross First Class for meritorious duty in the war was Jewish. Hitler wore this medal until the day he died, and it can be seen in countless photographs.

In 1920, Hitler joined the Nazi Party. He quickly rose to head the party and he increased membership dramatically. Hitler personally chose the swastika as the party's symbol and he also formed the Storm Troopers, a Nazi militia that was the forerunner of the elite SS, the ruthless and powerful quasi-military unit of the Nazi party that served as Hitler's personal guard and as a special security force in Germany and the occupied countries.

In 1923, Hitler was convicted of treason against the German government and sentenced to five years in prison for leading two thousand Storm Troopers in a failed attempt to overthrow the Bavarian government in southern Germany. He ultimately served only thirteen months (November 11, 1923—December 20, 1924). While incarcerated, he dictated to Rudolph Hess the words and thoughts that would become *Mein Kampf (My Struggle)*.

Hitler began rebuilding the Nazi Party when he got out of prison, and by 1932, the Nazis were the strongest political party in Germany. The following year Hitler was appointed Chancellor and within a short time had transformed his position into that of dictator. He gave himself the title of *Führer*, German for "absolute leader."

Hitler immediately disbanded every other political party or group in Germany and took all powers away from the individual German states. Nazis were appointed governors of these states and personal freedoms were, de facto, abolished.

Following his rise to power, the persecution of Jews began in earnest.

Jews were stripped of their German citizenship, which meant that they could no longer hold office, vote, farm, teach, work as civil servants, or practice medicine or law.

Hitler started World War II in 1939 when he invaded Poland and, for the next six years, worked to implement his Final Solution. He built concentration and extermination camps, and, with no qualms, he began the assembly-line massacre of six million Jews, as well as the slaughter of between six and nine million others deemed as undesirable and expendable as the Jews.

Hitler committed suicide on April 30, 1945, when Germany's defeat was looming and, a week later, Germany surrendered. Three months later, on August 6, 1945, the United States dropped the atomic bomb on Hiroshima and World War II was over.

To this day, the questions are still asked: "How could he?" and "Why did he?"

The answers are complex and daunting, and speak to the dark truth that human nature can not only conceive evil, but also embrace it.

Adolf Hitler viewed certain of his fellow humans as vermin, as an infestation that needed to be eradicated from the earth—for the greater good of Germany. When Hitler was climbing to power, he mesmerized, seduced, and mustered the masses. His acolytes saw in Hitler the face of a hero, the visage of a savior.

What they did not see, and what we today see all too well, was the face of pure, honed evil.

2

Joseph Stalin

(1879–1953)

*He knew that he was one of the cruelest, most despotic figures
in history. But this did not worry him a bit for he was
convinced that he was carrying out the will of history.*
  —Yugoslavian leader Milovan Djilas, talking about Stalin in
    his 1962 book, *Conversations With Stalin*

Liquidate the kulaks.

—Joseph Stalin

In 1956, three years after Stalin's death, Nikita Khrushchev used the opportunity of an address before the 1956 Soviet Twentieth Party Congress to publicly describe Stalin as "a mass murderer and a torturer."

After Khrushchev began revealing the truth about what historian
Andrew Evart calls Stalin's "fantastic evil," Stalin was christened the "New
Satan" by Yugoslav Communist rebel Milovan Djilas and described as "the
greatest criminal known to history." Stalin was relentless in abolishing individual freedoms during his reign and it is quite possible that he exercised more
political power during his time in office than any other leader in history.

Absolute power corrupts absolutely and Stalin was, in many ways, the quintessential definition of corruption: immoral, perverse, and depraved.

Joseph Stalin was born in 1889 in Gori, Georgia, Russian Empire (which means he was *Georgian*, not Russian, a fact that embarrassed him his entire life).

Interestingly, he had a doting mother and a physically abusive, drunkard father, which is a family profile that matches that of many serial killers and mass murderers, especially Kenneth Bianchi and John Wayne Gacy. In addition, Stalin's mother wanted him to become a priest, which is interestingly the same wish Mussolini's mother had for *her* son.

Stalin was known to be sadistic and cruel. He belittled his comrades in public and played malicious practical jokes on them. He experienced pleasure from inflicting pain and embarrassment on others. Many psychologists would say that these types of personality traits are indicators of an evil-natured person.

Khrushchev later revealed "revolting details of Stalin's sexual aberrations," claiming that in Stalin's later years, "his sexual obsessions degenerated into sadism against young girls. A number of minors and other girls disappeared." Stalin would have Lavrenti Beria, the head of the KGB, pick up underaged girls on the street and bring them back to Stalin for him to do with as he pleased. Beria would tell the girls that their families would be killed if they did not go with him. They obeyed, and Beria and Stalin indulged themselves in countless "Lolita" orgies.

Stalin was also vain. He regularly wore high-heeled shoes because he was insecure about his height. He also hated to be photographed because he was embarrassed about the pockmarks and scars that remained on his face from childhood smallpox.

Joseph Stalin was the successor of Vladimir Lenin and served as general secretary of the Communist Party in Russia from 1922–1953 and as Premier of the USSR from 1941–1953.

Stalin is ranked number 2 in *The Evil 100* because he was directly responsible for the death of at least twenty-five million Soviets—*his own people*—and some sources "credit" him with possibly as many as fifty million deaths.

Stalin's body count alone (the number of needless deaths attributed to his orders and policies) would warrant a high ranking for the maniacal despot, but other elements of his personality and history that mandate such a high ranking are his heartlessness and complete disregard for human life.

Stalin's policies caused famine and starvation, a colossal number of deaths, rampant societal pandemonium, and civil war. His collectivization policies, which abolished the private ownership of farms in Russia, caused massive famines. Soldiers were ordered to kill with machine guns any peasants (sometimes entire villages) that resisted or refused to abide by Stalin's orders to relinquish their properties, crops, and livestock. Sometimes there was resistance: Stalin himself revealed that by 1933, eighteen million of the country's horses and fifteen million of the country's cattle had been slaughtered, and thousands of acres of crops had been deliberately burned by farmers. Nevertheless, uncooperative peasants who resisted Stalin's orders were arrested, exiled, worked to death in concentration camps, or executed.

As millions were starving, Stalin was exporting the grain of his country's harvest all over the world, reaping an enormous financial bounty, none of which went to help his people.

Stalin ruled Russia from 1929 until his death in 1953, but his worst reign of terror consumed the decade 1929 through 1939. According to the accepted historical accounts, during this period, one million Russians were slaughtered as enemies of Stalin and the state; eight million perished from the famines brought about by Stalin's policies; eight million died in forced labor camps in the Arctic and Siberia set up by Stalin; and there were another eight million reported as simply "missing" from official Soviet population records. Also, after Germany was defeated at the end of World War II, Stalin and his Red Army tortured and killed millions in Europe and Asia in concentration camps that were as horrible as Hitler's.

Twenty-five million lives were lost and Stalin figuratively dug the grave of every one of the victims.

Stalin was also directly responsible for the deaths of twenty thousand Polish prisoners in the Katyn Forest in western Russia in April 1940. In March of that year, as part of a secret deal with Hitler, Stalin ordered the invasion and occupation of eastern Poland. His soldiers transported between fifteen and twenty thousand Polish prisoners—reservists who had been called up to fight after Russia's invasion, including doctors, lawyers, scientists, and businessmen—to the Katyn Forest near Smolensk in western Russia, then carried out Stalin's personal orders to execute them all. Stalin had commanded Lavrenti Beria to mete out to the Polish prisoners the "supreme measure of punishment—shooting"; that is, kill them all. Beria did as ordered, but only after he made the prisoners dig their own graves. The mass graves were discovered in 1943 by occupying Nazi forces, and in 1990 the Soviet government accepted responsibility for the massacre.

Stalin died in 1953 from complications following a cerebral hemorrhage. By this time in his life, he was extremely paranoid (some experts think he may have actually suffered from paranoid schizophrenia) and he was planning to have his aides and doctors killed because he no longer trusted them. Because of this, some historians suspect that medical care may have been withheld from Stalin long enough for him to worsen beyond recovery.

If this were true, it would be fitting vengeance against the man who cared more about his complexion than the lives of twenty-five million.

3

Mao Zedong

(1893–1976)

After our armed enemies have been crushed, there will still be our unarmed enemies, who will try to fight us to the death. We must never underestimate their strength. Unless we think of the problem in precisely those terms, we will commit the gravest of errors.

—Mao Zedong, speaking at the Seventh Congress
of the Chinese Communist Party in March 1949

Chinese Communist leader Mao Zedong is ranked in the top five of *The Evil 100* because of his passionate embrace of ruthless, "revolutionary violence" in the service of a totalitarian government, a policy that led to the death of between twenty and thirty million of his countrymen from execution and starvation during his reign. Dr. Michael Hart, author of the seminal *The 100,* described Mao's reign as "perhaps the bloodiest in all human history," noting that only Hitler, Stalin, and Genghis Khan can dispute Mao's ignoble claim to infamy.

Mao was born on December 26, 1893, in Shao-shan in the Hunang province of China, the son of a wealthy peasant. He was forced into marriage at the age of fourteen by a father he hated. Mao became involved in the pro-communism movement in his early twenties, helping to found the Chinese Communist Party in 1921. He was the People's Republic of China's first head of state from 1949 to 1959, and he remained party chairman until his death in Peking in 1976.

Mao is solely responsible for implementing two ill-conceived socio-political programs—The Great Leap Forward and The Great Proletarian Cultural Revolution—which, in toto, did tremendous damage to China and caused millions of deaths. Granted, failed political programs do not necessarily impugn their architects as evil; however, in Mao's case, his total disregard for human suffering is why he is included here.

The Great Leap Forward

Mao's "Great Leap Forward" program (1957–1960)—which centralized all agricultural production into grossly inefficient communes—caused famines of such magnitude that there are confirmed accounts of parents killing and eating their children, such was their devastating hunger.

Historian Jasper Becker, in his 1996 book *Hungry Ghosts: Mao's Secret Famine* (Free Press), wrote:

> There are enough reports from different parts of the country to make it clear that the practice of cannibalism was not restricted to any one region, class or nationality. Peasants not only ate the flesh of the dead, they also sold it, and they killed and ate children, both their own and those of others. Given the dimensions of the famine, it is quite conceivable that cannibalism was practised on a scale unprecedented in the history of the twentieth century. Moreover, it took place with the knowledge of a government which is still in power and which wields considerable influence over world affairs.

The Great Leap Forward was conceived and designed by Mao himself and it now stands as one of history's clearest examples of shortsighted, unrealistic, ignorant thinking. Ostensibly a program intended to revitalize the Chinese economy, the specifics of the Great Leap Forward actually resulted in great leaps *backward*.

The program's decentralization mandates drastically reduced the production efficiency that is typically one of the benefits of centralized production facilities.

The program's dependency on enormous pools of peasant labor obliterated the benefits of mass production.

And adding to the damage done was Mao's insistence on implementing plainly ridiculous ideas, such as replacing large efficient steel mills with thousands of inferior "backyard" furnaces.

Mao's "Great Leap" communization of production in 1957 and 1958 led to an almost total neglect of the 1959 and 1960 Chinese harvests and, thus, the result was devastating mass famine on a scale never before experienced in China. An estimated twenty million or more died as a result of the Great Leap Forward.

Mao's refusal to rescind the program, even after witnessing the toll in human suffering and the deaths of his own people, all for the perpetration of a false ideology, crosses the line and transforms his enormously incompetent acts into crimes against humanity. Some Maoists today assert that unexpected and deadly floods caused the famines that killed so many of Becker's "Hungry Ghosts," but a close study of the Great Leap Forward makes it clear that the deaths are the responsibility of Chairman Mao himself.

The Great Proletarian Cultural Revolution

Much as the Great Leap Forward was anything *but* a progressive plan of improvement, the Cultural Revolution (initiated in large part to eliminate Mao's enemies and implemented after the country had begun to recover from the debacle of the Great Leap), turned China's status quo upside down.

The Dictionary of Global Culture (Knopf) states unequivocally that Mao's Cultural Revolution, which was launched in the mid-'60s, "resulted in ten years of political turmoil, massive human suffering, and almost total economic collapse." Little wonder, when the specifics of this absurd "revolution" are analyzed.

In an attempt to paint all of Chinese society with the brush of communist ideology, it somehow actually made sense to Mao to "abolish the distinction between mental and manual labor," and to put professors to work in the fields and peasants in the schools to learn and teach. Resistance was considered counterrevolutionary and proponents were imprisoned, tortured, and killed.

Mao also established the sadistic and almost completely autonomous Red Guard, a group consisting of millions of young people who were given free reign to enforce Mao's doctrines and who did so by killing teachers, burning art, and destroying temples. This kind of "revolutionary violence" was not only condoned, but was encouraged by Mao, who became a cult figure to hotheaded Maoists.

The chaos, damage, and pain caused by the Cultural Revolution and its vicious Red Guard were profound. Mao was devoid of any sympathy for the millions of suffering and dying. At the time of his death he had carved out a legacy comprised of stupid ideas that resulted in millions of deaths, which was made truly heinous by the fact that, as Philip Short (2000) writes in *Mao: A Life*, to him, "the cost in human suffering had become irrelevant."

4

Genghis Khan

(c. 1162–1227)

*To crush my enemies, to see them fall at my feet, to take their
horses and goods, and hear the lamentation of their women . . .
that is the greatest happiness of all.*

—Genghis Khan

When Genghis Khan died in 1227, his loyal Mongols embarked on a mission to bring his body to the Gobi Desert for burial. To keep the death a secret and prevent revolt, the Mongols executed every living being they came upon as they carried the exalted Khan's coffin across the miles of their ruler's conquered territories. The death toll of the funeral march is not known, but the body count easily numbered in the hundreds of thousands, if not millions. Historians estimate that Khan was ultimately responsible for eighteen million deaths in China alone—almost half of the thirty-five million deaths attributed to Khan and his Mongol warriors during his bloody reign.

Genghis Khan is thought of by many today as one of the greatest military leaders and conquerors of all time, but he is included in *The Evil 100* for the same reason that many of his ignoble colleagues have been included.

Genghis Khan himself espouses this justification and secures his place here in the epigraph that introduces this chapter: Khan experienced over-whelming feelings of happiness—an unabashed, albeit macabre delight and joy—at the devastation and torment he and his troops inflicted on their con-quered victims. Such delight in the suffering of others can arguably be con-sidered one of the primary elements of true evil, and Genghis Khan, for all his brilliant military strategizing and expansionistic maneuvering, took "great happiness" from—and full responsibility for—cities in cinders and mountains of corpses and skulls reaching to the sky. Upon learning of the evil Mongol atrocities, Roger Bacon, the thirteenth-century scientist, philosopher, and friar, stated that he believed that Genghis Khan and his Mongol warriors were soldiers of the Antichrist.

Genghis Khan was named Temujin at birth after one of his father's con-quered enemies. Legend has it that Temujin came into the world holding a clot of blood in one of his little hands, an event many at the time interpreted as a portent of things to come, and a sign that the child might be of divine origin.

At the age of thirteen, Temujin succeeded his father as warlord, and in 1206, after a childhood of extreme poverty, internecine conflicts, and a slow rise to clan power and control, a conclave of Mongol warlords bequeathed Temujin the title "Genghis Khan," which translates to "universal emperor." Genghis Khan and his Mongol warriors massacred millions as they swept across northern China, Central Asia, Iran, and southern Russia in their cam-paign of brutal annexation.

Khan's influence was enormous: He conquered and ended up control-ling enormous portions of the world, becoming, as many historians have de-scribed him, the most powerful man in the world. His dynasty and his centuries of influence began in the early thirteenth century, when he united various Mongol tribes under his leadership and began systematically raiding and conquering neighboring kingdoms and lands.

When Khan's Mongol warriors invaded a city, they wreaked unbeliev-able torment and destruction. They gleefully tortured the elderly, slaughtered the children, and raped the women, before plundering the place of anything and everything of value and then burning the city to the ground, leaving smoking piles of carrion in their wake. Once, Khan learned that some of the inhabitants of cities he conquered were lying down among the piles of the dead in order to escape being slaughtered themselves. Khan was livid over being outsmarted by these desperate attempts at survival and immediately is-sued an order that added to his troops' workload: Every single resident of an invaded city must, from this point on, be beheaded—one of the surest ways of assuring their demise.

After years of such butchery and debauchery, Genghis Khan's chief ad-viser Ye Liu Chutsai suggested to his leader, "It is time to make an end of killing." Khan may have been assessing his and his hordes' behavior at that time, for he responded, "I have pondered the wisdom of the sages and I can see that I have slain without knowledge of what to do rightly." But his cold heart ultimately heard nothing that engendered compassion or self-doubt. His eventual reply to his adviser was filled with venom: "But what do I care for such men—or their views?"

Even though he could not write, Genghis Khan drafted a series of fifty laws, less than half of which have survived. Renowned historian Harold Lamb, in his seminal 1927 biography of Khan, recounts twenty-two of Khan's laws, including:

- Spies, false witnesses, all men given to infamous vices, and sorcerers are condemned to death.
- Adultery is to be punished by death, and those guilty of it may be slain out of hand.
- The law of marriage orders that every man shall purchase his wife . . . a man may marry two sisters, or have several concubines.

At the peak of its power, Genghis Khan's Mongol Empire stretched from the Pacific Ocean to the Black Sea. This enormous realm was acquired through savagery and the complete annihilation of entire populations in Asia and Europe. Khan once proclaimed, "I will carry slaughter and cause devastation to my enemy . . . so my name will live." It would be centuries, and it would take the madness of Adolf Hitler, before another such attempt at world domination would occur.

5

Ivan the Terrible

(1530–1584)

*Weaken not beating the boy, for he will not die from your strik-
ing him with the rod, but will be in better health: for while you
strike his body, you save his soul from death. If you love your
son, punish him frequently, that you may rejoice later. . . . Do
not smile at him, or play with him, for though that will dimin-
ish your grief while he is a child, it will increase it when he is
older, and you will cause much bitterness to your soul.*
   —from the mid-sixteenth-century guide *The Domostroi*,
      used to advise parents on how to raise children,
      including Ivan

Ivan Vasilyevich—Ivan IV—was a Russian tsar who took his title in 1547 and
who was so well known for his cruelty that the word "Terrible" became part of
his name.

In an essay titled "The Terrible Ivan," Professor Gerhard Rempel of
Western New England College tells us that "insatiable cruelty and extreme
depravity were perhaps [Ivan's] outstanding characteristics."

Like many a despot with unlimited power (Ivan was greatly admired by
Joseph Stalin) and no one (foolish enough) to challenge his decisions, Ivan indulged his darkest whims with impunity. He was certainly a literate and edu-

cated man, but education in and of itself does not deter action in the service of evil.

As a youth, Ivan tortured animals for fun, threw dogs off balconies, and once had a nobleman's tongue cut out in public because he did not like something he said. Ivan killed for the first time when he was thirteen; he ultimately stabbed and strangled to death his favorite son; and he was merciless in his horrific brutalization of those he called his enemy.

Ivan was only seventeen when he was proclaimed Tsar of Russia (he had inherited the throne at the age of three), and it wasn't long before he established his own thousand-strong secret police force called the Oprichnina ("The Ones Who Serve"), who wore threatening-looking black robes and were given free reign in ferreting out and disposing of the Tsar's enemies. Countless suspected enemies of the Tsar were arrested and, without a trial, whipped to death, impaled, drowned, tied to a log and roasted over a spit like a pig, or fried alive in enormous cast-iron skillets. Some were boiled to death in oil; others were made to lie naked in the snow; and some had their hair set on fire.

Sometimes Ivan would order that tortures be carried out as he watched, and there are many accounts of the Tsar exhibiting great glee while viewing the most abominable torments.

In 1570, Ivan had the sixty thousand residents of the town of Novgorod butchered in the period of one week: His soldiers slaughtered one person every ten seconds, every minute, every hour, around the clock, for seven straight days. Perhaps the most horrible aspect of the Novgorod massacre was how the Oprichnina slaughtered the babies of the town: They beat them to death and made their parents watch.

Ivan loathed the Russian boyars (the Russian ruling-class noblemen) and spared no effort in mistreating them and their families at will. One favorite pastime was to abduct a group of boyars' wives, strip them naked, and let the women loose in a forest where his Oprichnina would hunt them like wild animals. Ivan was a big fan of orgies and would plunder villages and order the women brought back to his palace where he would rape and torture them in his elaborately designed basement torture chamber.

Interestingly, there is the possibility that Ivan felt a little guilty about his horrendous deeds. (If so, does this exculpate him for his atrocities? Hardly.) After Ivan had tortured and killed a large number of "traitors," he would send their names to local monasteries. He would include sums of money to be used to pay the monks to pray for his victims. Was this an attempt to clear his conscience? Or was it blatant hypocrisy, designed to demonstrate his compassion and justify his deeds as politically necessary, but regrettable? Ivan's habitual actions would suggest the latter.

Ivan died in 1584, and it is rumored that on his deathbed he took the religious vows of a monk. Did this human horror, this bringer of death and suffering, truly believe he had a chance at escaping the eternal fires of Hell by taking monastic vows?

6

Attila the Hun

(406?–453)

He was a typical Hun: short, broad-chested, with a big head, small deep-set eyes, and flat nose. He was swarthy, almost black-skinned, and wore a sparse beard. Terrible in his rages, he used the fear he inspired as a political weapon.
  —Gothic historian Jordanes, cited in *The Emperor of the Steppes* by Rene Grosset

Why is Attila the Hun ranked so high on this list? Because of his legacy of mass destruction of human life for territorial conquest, and his *complete* disregard for human life. The Huns had a reputation for horrifying cruelty, and Attila instilled in his warriors a terrible passion for killing and destruction.

The words used to describe Attila the Hun in books and articles are pointed and relentlessly harsh. *Barbaric, cruel, dangerous, ferocious, notorious,* and *savage* are common, as are his ignoble titles, "Scourge of God," and Dante Alighieri's derisive description, "Scourge of the Earth."

The Roman writer Marcellus excoriated Attila and his Huns as "two-footed beasts," and Attila has also been described as a "fury," "the most feared person in the history of the world," a "killer of babies," a chieftain responsible for "wholesale destruction," and as "evil incarnate." The Romans believed that no one capable of the death, destruction, and atrocities Attila was guilty of could be of this earth, and they described him as "not human."

From approximately A.D. 433 through A.D. 453, Attila conquered close to 1,450,000 square miles and ruled an empire encompassing central and eastern Europe and the western Russian plain. He ravaged much of the European continent during the fifth century, but failed to conquer Gaul, an area corresponding roughly to modern-day France, Belgium, and northern Italy.

Attila's siege of Thrace (a region comprising the southeast Balkan Peninsula north of the Aegean Sea) was so lethal that the *dead could not be counted.*

Between 441 and 442, Attila and his soldiers devastated the city of Naissus, about a hundred miles south of the Danube River. Attila and the Huns achieved new levels of bloodlust and cruelty there. The invaders raped, plundered, killed, and dismembered people at will. When Roman ambassadors visited Attila in Naissus several *years* later, they had to stay outside the city because of the still-powerful stench of death. The riverbanks were completely covered with human bones.

During a rampage against the Eastern Empire in 447, Attila and his men are believed to have destroyed more than seventy towns and fortresses, raping, burning, and killing as they moved through towns and villages like locusts, destroying everything that was in their path.

In 452, Attila also laid siege to and obliterated Aquileia in northern Italy. When Pope Leo learned that Attila's next target was Rome, the pontiff asked him to leave Italy. At first Attila was obstinant and rejected the request. Then a miracle reportedly occurred. According to Attila, none other than St. Peter and St. Paul appeared to the conqueror and told him to obey Pope Leo. This was likely a face-saving fiction. It is probable that the real reason Attila left Italy was threefold: His Huns had been struck with a plague and were suffering and dying, making a rampage a difficult challenge; he had not recovered from the loss of the Chalons battle the previous year and finally, Italy was suffering through a famine and Attila knew it would be almost impossible to find enough food to feed his hordes, no matter how many villages or farms he might seize.

When Attila came to power in 433, he shared the throne in an uneasy partnership with his brother Bleda. After twelve years of joint rule, Attila murdered Bleda and became sole monarch of the Huns.

As omnipotent leader, Attila was able to indulge fully his basest desires. He was a voracious drinker and would regularly mount huge feasts that ended up as drunken orgies. There is also some historical evidence that Attila was a cannibal and that at one point he ate two of his sons. Attila reportedly died in 453. He was found dead in bed the morning after marrying his new young wife Idilco. (He married her even though he already had dozens of other wives. It is said she was beautiful and that Attila could not resist her.) Perhaps he had a stroke or broke a blood vessel and choked to death on his own blood. Because he was found in his honeymoon bed, it is assumed Attila was having sex with his new bride when he expired, but this cannot be confirmed. Reports from the fifth century are often conflicting and inaccurate; for example, another account of his death indicated that Attila died from a heart attack while gorging himself during the wedding feast.

Attila was buried in three coffins—gold, silver, and iron—and was eulogized as a great leader at his funeral. Nothing was mentioned of the unspeakable pain and devastation he was responsible for.

Attila's six surviving sons took over his leadership, but in 454, the year after their father's death, they could not overcome a revolt by Germanic tribes (including the Ostrogoths). The once-fearsome Huns splintered and died.

Pol Pot

"THE BUTCHER OF CAMBODIA"

(1924/25/28–1998)[1]

My conscience is clear.

—Pol Pot

Pol Pot, the architect of the "Killing Fields," was the Cambodian political leader whose Khmer Rouge guerilla communist movement overthrew the Cambodian government in 1975.

Under Pol Pot's regime, executions (often preceded by torture) and famine killed between 1.7 and 3 million Cambodians in the years 1975 to 1979. Pol Pot fled the capital in 1979 when Vietnamese forces overthrew his government.

Pol Pot instituted one of the worst campaigns of genocide ever. His reprehensible legacy is that he is the only dictator in world history to have annihilated a fourth of his country's total population.

The Khmer Rouge, acting on Pol Pot's orders, were ruthless. They bru-

[1] The year of Pol Pot's birth is uncertain. Different sources use different years, 1924, 1925, and 1928. The year of his death, 1998, however, is confirmed.

tally tortured men and women. Even children were not spared their barbarism. One of the Khmer Rouge's favorite forms of execution was to bury children alive while their parents watched or to kill parents as their children stood by and watched in horror. Children were also killed by having their heads repeatedly smashed against trees. The guerillas used hoes to smash the skulls of men and sharpened palm leaves to slit the throats of women.

Work details were eighteen hours long and it did not matter whether someone was sick. If they could not work, they were beaten to death with pick handles. Villages were raided and the villagers were buried alive in the Cambodian swamps. Some were buried up to their necks in the sand and then their heads were beaten until they died. The heads were then hacked off, stuck on spikes, and displayed as a warning to any Cambodians who were even thinking of resistance.

Pol Pot's Khmer Rouge communist guerillas killed army officers, government officials and their wives, villagers, farmers, peasants, merchants, children, and the elderly—all indiscriminately and often with unspeakable brutality. There are accounts of Khmer Rouge guerillas killing a grandmother by machine-gunning her in the eyes.

The Khmer Rouge guerillas were also very strict about ensuring that their torture techniques were as "efficient" as possible. They insisted that torture victims be kept alive until they confessed, but even a confession could not save the hapless victims. Once someone confessed, he was killed.

Pol Pot and the Khmer Rouge wanted to return Cambodia to the Middle Ages, using an extreme application of Mao Zedong's failed philosophy of social engineering, Maoism. Mao's ludicrous program did not work for him, and neither did it work for Pol Pot, who implemented inane policies, such as making everyone in Cambodia wear black pajamas to create "instant Communism." Pol Pot did far worse. He targeted for execution intellectuals, people who spoke a foreign language, and even people who wore glasses. The BBC wrote that Pol Pot "quickly set about transforming the country into his vision of an agrarian utopia by emptying the cities, abolishing money, private property and religion and setting up rural collectives." Pol Pot admitted as much when he declared after seizing power that he wanted to create a pure Communist society and set the clock back in Cambodia to "Year Zero."

And, much like later attempts by the religious dictatorship of the Taliban to suppress diversity in Afghanistan, the government of Pol Pot destroyed Buddhist temples in Cambodia. Pol Pot shut down schools and businesses and forced modern city dwellers to move from their homes and become rice farmers in the hinterlands. By putting everyone to work producing food, Pol Pot thought the country would not need to depend on foreigners for anything. The only problem with this strategy is that Cambodia's entire economy depended on exports and foreign dollars. Within a very short time, the ruthless Maoist parrot scrapped his country's system of laws and judicial review, skewed the normal male to female ratio by killing so many men, and destroyed Cambodia's economy. The soldiers and the police did not have to explain their behavior, arrests, or treatment of detainees to anyone, except, of course, the Khmer Rouge upper echelon, which was the source of the corruption, abuses, and death sentences.

Like many communist regimes, Pol Pot's regime was strictly "anti-pleasure." Smoking, drinking, games, sex, even laughing—anything that was fun—was frowned upon. Adultery was punishable by execution.

Pol Pot was born Saloth Sar, the son of a landowning farmer, in Cambodia in the mid-1920s. Sar studied at a Buddhist monastery and a Roman Catholic school, but he was not a very bright student. After he could not get into high school because he failed the entrance exam, he studied carpentry for a year and then went to France to study radio electronics. It was there that he met a group of left-wing Cambodian nationalists who would later become the leaders of the Khmer Rouge. Sar flunked out of school in France and returned to Cambodia in 1953 where, incredibly, he was deemed qualified enough to be a teacher, and he taught school from 1954 to 1963.

In 1963, he took the name Pol Pot and devoted the next dozen years to building up the Cambodian Communist Party. In 1975, the Khmer Rouge overthrew the regime of Lon Nol and Pol Pot named himself prime minister.

The next four years in Cambodia were marked by starvation, malnutrition, malaria, dysentery, massive outbreaks of epidemic, illness, and many deaths from torture and execution—all as a result of Pol Pot's heartless policies and complete apathy concerning the deaths of his own people.

Pol Pot's government was overthrown by the neighboring Vietnamese government in 1979. (The Vietnamese had been aghast at what Pol Pot had done to his country.) Pol Pot went into hiding, but maintained a leadership position in the Khmer Rouge, surviving financially through gem smuggling.

The Khmer Rouge ousted Pol Pot in 1997 and placed him under house arrest. Pol Pot died in 1998 of heart failure before he could be forced to stand trial for his crimes.

8

Osama bin Laden

(1957–)

This enemy hides in shadows and has no regard for human life. . . . The evildoers will not be able to terrorize America.

—President George W. Bush

I'm fighting so I can die a martyr and go to heaven to meet God. Our fight now is against the Americans. . . . Issue a call to the young generation to get ready for the holy war and to prepare for that in Afghanistan because jihad in this time of crisis for Muslims is an obligation of all Muslims. . . . We—with God's help—call on every Muslim who believes in God and wishes to be rewarded to comply with God's order to kill the Americans and plunder their money wherever and whenever they find it.

—Osama bin Laden

If the present injustice continues with the wave of national consciousness, it will inevitably move the battle to American soil . . . This is my message to the American people.

—Osama bin Laden, in 1998

What kind of God would tell Osama bin Laden to do what he did to America?

Who is this Allah that wants Osama and his followers to kill innocents in his name?

How dare Osama bin Laden speak for God?

These are the questions Americans, and many others around the world, have been asking since the morning of the attacks.

On Tuesday morning, September 11, 2001, four commercial airliners (two from United Airlines and two from American Airlines) were hijacked by nineteen fanatical followers of Osama bin Laden.

The hijackers were suicide terrorists who were willing to die to carry out their horrible mission. After taking over the aircraft, two of the planes were flown at high speed into the World Trade Center in New York City, destroying both towers and killing close to four thousand people; one intended for the White House was crashed into the Pentagon, killing more than eight hundred people; and the fourth plane, believed to be headed for the Capitol building or Camp David, did not hit its target (thanks to the efforts of several heroic passengers) and instead crashed in a wooded area outside of Pittsburgh.

It was later learned that the president's plane, Air Force One, was also a target of the terrorists. The total death count of the four planes, not counting the terrorists, was 266 people, including eight pilots.

This was the single worst act of terrorism in the history of the United States, marking that day with the second highest death count in American history—surpassed only by the twenty-two thousand dead in one day, September 17, 1862, in the Battle of Antietam during the Civil War.

Motivated by a deep and unfathomable hatred toward the United States (deep enough that terrorists would be willing to commit suicide while carrying out their missions), the attack was described by experts as "low tech, high concept." Essentially, what the terrorists did was use the American planes as guided missiles. The planning was extensive and shrewd enough to target Los Angeles–bound planes, all of which, departing from the East Coast, would be carrying maximum loads of fuel.

General Norman Schwarzkopf, speaking on the *Today* show the following day, called the perpetrators "bastards," and he explained that there was a huge difference between the 1941 Japanese attack on Pearl Harbor and the suicide attack on the World Trade Center. The Pearl Harbor sneak attack targeted military personnel and a military base. Soldiers accept specific levels of risk and the standard rules of engagement when they join the Armed Forces and know that they may be attacked at any time by the enemy. The World Trade Center attack targeted *innocent civilians*, in their offices, using *innocent civilians*, on non-military airplanes, as the offensive weapons.

Osama bin Laden is known to have been responsible for other acts of violence and terrorism against the United States, but his masterminding of the September 11th attacks drastically elevated his ranking on *The Evil 100;* frankly, even if the only act of terrorism he ever conceived was the September World Trade Center attack, he would be assured a spot on the list.

The United States gave Afghanistan's ruling religious militant faction, the Taliban, an ultimatum: turn over Osama bin Laden or suffer the consequences. They refused, demanding concrete evidence before they would acquiesce to the demands.

A month after the World Trade Center tragedy, the United States began an air offensive on Afghanistan. Within days, America took out the Taliban's planes, missiles, radar centers, terrorist training camps, communications installations, as well as rendered unusable their airports and other facilities. By contrast, America also dropped thousands of individual food packages, in an attempt to make it clear to the Afghan people that the war was not with them, but with Osama bin Laden, al Qaeda, and the Taliban.

The Taliban was decimated by November 2001.

Osama bin Laden was born in Riyadh, Saudi Arabia, in 1957, the son of a wealthy construction magnate. The Bin Laden Group is responsible for all the construction in Islam's two holiest cities, Mecca and Medina. Osama bin Laden has fifty-one brothers and sisters (including some in the United States), all of whom have denounced and disowned him.

Bin Laden has four wives and upward of a dozen children. His eldest son, nineteen-year-old Mohammed, serves as his father's bodyguard and carries an AK-47 to protect the elder bin Laden. Mohammed was given instructions to kill his father if there was a risk of Osama being captured by Americans.

Bin Laden graduated from King Abdullah Assize University in Jeddah, Saudi Arabia, in 1979 with a degree in civil engineering. In December of that year, the Soviets invaded Afghanistan and bin Laden left Saudi Arabia to join the Afghan anti-Soviet forces. In 1988, bin Laden formed the terrorist organization al-Qaeda ("The Base") and after the Soviets retreated from Afghanistan, bin Laden returned to Saudi Arabia where he worked in his father's construction firm.

Within six weeks of the World Trade Center attacks, a spate of anthrax contamination struck the United States, including in the U.S. Capitol's ventilation system, and in letters sent to various media outlets, including the *New York Times* and NBC. Bin Laden or Saddam Hussein were initially suspected of being responsible for the anthrax attacks, but a domestic terrorist taking advantage of the war climate was not ruled out.

Osama bin Laden is on the FBI's 10 Most Wanted List and there is currently a $25 million reward for information leading to his capture. He is wanted in connection with the 1998 bombings of the U.S. embassies in Kenya and Tanzania; the bombing of the USS *Cole* in Yemen, and a millennium bombing plot to bomb Los Angeles International Airport.

The following is from an interview aired on PBS. This question was asked of bin Laden by one of his followers and submitted to reporter John Miller as part of the final interview. Miller then asked bin Laden his own questions. (The complete transcript of Miller's interview can be found on the PBS Web site at http://www.pbs.org.)

Q: What is the meaning of your call for Muslims to take arms against America in particular, and what is the message that you wish to send to the West in general?

Osama bin Laden: The call to wage war against America was made because America has spear-headed the crusade against the Islamic nation, sending tens of thousands of its troops to the land of the two Holy Mosques over and above its meddling in its affairs and its politics, and its support of the oppressive, corrupt, and tyrannical regime that is in control. These are the reasons behind the singling out of America as a target. And not exempt of responsibility are those Western regimes whose presence in the region offers support to the American troops there. We know at least one reason behind the symbolic participation of the Western forces and that is to support the Jewish and Zionist plans for expansion of what is called the Great Israel. Surely, their presence is not out of concern over their interests in the region. . . . Their presence has no meaning save one and that is to offer support to the Jews in Palestine who are in need of their Christian brothers to achieve full control over the Arab Peninsula, which they intend to make an important part the Great Israel.

Osama Bin Laden decided that America was his worst enemy during the Gulf War in 1990 when Saudi Arabia allowed U.S. troops (including women) on Saudi land to expel Iraq's occupation of Kuwait. U.S. troops have maintained a presence in Saudi Arabia since the war's end and bin Laden considers their presence sacrilegious and a blasphemy against Islam. Saudi Arabia is home to the two holiest sites in Islam: Mecca, the birthplace of Mohammed, and Medina, where Mohammed's tomb, the Mosque of the Prophet, is located.

Through mid-April 2002, bin Laden's whereabouts were still unknown. Varying reports from Afghanistan and Pakistan offered conflicting stories, including that bin Laden had been wounded by U.S. bombs, had been killed, had escaped to Pakistan, was hiding in the mountains of Afghanistan, and other accounts that could not be verified or confirmed.

Note: also see page 85, "The Taliban."

9

Vladimir Ilich Lenin

(1870–1924)

Power is a poison well known for thousands of years. . . . That's when interrogators spit in the open mouth of the accused! And shove his face into a full cuspidor! That's the state of mind in which they drag priests around by their long hair! Or urinate in a kneeling prisoner's face!
—Alexander Solzhenitsyn, *The Gulag Archipelago*

When considering the deeds of Lenin for the purposes of this book, the convolutions of political ideology must, necessarily, take a backseat to a simpler evaluation that ignores rhetoric and concentrates on the core of Vladimir Lenin the man, as well as on the subsequent results of his policies, beliefs, orders, and actions.

That brings us to an uncomplicated, painful truth: In the years of Lenin's reign as head of the U.S.S.R. from 1917 to 1924, millions of innocent people died in what *The Black Book of Communism* called Lenin's Soviet Union's "venture into planned, logical, and 'politically correct' mass slaughter."

Famine, executions, incarcerations, torture, brutality, terror, and repression were the hallmarks of the Soviet Union first, under Lenin and his Bolsheviks, and then (with even worse abuses), under his successor Joseph

Stalin (see page 7). As Robert C. Tucker notes in his Introduction to the "On Revolutionary Violence and Terror" chapter of *The Lenin Anthology,* "Lenin himself furnished the original inspiration for the practices which were to evolve under Stalin in the 1930s into a monstrous slave-labor empire operating by systematic cruelty and inhumanity on a huge scale."

Lenin believed in the exile or extermination—a "radical cleansing"—of all those branded an enemy of the state. This included (and targeted) the intelligentsia—writers, journalists, politicians, economists, university lecturers, and, after a time, anyone who graduated from a university.

In 1922, Lenin oversaw a new penal code, which permitted the use of *all necessary violence* against political enemies. This de facto legalized political violence. He said, "Not a single problem of the class struggle has ever been solved in history except by violence."

Lenin insisted that the courts not suppress or limit the use of terror in any way, and he continually stressed the need, value, and importance of violence in the governmental process. Alexander Solzhenitsyn, writing in *The Gulag Archipelago,* attested to Lenin's "enthusiasm" for state-sanctioned violence and murder: "Lenin justly ridiculed the idealism of his comrades. He, at any rate, knew that without capital punishment there would be no movement whatever in the direction of the new society."

The system of prisons known as the Gulag Archipelago was begun under Lenin and the Bolsheviks and "perfected" under Stalin. In August 1918, less than a year after coming to power, Lenin issued orders to intern "kulaks, priests, White Guards, and other doubtful elements in concentration camps." The following month, the Red Terror movement was initiated, legalizing terror in defense of the state and leading to unspeakable atrocities and enormous numbers of deaths as the Soviet Republic did away with any and all "doubtful elements." Any form of opposition was considered an act of war against the state; and the Bolsheviks were liberal in their identification of who was an enemy of the state.

At any given time, millions languished in the Gulag's horrific prison camps. Prisoners were kept in airtight cells lined with cork that, once the door was closed, had almost no ventilation or air. Prisoners would literally sweat blood. The spectrum of tortures was limited only by the imagination of the torturer. Prisoners were thrown into pits filled with feces and urine or burned all over their bodies with cigarettes.

Lenin was committed to the tenets of Marxism; a harsh doctrine set forth by Karl Marx and Frederick Engels, which called for a classless society where all means of production were commonly owned. This translated into a simple dictum: The Party was everything. Individuals and individuality mattered nothing.

It was a short leap to the elimination of millions of people.

Vladimir Lenin was born Vladimir Ulyanov in 1870 in the town of Ulyanovsk (then Simbirsk) in Russia. He had embraced Marxism by the time he was twenty-three and was exiled to Siberia for three years by the Czar for his revolutionary activities. He lived in Europe for seventeen years and returned to Russia in 1917 after the Czarist government was overthrown. In November of that year, Lenin became head of state.

Lenin had a stroke in 1922 and, although he lived until 1924, he was almost completely incapacitated. It didn't matter, though, for he had set the stage for the deaths of millions, the establishment of the Gulag, the abolishment of civil liberties, and the conditions for what would come to be called the cold war.

After Lenin's death, his body was embalmed and displayed in a mausoleum near the Kremlin.

Even today, pro-Leninists believe that Lenin was a great man who did great things for the Soviet Union. He did make Russia a superpower, but the price for the Russian people was dear, indeed.

Vlad III Dracula
"The Impaler"

(1431–1476)

Here begins a very cruel frightening story about a wild blood-thirsty man Prince Dracula. How he impaled people and roasted them and boiled their heads in a kettle and skinned people and hacked them to pieces like cabbage. He also roasted the children of mothers and they had to eat the children themselves. And many other horrible things are written in this tract and in the land he ruled.

—from a pamphlet about Dracula
printed in Nuremberg in 1499

Count Vlad Dracula was born in Transylvania, Romania, in 1431, the son of Basarab the Dragon.

The name "Dracula" is one of the ten most recognized words of the English language. *Dracul* means "dragon" in Romanian and *adding* an "a" denotes "son of." At the time, Romania was Roman Catholic but the Muslim Turks wanted to take it over. There was tremendous political instability in the area, including internally in Romania, and Dracula ultimately lost and regained power three separate times.

Dracula's reign of terror lasted from 1456 to 1462, during which period he is believed to have tortured, impaled, and killed close to one hundred thousand before being deposed and imprisoned. Dracula killed for several reasons. Most of his victims were enemies, either Ottoman Turks or domestic traitors and insurgents, but he also tortured and killed for fun, or because he was bored.

The astonishingly cruel Count Dracula loved using impaling as a form of execution and once had twenty thousand Turkish prisoners impaled and lined up around his castle as a sign to the invading Ottomans that this could be their fate, too, if they did not retreat immediately. The Turks turned and ran, many of them with a prayer to Allah on their trembling lips.

While being held hostage by the Turks as a young man, Dracula learned the art of impalement watching from a prison cell window. He watched as his enemies executed *their* enemies in the yard outside his cell, impaling men and women alike. During this period, Dracula was confined to a stone hole in the dungeon, being beaten and whipped every day, burned with hot pokers, and deprived of food and water. Prisoners were also hanged, shot with arrows, crushed under heavy wheels, or eaten alive by wild animals. Impaling was one of the worst forms of torture execution at the time and Dracula was fascinated by its barbaric cruelty.

The English novelist Bram Stoker used the historical Count Dracula as the model for his fictional character Dracula, the vampire in the novel of the same name, but the real Count Dracula never practiced vampirism. There is, however, an historical account of Dracula dipping his bread into the blood of some of his victims.

On St. Bartholomew's Day during his second reign, Count Dracula had his troops storm and seize the city of Brasov, a central Romanian city in the foothills of the Transylvanian Alps.

First, Dracula had his armies round up all the townsfolk and bring them to the top of Timpa Hill. He then had Brasov torched and burned to the ground.

Under his watchful eyes, Count Dracula then had some of the thirty thousand of Brasov's merchants and nobles agonizingly impaled and staked into the ground of Timpa Hill.

While this was going on, the count engaged in a sumptuous feast laid out on a long table at the crown of the hill. As he ate, he watched as his soldiers slaughtered the remaining citizens of Brasov by chopping them up with axes and swords, limb by limb, while they were all still alive and conscious.

A mountain of dismembered arms, legs, heads, and torsos grew before him as he enjoyed his repast, delighting in the glorious horrors of the city burning beneath him, the writhings and screams of agony of the impaled, and the bloody butchering of men, women, and children taking place on the hill. The ground was soon so soaked with blood, it was as though the skies of hell had opened and rained down torrents of red.

One of Dracula's noblemen made a crucial mistake during the feast. When a person is impaled, their bowels release and they hemorrhage huge amounts of blood. The combined smell of the blood and feces of thirty thousand people was probably a little overwhelming for the nobleman, who almost certainly reflexively, held his nose. When Dracula saw him doing this, he was livid. He immediately ordered the nobleman impaled. "Let him join these others," Dracula proclaimed, "but because he had been loyal until today, hoist him higher than the rest that he does not have to smell his company!"

There are many other examples of Dracula's evil cruelty:

- When one of Dracula's mistresses lied to him about being pregnant, he cut her open from her breasts to her groin in order to show everyone "where he had been" and then left her to die in unspeakable agony.
- When Dracula learned of all the poor, sick, and homeless in his kingdom, he invited hundreds of them to his castle for an enormous feast. They were told they could eat and drink as much as they liked. When they were finished, he had all the doors and windows locked and bolted and then had his soldiers shoot flaming arrows into the room, setting fire to the curtains and burning everyone alive. No one survived. Dracula remarked, "The poor unloved creatures, it is best that they leave this world now, on a full stomach."
- Dracula liked to have people stripped naked and then buried in the earth up to their waists. Unable to flee or even fall down, they were then stoned and shot at with rifles. (Dracula was one of the first in Europe to use the new invention gunpowder for murder.)
- Dracula also liked to roast people alive and then remove their skin while they still lived.
- Dracula was inventive. He instructed an enormous pot to be built that could hold several people at one time. He also ordered a heavy board to be built with holes in it large enough for a human head. He would have his victims stripped naked, placed in the pot after it had been filled with water, and then have their heads put through the holes in the board. Once the board was put in place on top of the pot, preventing the victims' escape, a fire would be lit under the pot and the water would be brought to boiling and kept there by regularly feeding and stoking the fire. All the people in the pot would literally be boiled to death.
- When three hundred gypsies strolled uninvited into his realm, Dracula picked three of them, had them slaughtered and cooked, and then made the remaining gypsies dine on their fellow wanderers.
- Dracula's punishment for female adulterers was especially horrific. While fully conscious, her sexual organs would be hacked out with a knife. The woman was then skinned alive and her flayed body was im-

paled in the public square. Her skin was hung from a separate pole standing next to her.

Dracula died in 1474 when he was beheaded in a battle against the Turks.

11

Talat Pasha and Enver Pasha

(1874–1921) (1881–1922)

*Turkey is taking advantage of the war in order to thoroughly
liquidate its internal foes, i.e., the indigenous Christians, without being thereby disturbed by foreign intervention.*

—Talat Pasha

*The Ottoman Empire should be cleaned up of the Armenians
and the Lebanese. We have destroyed the former by the sword,
we shall destroy the latter through starvation.*

—Enver Pasha

The abomination known as the Armenian Genocide of 1915–1918 (followed by a resurgence of hostilities from 1920 to 1923) was implemented and carried out by the Central Committee of the Young Turk Party, led by two brothers, Talat Pasha and Enver Pasha.

The Young Turks decided that they would kill all the Armenians because the Armenians were Christians, the Turks were Moslems, and as we have learned from recent history, infidels cannot be allowed to live.

As evidence of just how despicable the actions of Talat Pasha and Enver Pasha were, none other than Adolf Hitler used the resultant Armenian slaughter as evidence that the world would meekly stand by and allow a Jewish genocide. "Who, after all, speaks today of the annihilation of the Armenians?" Hitler asked his advisers.

Prince Abdul Mecid, the heir-apparent to the Ottoman throne, when asked about the Armenian Genocide, said:

> [T]hose awful massacres . . . are the greatest stain that has ever disgraced our nation and race. They were entirely the work of Talat and Enver. I heard some days before they began that they were intended. I went to Istanbul and insisted on seeing Enver. I asked him if it was true that they intended to recommence the massacres . . . The only reply I could get from him was: "It is decided. It is the program."

A letter from the 1915–1916 period, from an unknown Armenian to an Armenian minister, succinctly summed up the Turks' eventual goal: "Armenia without the Armenians—such is the plan of the Ottoman Government, which has already begun to install Moslem families in the homes and property of the Armenians."

It started with gendercide. All young Armenian soldiers in the Turkish army were demoted to workmen; all Armenian men not in the military were drafted to similar service. Being a workman meant, essentially, being a mule. These men were overloaded with supplies and forced to trudge miles on almost no food. They were beaten and whipped, and then shot when they were unable to continue.

This systematic annihilation of the strong Armenian male class left towns filled with women, children, and old men, who were all forced to leave their homes and make a nightmarish journey to concentration camps in Syria.

The vast majority did not survive the trip (that is, they were not *allowed* to survive). They were brutalized the entire way by the soldiers—by Turks who waited for them to pass through town so they could rape and beat them, and by convicts who had been released by the government specifically to perform as "good Moslems," which meant beating, raping, robbing, torturing, and killing the Armenian refugees.

As days passed and the women, children, and old men dragged themselves under the hot desert sun, they got weaker and sicker, and many would fall to the ground, unable to continue. The Turkish solders would simply bayonet them as they lay there and move on.

Henry Morgenthau, U.S. Ambassador to Turkey at the time, in his 1915 book, *Murder of a Nation,* described the annihilation of the men from one town in Turkey:

At Angora all Armenian men from fifteen to seventy were arrested, bound together in groups of four, and sent on the road in the direction of Caesarea. When they had travelled five or six hours and had reached a secluded valley, a mob of Turkish peasants fell upon them with clubs, hammers, axes, scythes, spades, and saws. Such instruments not only caused more agonizing deaths than guns and pistols, but, as the Turks themselves boasted, they were more economical, since they did not involve the waste of powder and shell. In this way they exterminated the whole male population of Angora, including all its men of wealth and breeding, and their bodies, horribly mutilated, were left in the valley, where they were devoured by wild beasts.

Morgenthau went on to describe what happened to the women left behind who were subsequently forced to go on their own death march:

The whole course of the journey became a perpetual struggle with the Moslem inhabitants. . . . attacks in the open would find new terrors awaiting them in the Moslem villages. Here the Turkish roughs would fall upon the women, leaving them sometimes dead from their experiences or sometimes ravingly insane. After spending a night in a hideous encampment of this kind, the exiles, or such as had survived, would start again the next morning. The ferocity of the [soldiers] apparently increased as the journey lengthened, for they seemed almost to resent the fact that part of their charges continued to live. Frequently any one who dropped on the road was bayoneted on the spot. The Armenians began to die by hundreds from hunger and thirst. Even when they came to rivers, the [soldiers], merely to torment them, would sometimes not let them drink. The hot sun of the desert burned their scantily clothed bodies, and their bare feet, treading the hot sand of the desert, became so sore that thousands fell and died or were killed where they lay. Thus, in a few days, what had been a procession of normal human beings became a stumbling horde of dust-covered skeletons, ravenously looking for scraps of food, eating any offal that came their way, crazed by the hideous sights that filled every hour of their existence, sick with all the diseases that accompany such hardships and privations, but still prodded on and on by the whips and clubs and bayonets of their executioners.

Estimates are that three of every four Armenians forced to make the death march to Syria did not survive. One convoy that consisted of eighteen thousand people whittled down to 150 survivors at the end of the journey.

❖   ❖   ❖

The Armenian Genocide is now considered the first twentieth-century holocaust. The nations of the world today all acknowledge the complete elimination of the Armenian race from Asia Minor by 1923.

Turkey's official position on their actions during the World War I years is that the Armenians died in a civil war. They do not admit that the Ottoman Empire set in motion, and carried out, the mass extermination of the Armenian people.

Enver Pasha and Talat Pasha were tried in absentia in 1919, found guilty of genocide, and sentenced to death. Enver Pasha was killed while leading an anti-Bolshevik revolt in Turkestan in 1922, and Talat Pasha was killed by an Armenian assassination squad.

12

Tamerlane
"Timur the Lame"

(1336–1405)

Timour—he
Whom the astonished people saw
Striding o'er empires haughtily
A diadem'd outlaw!

—Edgar Allan Poe, "Tamerlane"

H e was born "Timur" and known as the "Lame" because he was partially paralyzed on his left side. His legacy is that of a great conqueror, yet history also unblinkingly tells us that Tamerlane was one of the cruelest, most sadistic, heartless, and yes, evil men of all time. His body count is staggering.

Colin Wilson, the acclaimed author of many books on murder and crime, describes Tamerlane as "the most spectacular sadist in world history." Even a cursory review of the actions of Tamerlane reveals a vanquisher who took pleasure in mass annihilation; a "diadem'd outlaw" reveling in atrocities.

In 1383, Tamerlane invaded and conquered Zirih in Turkey and took five thousand prisoners. Shortly thereafter, Tamerlane decreed that the heads of all five thousand prisoners be chopped off and, as each head was removed, it should be placed in a pile, which resulted in a macabre pyramid of decapitated heads climbing to the sun.

That same year, Tamerlane invaded Sabwazar and took two thousand prisoners. He ordered these men to pile on top of each other, many of them having to climb up writhing bodies to get to the top of this living mound. And then, when all two thousand were in the mass of bodies (many of whom had already been crushed to death at the bottom), he ordered his soldiers to carefully encase the mound in brick, creating a tomb for the living that would eventually be their final mausoleum.

In 1386, Tamerlane invaded the city of Luri and rounded up thousands of prisoners. He then ordered them executed by having them all thrown off an extremely high cliff. As might be expected, there were no survivors.

Several years later, in 1398, Tamerlane traveled to India and invaded Delhi, apparently strictly for the booty. Once he had dominion over the city, his warriors, on Tamerlane's orders, massacred by sword an incredible one hundred thousand people and then leveled the city. When Tamerlane and his Mongol troops withdrew from Delhi, they left behind nothing but corpses and rubble.

In 1400, Tamerlane and his men invaded the area of Turkey in western Asia known as Anatolia and completely overpowered the four thousand Christians manning the garrison at Sivas. Tamerlane's Mongol soldiers ordered the captured Christians to dig enormous trenches, and they had no recourse but to comply, or die instantly.

Once the holes, which were really mass graves, were deep enough, Tamerlane's men hurled their prisoners into them and began covering them with dirt. The Mongols did not bestow the mercy of death upon the Christians before they buried them.

Tamerlane's army was made up of Turks and Mongols and, during his forty-year siege, from 1362 to 1402, Tamerlane invaded and conquered much of Persia, Turkey, Russia, and India. He was almost always at war.

In 1370, he established Samarkand in south central Asia in Uzbekistan as the capital of his empire and, from there, he reached out to terrorize, kill, and destroy.

Tamerlane believed wholeheartedly that the sacred duty of an emperor/conqueror such as himself was to kill on as massive a scale as possible. The more deaths, he believed, the better he was fulfilling his holy mission.

Tamerlane was the last in a long line of nomadic Mongol conquerors, and he professed that he was a devout Sunni Muslim. (The Sunni Muslims believe that the first four caliphs of Islam were the rightful successors to the prophet Mohammed.) Tamerlane's commitment to Islam did not, however, dissuade him from indulging in sadism for the sake of sadism, and indiscriminate slaughter that rivaled the atrocities of his ancestor Genghis Khan (see page 13). (Ironically, the aforementioned Samarkand had been visited in 1220 by Tamerlane's forbear Genghis Khan. Khan did not occupy Samarkand, however. He destroyed it.)

There was an odd paradox to Tamerlane's personality. There is no denying that he loved great art and delighted in literature, and yet he embraced none of the higher ideals of art when it came to his military objectives. It is a given that massacring entire populations was part of the dynamic of twelfth- and thirteenth-century empire building; Tamerlane did not shirk in this aspect of his perceived mission. However, the cruelty he exhibited in his endeavors (bricking up living prisoners, burying men alive) was clearly a willing embrace of his baser impulses.

Tamerlane died in his sixties while making plans to invade China. He left his abundant riches to his sons and grandsons, who continued their progenitors' life's work by killing, plundering, and destroying.

A Russian scientist exhumed Tamerlane's skeleton in 1941. The scientist learned that Tamerlane was 5 feet, 8 inches tall, and he confirmed Tamerlane's left-side paralysis. From the long-dead conqueror's skull, forensic experts were able to reconstruct an accurate likeness of his face.

13

Tomás de Torquemada

(1420–1498)

"In the shadow of every religion lurks a Torquemada. He was an obscenity. He made living torches out of people who disagreed with him."
　　　　—Leto II from *God Emperor of Dune* by Frank Herbert

Tomás de Torquemada was the Adolf Hitler of the fifteenth century, and the Inquisition is a detestable stigma on the history of the Roman Catholic Church.

Begun in the fifteenth century during the reign of the Catholic monarchs Ferdinand and Isabella, and continuing through the nineteenth century, the Inquisition was a court established by the Catholic Church to try cases of heresy and other affronts against the church. What it *really* was was a pogrom against Jews—deliberate persecution against even those Jews who had converted to Christianity—(and an insidious way of filling the church's treasury with seized property and goods). The stated goal of the Inquisition was *sangre limpia—pure* (that is, white, Christian) *blood* for all of Europe, but especially Spain. The Inquisition was a heinous tool used to inflict unspeakable cruelty, torture, and death on Jews, and it was motivated and fueled by religious fanaticism and anti-Semitic bigotry.

The Inquisition's premier architect was the despicable Tomás de Torquemada, a man who had Jewish roots, but whose family converted to Christianity before his birth and never looked back. Torquemada was a Dominican priest prior to becoming Grand Inquisitor, and he was Isabella's confessor. He convinced her that the Catholic Church was seriously threatened by Jews in Spain and persuaded her to establish a court to try suspected heretics. She agreed that such a court was necessary and Torquemada was given free reign to exercise all manner of torture and execution, resulting in centuries of some of the most evil deeds ever perpetrated in the name of God. A striking illustration of the hypocrisy of the acts of the Inquisition is the fact that the public torture and execution of Jews and heretics was called an *auto-da-fé*, which is Portugese for "act of faith."

Several types of torture and punishment were devised and carried out during Torquemada's reign as Grand Inquisitor, many of which were conceived by Torquemada himself. These included torture by fire, water (the *toca*), the rack (the *garotte*), and the hoist (the *garrucha*).

The fire torture involved covering heretics' feet with lard and roasting them in a blazing fire.

For the water torture, the victim was placed on a tilting table so that his head was below his feet, his nostrils were plugged up, a gag of cloth was placed in his mouth, and water was then continuously poured into his mouth, giving him the excruciating experience of drowning and suffocating, all while fully conscious.

The rack was a stretching table that would pull the victim apart in gradual degrees. Each turn of the wheel further opened the table and brought unspeakable agony.

The hoist was an agonizing torture that required nothing but a rope and a pulley attached to the ceiling. The apostate's hands were tied behind his back and he was lifted up off the ground by a rope tied to his wrists. This was done slowly until his entire body weight was suspended by his shoulder joints. He was then asked to confess to heresy and all other types of "sins." If he refused, he was elevated almost to the ceiling, and then dropped suddenly to a foot or so above the ground. This jerking would often dislocate his arms out of their shoulder sockets and cause unbearable agony. He would then be asked again to confess. If he was able, through some incredible strength of will, to again refuse, heavy weights would be suspended off his feet to increase the pressure on his dislocated arms. Prisoners were often left hanging like this for hours until they either confessed or died. The most horrifying part of this whole ordeal, though, was what would happen *after* the heretic confessed (and at some point they *would* confess to anything just to stop the torture): he would then qualify for punishment, which often involved dismemberment, disembowelment, and burning alive.

Sometimes Jews were targeted for persecution because of their standing and possessions. One of the benefits of the Inquisition to the Church was the confiscation of all property of the heretics, adding greatly to the Church's (and Torquemada's) coffers.

A victim (often a respected businessman or town elder) would be dragged from his house and everything he owned taken from him. He would then be humiliatingly paraded through the streets wearing only a short yellow tunic of penance (the *sanbenito),* leaving him naked from the waist down and exposed to the townfolk. He would be marched to a church where he would be publicly flogged, often to the point of death, and then he might be burned alive at the stake, or imprisoned, never to be seen again.

Torquemada codified his brutality in a number of "Articles," one of which actually granted him and the church the authority to convict someone *forty years dead* of heresy and then seize all property and possessions of his grandchildren and other descendants.

Torquemada is ranked high on this list for several reasons, including the duplicity with which he deferred the responsibility for his horrendous deeds to God; his blatant (and blatantly *non*-Christian) bigotry; and the obvious sadistic delight he took in devising all manner of torment and thievery in the name of his demonically single-minded "spiritual" mission.

14

Caligula
(Gaius Caesar)

(A.D. 12–41)

"Strike so that he may feel that he is dying."
—Caligula, issuing an execution command

"Off comes this beautiful head whenever I give the word."
—Caligula, to his wife

"Let them hate me, so they but fear me."
—Caligula, quoting Accius

Public torture, rampant cruelty, willful executions; rape, pedophilia, incest; indiscriminate assassination; capricious appropriation of citizens' property and money; cavalier adultery; and a persistent, sadistic psychopathological megalomania—these were all hallmarks of Caligula's tyrannical reign as emperor of Rome from A.D. 37 to A.D. 41.

Caligula's reprehensible behavior is now believed to have been caused by schizophrenia and epilepsy; this does not, however, mitigate the horror and evil of the atrocious deeds carried out on his orders and in his name.

The story is told of a time that Caligula became displeased with the performance of one of his games supervisors, a loyal servant who also was in charge of the beasts used in the gladiatorial contests in the arena. Caligula had the man brought before him and then ordered him flogged with heavy chains, nonstop, for days. The flesh was ripped from the man's body, his bones were shattered and broken, and his head and skull were torn open by the blows of the chain. Caligula refused to order the man put to death (and out of his misery); only when the smell of the man's gangrenous brain became so offensive to Caligula that he couldn't stand it anymore was the man allowed to die.

Caligula insisted on a certain number of participants for his bloody games (a number that always translated into a body count after the lions got into the act), and he would not tolerate a smaller number of victims than he felt appropriate. If there were not enough slaves to satisfy his blood lust, he would have his soldiers randomly grab people from the stands and throw them into the arena, where they would be torn to shreds and eaten by the lions. No one was safe from Caligula's evil insanity.

Other examples of Caligula's cruelty stain the historical record. Sometimes, just to prove his power over his subjects, he would close the granaries and allow countless people to starve to death. He would take great delight in forcing people with handicaps or infirmities to fight one another to the death. To conserve valuable cattle, he would, instead, feed human prisoners to his arena beasts. Once, Caligula ordered a poet burned alive in public because he did not like the possible meaning of one of the poet's lines of verse. Caligula had high-ranking officials branded with his sign and then cut into pieces or caged like animals. He had a Roman senator he suspected of treason stabbed to death on the steps of the Senate, disemboweled, and dismembered into several pieces, and then had each piece dragged through the streets of Rome. To punish a slave caught stealing, Caligula had the man's hands cut off, threaded onto a piece of chain, and draped around the slave's neck to show others what happened to thieves under Caligula's rule.

Caligula was one of the twelve Caesars of ancient Rome and he succeeded his adoptive father, Tiberius, to the throne. (The Caesars' family reign began with Julius Caesar in the first century B.C.) Caligula's biological father was Germanicus Caesar (15 B.C.–A.D. 19), who was also the grandfather of Nero (see page 64). Caligula's mother was Agrippina (B.C. 14–A.D. 33).

As a child, Caligula was a favorite of his father's troops, who gave him the nickname "Caligula," which means "little boots," after the small military boots he favored wearing.

As an adult, Caligula was tall, thin, and bald. He was hypersensitive about his lack of hair and would not allow anyone to look down onto his glabrous pate. He suffered from insomnia, hallucinations, delusions, and often heard the spirit of the ocean speaking to him.

In the initial months of Caligula's reign, there was little indication of the sadism and cruelty that would soon mark his time in power. But when Caligula was twenty-five, his influential grandmother Antonia died, followed by Caligula himself becoming gravely ill. Many historians believe that it is likely that Caligula contracted encephalitis, an inflammation of the brain that is often caused by a virus or lead poisoning (a likely possibility since many drinking vessels of the time were made with lead), and which can cause permanent brain damage. Following his recovery, Caligula's insanity became obvious, and his sadistic tendencies and megalomania were subsequently indulged completely.

It was after his recovery that his bizarre behavior surfaced, including dressing in women's clothes and practicing grimaces and ugly facial expressions in the mirror that he would then use later in public.

In A.D. 40, the third year of his time in office, the Roman people had had enough. A successful assassination plot against him was carried out on January 24, 41, at the Palatine Games, when two of his own Praetorian guards murdered Caligula, Caligula's wife, Caesonia, and their daughter. By this time Caligula was so hated, that once he fell to the ground, mortally wounded, many guards began stabbing him continuously, some even plunging their swords into his genitals. His wife also died by the sword, but his daughter was killed by having her head smashed against a wall until her brains were a bloody pulp.

Caligula's death marked the end of the reign of the Caesars in ancient Rome.

15

Basil II
"THE BULGAR SLAYER"

(c. 957–1025)

If you want to know someone, give him power.
—Bulgarian proverb

An eye for an eye—and everyone is blind.
—Gandhi

B asil knew it would take a great many soldiers to carry out his order, but he believed the expenditure of time and men was justified and necessary.

Basil had already decided to let his fourteen thousand Bulgarian prisoners go. He did not want to kill them, but he did not want to take care of them either. Basil had ended a thirty-year war with the Bulgars with a mass capture in 1014 after a bloody battle in the upper valley of the Struma River, and even though the Bulgar leader, Tsar Samuel, had escaped, Basil knew that he was victorious and could afford to let his prisoners of war go. However, these men were not going to simply walk away. They would have to pay a price for their loyalty to Samuel and for having Basil as their enemy—that price was their sight.

With unimaginable cruelty and stony reserve, Basil II commanded his soldiers to gouge out the eyes of every single Bulgar prisoner, with the edict to leave one eye in every hundredth prisoner. Those "lucky" 140 men would be given the dark and terrible duty of leading their blinded comrades home to Samuel's fortress of Ochrid (in modern Macedonia), each man holding on to the belt of the man in front of him.

Imagine the scene. Hundreds of Basil's troops, probably bearing short-blade knives and perhaps red-hot pokers, moving as rapidly as possible through the hordes of Bulgar prisoners, stabbing each man in the eyes, leaving them bloody and screaming, clutching their faces, suddenly and permanently blinded, helpless cripples and no longer soldiers.

It is believed that thousands of these maimed Bulgars died during the trek back to their homeland. Two days after Tsar Samuel saw his mutilated army stagger pathetically back into his realm, he had a massive heart attack and died. Tsar Samuel had escaped capture at the hands of his enemy, the Byzantium emperor Basil, now known as the Bulgar Slayer; but Basil had ultimately succeeded in not only defeating the Bulgarians, but destroying their leader as well.

This brutal "statement" to the Bulgars—the merciless blinding of fourteen thousand defenseless men—qualifies as what we would today call a war crime of the highest order. It was unspeakably cruel, was torture for the sake of torture, and this act alone warrants Basil's inclusion in this ranking, irrespective of the qualities of leadership he manifested or the acknowledged brilliance of his military strategies.

Adding to the profound malevolence of Basil's mass blinding, and further justifying his inclusion as a member of *The Evil 100,* was a similar act two years later. In 1016, during a military campaign in Macedonia, Basil had his troops, yes, again, blind every Bulgarian in their path. This time, however, Basil left no one sighted. And he did not limit his brutality to enemy soldiers. Basil also ordered civilians—including women and children—be blinded as well.

Basil II, son of Romanus II and Theophano, was only three years old when he was crowned co-emperor of the Byzantine Empire with his brother Constantine VIII, but he did not take actual control until he was eighteen.

Basil assumed leadership of the Balkans after successfully defeating his great-uncle, Basil the chamberlain, who had taken command on the death of Basil's father in 963.

In his late teens and early twenties, with the riches of the Byzantine Empire at his command, Basil was a hedonist, delighting in elaborate and debauched banquets and the sexual indulgences of multitudes of willing women.

However, by his late twenties, Basil became utterly committed to expansion of his kingdom and to territorial domination, with an especially vicious hatred toward Tsar Samuel and his Bulgarian kingdom. Basil was steadfast in his wrath toward Samuel and, year after year, he made inroads into Bulgarian territory. He forced his troops to advance and conquer year-round, summer and winter, until his crucial 1014 victory on the banks of the Struma. This crushing victory that made the Bulgarian Kingdom part of the Byzantine Empire.

Basil was uncultured and had no interest in scholarship of any kind, yet he was able to stir a crowd when he spoke and there are reports that he had a sense of humor. He was a lifelong bachelor and the historical record shows no evidence of Basil ever having fathered children. Basil was a full-time soldier, and is remembered as an often cruel, severe, hot-tempered despot.

Basil the Bulgar Slayer died on December 15, 1025 at the age of sixty-seven. With no one to follow in his footsteps, it wasn't long before his exploits and victories were all but erased from history.

16

Adolf Eichmann

(1906–1962)

I remember clearly the first time [Auschwitz Commandant Hoess] guided me around the camp. He showed me everything, and at the end he took me to a grave where the corpses of the gassed Jews lay piled on a strong iron grill. Hoess's men poured some inflammable liquid over them and set them on fire. The flesh stewed like stew meat. The sight made such an impression on me that today, after a dozen years, I can still see that mountain of corpses in front of me. [I told Hoess] "When I see your corpses, I think of those charred German bodies in the air-raid shelters in Berlin."

—Adolf Eichmann

To sum it all up, I must say that I regret nothing.

—Adolf Eichmann

The Fifteen Charges Brought Against Adolf Eichmann at the Nuremberg Trials

Charge 1:   He was ultimately responsible for the murder of millions of Jews.

`**Charge 2:**   He placed these Jews, before they were murdered, in living conditions designed to kill them.

Charge 3:   He caused them grave physical and mental harm.

Charge 4:   He took actions that resulted in the sterilization of Jews and otherwise prevented childbirth.

Charge 5:   He caused the enslavement, starvation, and deportation of millions of Jews.

Charge 6:   He caused general persecution of Jews based on national, racial, religious, and political grounds.

Charge 7:   He spoiled Jewish property by inhuman measures involving compulsion, robbery, terrorism, and violence.

Charge 8:   That all of the above were punishable war crimes.

Charge 9:   He deported a half-million Poles.

Charge 10:   He deported fourteen thousand Slovenes.

Charge 11:   He deported tens of thousands of gypsies.

Charge 12:   He deported and murdered one hundred Czech children from the village of Lidice.

The final three charges were for being a member of organizations judged to be criminal by the Nuremberg Trials: the SD, the Gestapo, and the SS.

One of the most somber, yet possibly gratifying moments in modern Jewish history was the day in 1962 when the state of Israel announced that it had executed Adolf Eichmann by hanging after finding the notorious Nazi war criminal guilty of crimes against humanity for his culpability in the deaths of six million Jews and six million non-Jews during the Holocaust.

Incredibly, after Eichmann was hunted down and captured in Buenos Aires, Argentina, by the Mossad, Israel's elite secret police force, he wrote from his jail cell that he had only been "obeying orders."

One still wonders if Eichmann, who once said, "The death of five million Jews on my conscience gives me extraordinary satisfaction," truly believed that he was not responsible for those millions of deaths and that he was just a bureaucrat doing his job. Or was he shamelessly dissembling in a last-ditch attempt to save his own life? It would seem that the latter is more realistic, since this was the man who, after all, arrogantly proclaimed himself a "Jewish specialist" (he spoke Hebrew and Yiddish) and who prided himself on keeping the death trains rolling as they carried their doomed human cargo to Auschwitz, Dachau, Bergen-Belsen, Treblinka, and the other places where the gas chambers operated twenty-four hours a day.

◦   ◦   ◦

Karl Adolf Eichmann was born into a Protestant family in Solingen, Germany, in 1906. As a child, Eichmann was teased about his dark hair and complexion and mockingly called the "little Jew."

Eichmann's father had a small mining company and thus, it made sense that young Karl would study engineering, which he did, and at which he failed. He worked as a traveling salesman (for an American company) and as a laborer, but Eichmann's real "career" began in April 1932, when he joined the Austrian Nazi Party. In November of that year, he joined Heinrich Himmler's elite SS, which then was serving as Hitler's bodyguards, but which would eventually oversee the smooth functioning of the concentration camps.

Although Eichmann was getting more involved with the growing Nazi Party at this time, he still worked as a salesman for the Vacuum Oil Company until early 1933. Eichmann was fired as part of a cutback, but he spread the story around that the man who fired him was a Jew and that he had lost his job because of his Nazi connections.

Between the mid-1930s and 1941, Eichmann moved up the Nazi ladder, earning promotions and assisting in the implementation of programs that would ultimately culminate in the Final Solution. At first, the "Jewish problem" was addressed through deportations, ghettoization, arrests and imprisonments, and the seizure and destruction of Jewish property and businesses.

October and November of 1938, however, marked a turning point in the pogrom against the Jews and set the stage for Hitler's 1941 order to eradicate the Jewish race.

In October 1938, fifteen thousand Polish Jews were thrown out of Germany with no warning and taken by train to the border of Poland, where they were unceremoniously dumped. In addition, in early November the same year, the terrible storm of destruction that would come to be known as *Kristallnacht* (Night of Broken Glass) took place in Germany and Austria.

When the war started in 1939, Eichmann was in charge of the Jewish problem. He went about solving it cold-bloodedly, with no hesitation, and with total devotion to his Führer and the Nazi Party.

After a short period, Eichmann began to worry about the stress on his troops if they were forced to shoot hundreds of thousands of Jews—not to mention the waste of so many bullets!—and thus he convened a meeting to find a "more elegant solution."

Hitler had recently issued the order to kill every Jew in the Reich and when the Führer gave an order, it was carried out. It was decided at the secret meeting that the solution to the problem of how to kill a great many Jews in the most efficient manner was to use deadly Zyklon-B gas in large quantities. This would allow them to wipe out hundreds of people at once.

Zyklon-B had been in use in Germany for some time: the German government used it to exterminate the mentally handicapped. Eichmann implemented its use on a large scale as part of the Final Solution. All the responsibility for organizing and carrying out the mass execution of all the Jews in the Reich was given to Eichmann—and he eagerly embraced the task.

✿   ✿   ✿

After Hitler's suicide, Eichmann escaped Germany and managed to elude authorities for fifteen years. He was eventually captured in 1960 by Israeli agents in Argentina, tried, and sentenced to death for crimes against humanity. He was hanged in 1962.

Dr. Josef Mengele
"THE ANGEL OF DEATH"
(1911–1979)

[I saw] an immense square chimney built of red bricks tapering towards the summit. I was especially struck by the enormous tongues of flame rising between the lightning rods. . . . I tried to realize what hellish cooking would require such a tremendous fire. . . . A faint wind brought the smoke towards me. My nose, then my throat were filled with the nauseating odor of burning flesh and scorched hair.

—Dr. Miklos Nyiszli, *Auschwitz,*
A Doctor's Eyewitness Account

The gas chambers were full and could not fit another Jew.

Dr. Mengele had a problem. Ten trucks filled with Jewish children—all of whom were *under five years old*—were on their way to Auschwitz and Mengele knew he needed dispatch them quickly when they arrived.

There may not be words to describe adequately the unspeakably evil horror of Mengele's solution. Dr. Mengele ordered long, deep trenches dug in the yards of Auschwitz. He then had these trenches filled with hundreds of gallons of gasoline and set ablaze.

When the trucks arrived, he ordered them to back up to the edges of the trenches and dump the screaming, terrified infants and children into the pits of fire. Mengele stood by and watched with satisfaction as Nazi soldiers picked up babies and threw them into the flames.

In what must have been one of the most horrific scenes ever to occur in the history of Man, some of the older children attempted to crawl out of the blazing pit. These children were on fire from hair to toe, and Mengele ordered his soldiers to kick them back into the raging inferno. The screams of burning children commingled with the roar of the flames to create an inhuman scene that literally created hell on earth.

It is likely that many of Dr. Mengele's physician subordinates, as well as Jewish prisoners, averted their eyes from the walls of his office if they happened to be summoned to the Angel of Death's sanctum. Pinned on Mengele's walls were eyes, specifically, the eyes of twins who died during many of Mengele's horrific experiments. (He injected them with dye to see if it would change the eye color.) A survivor named Vera Kriegel was one of those who saw Mengele's wall of eyes. She later said, "I thought I was dead and already living in hell." (In Posner's *Mengele: The Complete Story.*)

Dr. Mengele did not just mete out death sentences with a flick of his riding crop, he also performed medical experiments as part of his stated mission to unlock and understand the genetic code of inferior, "unworthy of life" individuals. Mengele believed that if he discovered the genetic variations that made people feebleminded, schizophrenic, manic depressive, epileptic, blind, deaf, physically deformed, or alcoholic, he would be able to ultimately "design" a superior German, with none of the flaws of the "inferiors."

Mengele's experiments consisted of barbaric, non-scientific tortures performed in the guise of medical research.

He operated on children—including performing castrations, the removal of internal organs, lumbar punctures, and limb amputations—without anesthesia.

He placed children in cages, then tortured them to see how long they would survive.

He injected twins with such deadly infectious diseases as typhus and then recorded their death agonies.

He stood full weight on the stomachs of pregnant women and timed how long it would take for their bodies to miscarry and expel the fetuses.

He performed a live dissection of a one-year-old.

He sterilized a group of Polish nuns with such enormous levels of X-rays that they were left with permanent, agonizing radiation burns.

He had twin brothers, one of whom was a hunchback, sewn together, back to back. Their wrists were also sewn together.

He operated, again without anesthesia, on the vocal cords of twins, one of whom could sing; the other who could not. Mengele inflicted equal damage on both sets of vocal cords to see whether the one who could sing would recover her singing voice.

In addition to his death orders and experiments, Mengele was also a case study of personal cruelty. He once grabbed an old man and split his skull open with repeated blows of an iron rod as everyone watched.

A Jewish female prisoner named Ibi was caught jumping off a truck headed to the gas chambers. Dr. Gisela Perl (1948), writing in *I Was a Doctor in Auschwitz,* recalls what happened next:

> "You are still here?" Dr. Mengele left the head of the column, and with a few easy strides caught up with her. He grabbed her by the neck and proceeded to beat her head to a bloody pulp. He hit her, slapped her, boxed her, always her head—screaming at her at the top of his voice, "You want to escape, don't you. You can't escape now. This is not a truck, you can't jump. You are going to burn like the others, you are going to croak, you dirty Jew," and he went on hitting the poor unprotected head. As I watched, I saw her two beautiful, intelligent eyes disappear under a layer of blood. Her ears weren't there any longer, maybe he had torn them off. And in a few seconds, her straight, pointed nose was a flat, broken, bleeding mass. I closed my eyes, unable to bear it any longer, and when I opened them up again, Dr. Mengele had stopped hitting her. But instead of a human head, Ibi's tall, thin body carried a round, blood-red object on its bony shoulders, an unrecognizable object, too horrible to look at; he pushed her back into line. Half an hour later, Dr. Mengele returned to the hospital. He took a piece of perfumed soap out of his bag and, whistling gaily with a smile of deep satisfaction on his face, he began to wash his hands.

Dr. Josef Mengele fled from Auschwitz in 1945 as the Soviets advanced toward Berlin. He remained in Germany for four years but then traveled to Argentina in 1949 when he determined that Europe was no longer a safe refuge for him.

Mengele died in Brazil in 1979 in a drowning accident. He was never arrested or tried for his crimes.

18

The Nazi Doctors

(1933–1945)

I will use treatment to help the sick . . . but never with a view to injury and wrongdoing. . . . In whatsoever houses I enter . . . I will abstain from all intentional wrongdoing and harm. . . .
—from the Oath of Hippocrates

All the experiments were conducted without anaesthetics or the slightest attention to the victims' sufferings. Amongst the ordeals to which they were subjected were intense air pressure and intense cold until the "patient's" lungs burst or he froze to death; the infliction of gas gangrene wounds; injections with typhus and jaundice; experiments with bone grafting; and a large number of investigations of sterilization (for "racial hygiene"), including castration and abortion. According to a Czech doctor who was a prisoner at Dachau and who personally performed some seven thousand autopsies, the usual results of such experiments were death, permanent crippling, and mental derangement.
—from Hitler: A Study in Tyranny (1962) by Alan Bullock

Individual Nazis are ranked elsewhere in this book, but the Nazi Doctors, as a group, are treated as a single entity, because these physicians, *as a group,* perpetrated horrors and torment on their "patients," as they not only performed abominable (and often fatal) experiments on them, but also used their medical training to carefully conceive and systematize the methods of mass extermination necessary to effectuate the Holocaust.

Who were the Nazi Doctors?

Auschwitz survivor Herman Langbein, quoted from Robert Jay Lifton's book, *The Nazi Doctors* (1986), described the three types of Nazi doctors:

1. "[Z]ealots who participated eagerly in the extermination process and even did 'extra work' on behalf of killing";
2. "[T]hose who went about the process more or less methodically and did no more and no less than they felt they had to do";
3. "[T]hose who participated in the extermination process only reluctantly."

The Nazi doctors were completely lacking in empathy. A lack of empathy is one of the defining features of the psychopathic personality. Does this mean that all the Nazi doctors were psychopaths? If we use the definition of psychopathic that employs complete amorality in decision making and actions, then the answer is, "Yes."

Roy Baumeister, writing in his 1999 book, *Evil: Inside Human Violence and Cruelty,* notes that "It appears that most people develop a capacity for empathy, and this capacity does deter cruelty."

Why didn't the Nazi Doctors feel guilt over their deeds? Lifton explains the actions of the Auschwitz physicians as a function of the psychological process he terms "doubling." His research into the psyches and actions of these men led him to the conclusion that a "division of the self" took place in which the Auschwitz doctors could perform their unspeakably cruel and, yes, evil acts, fully cognizant of what they were doing to innocent people, and yet still maintain a sense of self, a separate identity that did not have to deal with the consequences of their actions.

According to Lifton, every case of Nazi doubling was distinguished by five characteristics. First, the doctor had to create an identity that could function psychologically in the death camp environment, a world that was at total odds with their previous medical existence; second, the doctor's Auschwitz identity had to learn how to operate seamlessly within a complete and fully functioning system (that of the death camp and the medical labs); third, there was a strong survival component involved in the creation of a doubled identity—the doctors felt strongly that they were in a "kill or be killed" situation; fourth, in order to avoid the inevitable guilt and feelings of remorse from their actions, they could assign this burden to their "other" self; and fifth, the

Nazi doctors all felt a strong sense of transcendence, a feeling of operating outside themselves, distant from their usual range of perceptions. (Hitler's personal architect and minister of armaments, Albert Speer, reported experiencing this feeling of transcendence and a sense of being connected to a higher spiritual plane the first time he heard the Führer speak publicly.)

The actions of the Nazi Doctors were Kafkaesque in their surreal, clinical brutality. Euthanasia—medicalized killing—was a primary concern, as was the forced sterilization of Jews. Caustic chemicals were injected into the cervixes of female prisoners over a period of weeks to form adhesions that would block the fallopian tubes and prevent fertilization. Male prisoners were blasted with massive doses of radiation for X-ray castration (the genitals would agonizingly rot away), or they had to endure surgical removal of the testicles with little or no anesthesia.

Josef Mengele (see page 55), the personification of the "medical Auschwitz," was responsible for some of the most brutal experimentation in the camp, with a special interest in twins. Other names of Nazi doctors echo through history:

- Eduard Wirths, who ultimately committed suicide over his role as the doctor who designed the selection process and supervised the killing of four million prisoners.
- Johannes Goebel, who was responsible for sterilizing thousands of woman by direct injection into their wombs of the aforementioned caustic chemicals.
- Carl Clauberg, who conducted bizarre experiments in artificial insemination.
- Horst Schumann, who performed castrations and hysterectomies on conscious, unanesthetized prisoners.
- Karl Brandt, who developed efficient methods of mass euthanasia.
- Werner Heyde, who advised the Gestapo on torture methods.

And there are many, many more. What they all have in common is a total commitment to the Final Solution, and their willingness to pervert and debase their medical training in the service of cruelty, torture, and death.

19

Erzsebet Báthory

(1560–1614)

"More! More still! HARDER STILL!"
  —Countess Elizabeth Báthory, goading her servants to
  escalate their torture of her female victims

Erzsebet Báthory, also known as Elizabeth, gave new meaning, or should we say, *expanded* meaning, to the word "bloodbath."

The word's classic definition of a savage, indiscriminate massacre applies to Elizabeth, since she would regularly order dozens of young girls (usually virgins) tortured and killed.

The word's expanded meaning comes from what she would then do with these slaughtered innocents: she would have their bodies drained of blood, and when she had enough to immerse herself in, she would take long, luxurious baths in the blood, believing that this gave her renewed youth and made her skin glow with health.

Elizabeth's belief in the rejuvenating powers of female blood came after an incident in which she was having her hair combed by a servant girl and the girl accidentally pulled Elizabeth's hair too hard and caused her pain. Elizabeth struck the girl in the nose with such force that the girl's nose began spouting blood, some of which splashed onto Elizabeth's face and arm. When

Elizabeth wiped off the blood, she suddenly believed that she saw smoother, more radiant, *younger* skin. She, of course, did not, but her delusional belief that the blood had made her skin look younger was the impetus for her to begin bathing in the blood of virgins. Some historians claim that the "servant's nosebleed" story was embellished to come up with the story of Elizabeth bathing in blood, but if it is true that she found rejuvenative powers in a simple *splash* of blood, one could easily believe that she would wonder what a lot would do.

It wasn't bad enough that Elizabeth began rounding up young virgins from the surrounding towns, often on the pretext of offering them a servant's job, and then torturing and killing them for their blood; sometimes she would imprison girls and have them fed constantly, believing that the fatter the girl, the more blood she would eventually be able to harvest.

The truly evil nature of Báthory's personality manifested itself in what she would do to these poor girls *before* she killed them and drained their blood for her Satanic rituals and cosmetic uses. Elizabeth had an underground room outfitted in the depths of her castle that became known as "Her Ladyship's Torture Chamber." She would bring her servant girls and village girls there regularly, ostensibly to train them or punish them for making a mistake while carrying out a task or forgetting to complete a chore, but in reality, it would be to cruelly torture them for her own pleasure before killing and exsanguinating them.

Elizabeth was especially inventive when it came to concocting ways of inflicting torment on her victims. She greatly enjoyed sticking needles through the nipples and lips of her captives. She also delighted in ramming pins under the girls' fingernails and toenails and laughing as they screamed in agony. Slow tortures were her specialty. Records show that she would sometimes have a girl stripped naked, smeared with honey, and then tied up and left in the woods where animals and insects would devour her alive. Sometimes she would have a naked girl placed in a steel cage that would be suspended from the ceiling. Inside the cage were protruding razor-sharp spikes surrounding the victim and Elizabeth would have her lackeys poke the girl from beneath with red-hot irons and swords. As the trapped girl tried to evade the stabbings she would cut and sometimes impale herself on the "teeth" of the cage.

Once Elizabeth bit off a huge chunk of a girl's flesh, then made the virgin cook the piece of her own body and eat it.

Elizabeth would carry out anything her twisted mind could conjure up.

She would insert lighted candles up young girls' vaginas and she would use branding irons and sharpened pincers to burn and shred the doomed girls' bodies. She delighted in anything that would degrade a female, especially a young, virginal female. She also greatly enjoyed using her mouth to bite off parts of their bodies, and then drink the flowing blood. She was often seen with blood smeared all over her face and mouth.

Elizabeth was served well by a coterie of demons, including witches, a dwarf, and her nurses.

Elizabeth Báthory was not called the "Blood Countess of Transylvania" for nothing. In fact, many historians believe that Countess Elizabeth Báthory's deeds may have been additional inspiration (along, of course, with the history of Vlad III Dracula, the Impaler—see page 31) for Bram Stoker's literary Count Dracula.

Elizabeth came from a royal Hungarian family whose crest was the Order of the Dragon, as was Vlad III Dracula's. There was also a great amount of inbreeding in Elizabeth's family and many believe this contributed to her deviltry.

Elizabeth was stunningly beautiful. She had long, shiny black hair, alabaster skin, soft brown eyes, and a voluptuous and sensuous body. She was also a lesbian with a taste for the perverted aspects of sadomasochistic sex, taught to her by her favorite aunts, who were also lesbians and sadists. Elizabeth was married by contract at the age of fifteen, but her husband kept a low profile and tried to stay away from the castle as much as possible. With the count gone, the fiendish Elizabeth was able to indulge her worst impulses and sadistic tendencies.

Elizabeth was caught in the middle of a bloody orgy of sex and torture in 1610 by a neighboring count who was given the task of investigating the disappearances of so many nubile young ladies from the area.

Elizabeth's accomplices (many of whom participated in the horrors because they would be subjected to the same treatment if they disobeyed her) were found guilty, tortured mercilessly in front of the townsfolk, and executed by beheading. Two of her confederates, the witches Ilona Joo and Dorotta Szentes, suffered extremely terrible fates: their fingers were pulled off one by one and they were burned alive.

Elizabeth was sentenced to life in prison and died in her cell from unknown causes in 1614 at the age of fifty-four. It is estimated that she was responsible for the torture deaths of more than 650 young women.

20

Nero

(A.D. 37–68)

Qualis artiflex pereo!
What an artist dies with me!

> —Emperor Nero, from
> Suetonius, *Life of Nero*

Nero, born Lucius Domitius Ahenobarbus in A.D. 37, was a sadistically cruel and perverse emperor who ruled Rome from 54 until his death in 68.

The Roman historian Tacitus, writing in *Annals XV*, recounted how the Emperor Nero scapegoated the "Chrestiani" for the fire of Rome and described the extent to which he persecuted and savaged them:

> Neither human resources nor the emperor's generosity nor the appeasement of the gods sufficed to quell the suspicion that the fire had been instigated by Nero. To suppress this rumor he fabricated scapegoats and punished with the most refined tortures those who were popularly called "Chrestiani," who were hated for their crimes. The originator of this name was Christus who had been executed in the principate of Tiberius by the procurator Pontius

Pilate. Although suppressed by this for a while, the pernicious superstition broke out again not only in Judea, where the evil had
begun, but also in the city, where all disgraceful and shameful
practices from all over the world collect and flourish. First, those
who confessed [that they were Chrestiani] were arrested, and on
their information large numbers were convicted not so much for
incendiarism as for their hatred of the human race. Their deaths
were made objects of amusement; dressed in the skins of wild animals they were torn to pieces by dogs, or crucified or burned alive,
being used as torches when daylight ended. Nero provided his gar-
dens for the spectacle and exhibited displays in the Circus mixing
with the people dressed as a charioteer or standing on a chariot. As
a result, the victims were pitied although guilty and deserving the
harshest penalties, on the ground that they were being destroyed
to gratify the cruelty of one man rather than for the public good.

Legend has it that Nero knew and understood quite well the nature of
the Romans he ruled: they had a powerful bloodlust and he feared greatly the
possibility that he would be blamed for the fire of Rome and be set upon by
angry mobs of homeless and starving citizens. (He did, after all, play a lyre as
the city burned—fiddles and violins had not been invented in the first century.)

The Christians were the perfect answer to his problem. In the first century A.D., Christianity was still viewed with suspicion, and pagans viewed the
ritualistic consumption of what the Christians called the "body" and "blood"
of Christ as cannibalism.

The Romans also believed that Christians were abducting and killing babies to provide the body and blood used in their ritual masses. Thus, Nero decreed that the Christians had set the fire that had burned for six straight days,
and the brutal persecutions began.

Nero was savage and depraved in the tortures and abominations he ordered committed against Christians.

The emperor's beloved chariot races took place at night. Hundreds of
torches lit the road to Rome and the amphitheater where the races were run.
After deciding to launch a full-scale assault against the Christians, Nero came
up with an ingenious idea that saved wood used for the torches and also eliminated thousands of Christians.

Nero decided to use human torches to light the chariot races. Nero ordered hundreds of Christians to be rounded up, stripped naked, rolled in tar,
agonizingly impaled, and then lit on fire to illuminate the night. Impaling is
one of the most painful methods of execution known to humankind.

Nero also decreed that Christian children and the Christian elderly
were to be thrown into the center of the Colosseum to be torn to pieces by
animals during public spectacles.

Nero also ordered countless public crucifixions and other unspeakable tortures and deaths. He would sometimes line the road to Rome with his crucified victims.

Moreover, the heartless and sadistic emperor did it all with a complacency and an amoral arrogance that warrants—it actually demands—his ranking in *The Evil 100*.

After the fire of Rome, Nero had a spectacular palace built for his own pleasure and enjoyment, remarking that he could now finally begin to live like a human being.

Nero's savage persecution of the Christians was just the culmination of a life committed to heinous deeds. When Nero was twenty-one, he had his mother, Agrippina, murdered. Sometime after his mother's body was cremated, he then kicked to death his pregnant wife, Poppae Sabina, because she angered him. Legend also tells us that Nero ordered the executions of Christ's apostles Peter and Paul.

Nero was believed by Christians to be the Antichrist, such was his abominable legacy of persecution, torture, and murder. In addition, Nero's campaign of persecution continued even after his death: whenever there was a natural disaster or some kind of calamity, the Christians were blamed and again, tortured and executed. This continued until the Edict of Milan in 313, which granted official sanction to Christianity and put an end to the persecutions. For Nero's many victims, it was much too late.

21

Benito Mussolini

(1893–1945)[1]

*Here lies one of the most intelligent animals who ever appeared
on the face of the earth.*

—Mussolini's self-written epitaph

In an article in the June 25, 2001, edition of London's *The Guardian* titled "Italy's Bloody Secret," journalist Rory Carroll stated: "Benito Mussolini's invading soldiers murdered many thousands of civilians, bombed the Red Cross, dropped poison gas, starved infants in concentration camps, and tried to annihilate cultures deemed inferior." Carroll then goes on to quote James Walston, a historian at the American University of Rome, who said: "There has been little or no coming to terms with Fascist crimes [under Mussolini] comparable to the French concern with Vichy or even the Japanese recognition of its wartime and prewar responsibilities."

Mussolini is ranked in *The Evil 100* because of atrocities committed

[1] Some of the material about Mussolini is based on previously published material that appears in the book *The Italian 100* (1997) by Stephen J. Spignesi, also published by Kensington Books.

under his orders, because of his alliance—the Axis—with Adolf Hitler, and for eagerly embracing in 1938 Nazi Germany's heinous racial policies and his subsequent brutal persecution of Italian Jews.

Benito "Il Duce" (the Leader) Mussolini was born on July 29, 1893, in Predappio, Italy. He was a rowdy and unmanageable child and a troublesome student, and was expelled from a religious boarding school for stabbing a classmate in the buttocks with a pocketknife. In his teens and twenties Mussolini wrote for and edited Socialist newspapers, including *The Class Struggle* and *Avanti!* Gradually he developed the ideology of Fascism, which preaches extreme nationalism and suppresses individual freedoms in the name of a national unity that is often based on concepts of racial superiority. Unlike Communism, however, Fascism does not demand state ownership of the means of production, nor is Fascism committed to the achievement of economic equality.

During World War I, Mussolini edited the paper *Il Popolo D'Italia (The People of Italy)* and, even though the paper initially proclaimed itself Socialist in ideology, it wasn't long before Mussolini began calling for Italy's involvement in World War I on the side of the allies, shrewdly utilizing the country's growing nationalistic fervor through inflammatory exhortations to working-class Italians. Mussolini himself ultimately served in the army until he was wounded in 1917, a year before the war's end. Historian Dennis Mack Smith in his 1982 book, *Mussolini,* notes that, "for anyone prepared to read or listen, Mussolini made it obvious that he was becoming a nationalist with great ambitions for his country," and observes that Mussolini's ultimate goal was to "raise the flag of imperialism throughout the Mediterranean and make Rome once again the centre of European civilization."

After the war, Mussolini began to organize his followers into the black-shirted *Fasci di combate,* who took violent action against opponents such as Socialists and Communists. The Fascists marched on Rome on October 28, 1922, and this bold move was the catalyst for Mussolini's ascent to power.

Mussolini's reign as dictator of Italy began on Friday, October 31, 1922, when, at the age of thirty-nine, he was installed as the youngest prime minister in Italy's history. Italy's King Victor Emmanuel III, bowing to Mussolini's threats to take over the government by violence if necessary, surrendered authority to the young Fascist, and within a year, Mussolini had complete dominion over Italy and the Italian people. In 1928, Mussolini said, "The eighteenth and nineteenth centuries experimented with democracy. The twentieth century will be the century of Fascism." He also proclaimed that "Democracy is beautiful in theory; in practice it is a fallacy."

Much to Mussolini's delight, he was embraced by the Italian people as a savior. Il Duce was a consummate showman who, by using a highly theatrical blend of inflammatory oratory and rhetoric, was able to get things done. Roads were paved, labor strikes stopped, bridges and public buildings were built, and, most memorably, the trains ran on time. Mussolini is reported to have told a train station master, "We must leave exactly on time. . . . From now on everything must function to perfection." In 1929, Infanta Eulalia of Spain, writing in *Courts and Countries after the War,* noted, "The first benefit of Benito Mussolini's direction in Italy begins to be felt when one crosses the Italian Frontier and hears 'il treno arriva all'orario' ['the train is arriving on time']." Historian Valerio Lintner correctly notes, however, that "Fascism may have 'made the trains run on time', . . . but it also turned Italy into a vulgar, corrupt, cynical, and conformist society, in which fear and intellectual poverty dominated."

Mussolini's administrative brilliance was, in essence, a sham. Luigi Barzini, who knew the fiery dictator and once described him as "the master of make-believe" noted that "Behind the scenery of modernization and industrial investments, millions of Italians still lived a life of prehistoric squalor, and most of the fundamental problems of the country had been left practically untouched."

In October 1935, Mussolini made a huge miscalculation, one that stemmed from his megalomaniacal delusions of an Italian "empire" and his eagerness to believe the exaggeratedly flattering things the Italians and others in the world were saying about him and his purported accomplishments. With the advice and encouragement of his one European supporter, Adolf Hitler, Mussolini invaded the African country of Abyssinia (now known as Ethiopia) and seven months later, on May, 9, 1936, announced to a throng of 400,000 supporters that Italy had successfully begun the building of its empire.

The world was outraged by this blatant expansionism. The League of Nations imposed economic sanctions on Mussolini, but since the League did not restrict Abyssinian oil exports, the Italian occupation held fast. That same year, Mussolini and Hitler formed an alliance known as the Axis, with Italy playing a secondary role to Germany and its massive, well-organized military machine. (Japan joined the Axis in 1940.) In 1938, Mussolini embraced Nazi Germany's reprehensible racial policies and began the persecution of Italian Jews.

In April 1939, Mussolini misguidedly invaded Albania, forcing Germany to devote resources to the extrication of Italian forces, and on June 10, 1940, Italy officially entered World War II. Following the successful Allied landings in Sicily in 1943, Mussolini was forced from power by his followers on July 25 and placed under arrest in Rome. In September, German forces rescued Mussolini, and Hitler installed him as head of a puppet regime, the Italian Social Republic, in northern Italy. Two years later, after the Germans had essentially abandoned him to anti-Fascist factions, Mussolini was captured trying to flee to Switzerland in a German uniform. On Saturday, April 28, 1945, Il Duce and his mistress were shot; their bodies were hung upside down from the roof of a Milan gas station with the bodies of other captured Fascists. In 1932, Mussolini had told a friend, "Everybody dies the death that corresponds to his character."

22

Heinrich Himmler

(1900–1945)

We came to the question: what to do with the women and children? I decided to find a clear solution here as well. I did not consider myself justified to exterminate the men—that is, to kill them or have them killed—and allow the avengers of our sons and grandsons in the form of their children to grow up. The difficult decision had to be taken to make this people disappear from the earth.

—Heinrich Himmler, October 1943

Heinrich Himmler, born a Roman Catholic in Munich in 1900, ultimately served as Reichsfuhrer-SS (Reich SS Leader), head of the Gestapo and the Waffen-SS, Minister of the Interior from 1943 to 1945, and facilitated the mass murder of Jews in Adolf Hitler's Third Reich.[1] Himmler committed sui-

---

[1] Reich means "empire" in German and was the name Hitler assigned to his government, believing that his regime was the successor to first, the Holy Roman Empire, and second, to the German Empire formed by Chancellor Otto von Bismarck in the nineteenth century after the Franco-Prussian War.

cide in 1945 by biting on a cyanide capsule after a failed escape attempt to avoid standing trial for war crimes at the Nuremberg Trials.

Heinrich Himmler was the second most powerful Nazi after Adolf Hitler and was the overseer of the system of concentration camps and execution programs designed to rid the world of all the "inferior" races so that the German people could triumph and thrive.

In a January 1937 speech, Himmler's perverted philosophy shone through with a poisonous, clinical logic. Himmler proclaimed that "there is no more living proof of hereditary and racial laws than in a concentration camp. You find there hydrocephalics, squinters, deformed individuals, semi-Jews: a considerable number of inferior people."

Himmler was convinced that people who had any kind of physical deformities—including those who had to squint due to nearsightedness—were racially inferior. This kind of twisted reasoning prompted Himmler to establish the *Lebensborn* ("Spring of Life") institute, which put into motion Hitler's and the Nazi Party's concept of racial eugenics in their attempt to breed a "master race."

Beautiful Nordic young women were "institutionalized" at *Lebensborn* and served as human breeders for German soldiers and officials. The resulting babies—believed to be superior genetically, physically, and intellectually—were cared for by the state. Its scientific window-dressing aside, *Lebensborn* was nothing but a human stud farm, with legions of German men having as much sex as they wanted to with unwilling but compliant women, all in the name of German nationalism.

Himmler succeeded in defining the mission of the German people as "the struggle for the extermination of any sub-humans, all over the world who are in league against Germany, which is the nucleus of the Nordic race; against Germany, nucleus of the German nation, against Germany the custodian of human culture: they mean the existence or non-existence of the white man; and we guide his destiny."

Himmler believed that the Third Reich's mission to achieve Jewish genocide was a noble act and was evidence of his government's "integrity" (his word).

The essence of the evil of Heinrich Himmler is that he succeeded in redefining mass murder as a heroic act that effectively eliminated the personal responsibility of the perpetrators, even for the most heinous of crimes. The word "conscienceless" has never been more appropriately assigned than to Himmler from the late 1930s on.

Himmler started out as the head of the three-hundred-member SS (which at the time served solely as Hitler's bodyguards), quickly enlarging its ranks to more than fifty thousand men. At the age of thirty-six, he was appointed chief of the German Police, a position which incorporated all the enforcement powers of the German government, including the secret police, known as the Gestapo.

When ordered to carry out Hitler's "Final Solution" plan, Himmler conceived the notion of using poison gas, a practice which resulted in the deaths of approximately six million Jews and as many as six million non-Jews before the end of the war (and Hitler's and Himmler's suicides) in 1945.

If Himmler had lived to stand trial at Nuremberg, his defense would likely have been: "I was only following orders." The most detestable element of that defense is that it is true. Himmler obeyed his Führer's orders, never questioning, and never wavering from total submission to the perverse mission of the Third Reich.

23

Saddam Hussein

(1937–)

We're dealing with Hitler revisited.
—President George H. Bush of
Saddam Hussein, October 15, 1990[1]

In October 2001, Dr. Khidhir Hamza, the former head of Saddam Hussein's nuclear weapons research program in the early 1990s, told journalist Geraldo Rivera that the October 2001 wave of anthrax attacks in the United States were the work of Saddam Hussein.

"This is Iraq," he told Rivera. "This is Iraq's work."

Dr. Hamza, who defected to the United States in 1994 also said, "Nobody [else] has the expertise outside the U.S. and outside the major powers who work on germ warfare. Nobody has the expertise and has any motive to attack the U.S. except Saddam to do this. This is Iraq. This is Saddam."

Hamza also said that Saddam had weaponized anthrax before the Gulf War and that he had a "secret doomsday strategy" of which the post–World Trade Center attacks' anthrax mailings were only the first wave.

---

[1] Bush later retracted this statement under criticism that it minimized the Holocaust.

In 1991, when the United States forced Saddam Hussein to retreat from Kuwait, marking the end of the Persian Gulf War, the retreating Iraqi Army, on Saddam's orders, set fire to 613 Kuwaiti oil wells. The fires released sixty million barrels of oil and formed 246 oil lakes in the Kuwaiti desert. The "elite" Red Guard (which was anything but) also destroyed oil wells, oil refineries, storage facilities, desalination plants, power plants, transportation and communications systems, water and power lines, as well as manufacturing facilities. In addition, they plundered data archives, destroyed scientific data, and stole computers and other valuable scientific equipment.

All on Saddam's orders.

Saddam has gassed his own people. The U.S. Department of State's Bureau of Near Eastern Affairs, in a January 2001 report, stated, "Saddam's gassing of the Kurds in northern Iraq in 1988 was one of the largest chemical weapon attacks ever waged against a civilian population. Even today, Saddam continues to practice systematic torture, executions, forced displacement, and repression against the Iraqi people. The United States is currently seeking an indictment of senior regime officials for these atrocities."

Amnesty International issued a report in 2000 in which they detailed what goes on in Iraq—again, under Saddam's orders:

> Torture victims in Iraq have been blindfolded, stripped of their clothes and suspended from their wrists for long hours. Electric shocks have been used on various parts of their bodies, including the genitals, ears, the tongue and fingers. Victims have described to Amnesty International how they have been beaten with canes, whips, hosepipe or metal rods and how they have been suspended for hours from either a rotating fan in the ceiling or from a horizontal pole often in contorted positions as electric shocks were applied repeatedly on their bodies. Some victims had been forced to watch others, including their own relatives or family members, being tortured in front of them.
>
> Other methods of physical torture described by former victims include the use of Falaqa (beating on the soles of the feet), extinguishing of cigarettes on various parts of the body, extraction of fingernails and toenails, and piercing of the hands with an electric drill. Some have been sexually abused and others have had objects, including broken bottles, forced into their anus. In addition to physical torture, detainees have been threatened with rape and subjected to mock execution. They have been placed in cells where they could hear the screams of others being tortured and have been deprived of sleep. Some have stayed in solitary confinement for long periods of time. Detainees have also been threatened with bringing in a female relative, especially the wife or the mother, and

raping her in front of the detainee. Some of these threats have been carried out.

In Iraq, insulting Saddam Hussein is punishable by death.

Hussein is a germophobe. He is obsessed with cleanliness, to the point where people have to shower in front of his security people before they are allowed to enter into his presence.

Saddam Hussein professes love for his family, but had his two sons-in-law and his brother-in-law killed.

Saddam Hussein lets his people starve, while he has three meals a day cooked in most of his palaces and houses, whether he is going to be there or not.

Saddam Hussein implemented barbaric judicial punishments in Iraq, including hand and foot amputations, branding foreheads, and cutting off of ears. He is now overseeing the building of the world's biggest mosque: its shape will follow the contours of his fingerprint.

Saddam Hussein tells the world that Iraq has a Constitution that guarantees the Iraqi people civil rights and liberties, due process, and a say in their government; in reality, there are no freedoms or civil liberties in Iraq. Freedom of speech, movement, the press, and what have you are strictly controlled by Saddam Hussein's government; all of which the Iraqi people cannot change.

Political dissidents (anti-Saddam troublemakers) or women accused of prostitution are beheaded in front of their families, and the decapitated heads are displayed on stakes in front of their homes for several days. Also, relatives of people involved in anti-Iraq activities abroad have been tortured in Iraq as pressure to get their relatives to stop their efforts.

Saddam Hussein allows Iraqi men to commit "honor crimes": Men can beat a female relative to the point of death if they determine (or suspect) that the woman has been immodest or has committed sexual misconduct.

Saddam Hussein was born in 1937 in a small village in Iraq. In 1955, at the age of eighteen, he moved to Baghdad and joined the Arab Baath Socialist Party. Four years later, he masterminded an assassination attempt of Iraqi Prime Minister Abd al-Karim Qasim. The attempt failed and Hussein fled to Egypt, where he studied at the Cairo School of Law. When the Baaths seized power in Iraq in 1963, he returned to his homeland and was given the position of assistant secretary general of the Baath party.

The Baath party was soon overthrown, but regained control in a coup in 1968. Saddam became vice chairman of the ruling Revolutionary Command Council in 1969. Ten years later, Saddam Hussein was president of Iraq, the title used because despots do not declare themselves dictator of a country.

During his time as leader of Iraq, Hussein waged a ten-year war with neighboring Iran and, after that conflict was declared a stalemate, he proclaimed that Kuwait was a territory of Iraq and invaded the small country in 1990. The United States made quick work of removing him from Kuwait, but he left behind all manner of devastation, including physical, environmental, and psychological.

It is a certainty that Saddam Hussein will continue to be an enemy of the United States, and many other countries, for as long as he holds office.

24

Idi Amin

(1925?–2003)

*Germany is the place where when Hitler was Prime Minister
and Supreme Commander, he burned over six million Jews.
This is because Hitler and all German people knew that Israelis
are not people who are working in the interest of the world and
that is why they burned the Israelis alive with gas in the soil of
Germany.*

> —from a September 12, 1972, telegram from Idi Amin
> sent to United Nations Secretary General Kurt Waldheim
> and Israel Premier Golda Meir

Thomas Melady, the former U.S. ambassador to Uganda, writing in his 1977 book *Idi Amin Dada,* called Amin the "new Hitler" and the "Hitler of Africa," and described Amin's regime as the Holocaust of Africa.

In his book, Melady spelled out the similarities between the Amin rule and the Nazi regime, specifically citing "cruel tortures, the killer squads, the anti-intellectualism, the reprisals, the aggressive war posture, and above all, racism."

In 1999, the people of Uganda celebrated the twentieth anniversary of Amin's overthrow by chanting "never again," the same phrase used by the

Jews when talking about the Holocaust. Idi Amin once said of Adolf Hitler, "Although some people felt Adolf Hitler was bad, he was a great man and a real conqueror whose name would never be forgotten." During his reign, Amin was known to tell a Jew, "I like you, you are my friend," and then have him killed.

At the time of this writing, Amin is still alive and living in exile in Saudi Arabia, safe from the justice Ugandans seek.

Great Britain ruled Uganda until October 1962 when the African country, with a population of about thirteen million, achieved independence. Dr. Milton Obote was the first prime minister of Uganda, and he became president in 1966.

On January 25, 1971, Idi Amin, a former British colonial army sergeant and heavyweight boxer, seized control of the country in an armed military coup, deposing Obote. This was the beginning of Amin's eight-year reign of terror.

Idi Amin the dictator was pure evil. He was sadistic and cruel, and one of his trademark tortures was to decree that certain people had to die. He had them brought before him, crying and pleading for mercy and for their lives and, as they begged, he would mock them. When Amin tired of this amusement, he sent them off to be killed.

Once, Amin ordered his troops to detain Francis Walugembe, the former mayor of Masaka, Uganda. The soldiers took Walugembe to the Tropic Inn restaurant in Masaka. After the soldiers had drinks, they brought Walugembe outside the hotel, stripped him naked, tied his wrists and ankles and, in full view of tourists and passersby, one soldier chopped off Walugembe's penis with a knife and held it up in front of Walugembe's face. As Walugembe screamed in agony, the soldiers threw the naked former mayor into the back of a truck and drove off. Walugembe was never seen again.

In 1976, Palestinian terrorists hijacked an Air France plane in Uganda. Amin publicly supported the hijacking and actually hugged the hijackers. All the passengers, mostly Jews, were herded into the Entebbe terminal and held under armed guards by Palestinians and Ugandans. Shortly thereafter, the Israeli army raided the Entebbe terminal. In ninety minutes, they freed the hostages; killed, photographed, and fingerprinted the hijackers; and destroyed some Russian planes. Amin was humiliated in the eyes of the world.

Journalists, Peace Corps volunteers, and even tourists were often arrested in Uganda for no reason and held in abominable conditions. Amin also had an active "extermination policy," which he implemented arbitrarily, resulting in many needless deaths.

It is believed that Amin was personally responsible for the deaths of at least 500,000 Ugandans during his eight-year reign.

Amin was also ignorant and shortsighted. As part of his hatred of Jews and Asians, Amin launched an "Economic War" against Asian émigrés in Uganda. This "war" was a complete disaster, because the Asian people in

Uganda made up the bulk of the skilled workers in the country. On their way out of the country, many Asian émigrés were searched and robbed by Amin's military guards. Women were forced to strip completely naked for the searches and many were raped. Men and women were beaten for no reason. Departing Asians often had to pay exorbitant exit visa fees and wait for great lengths of time in lines and holding rooms. After expelling the Asians in 1972, Amin had to hire people in order to keep the Ugandan economy alive, but it was too late; the country slumped deeper into poverty and abominable living conditions.

As Amin committed his crimes against humanity, the rest of the world essentially ignored what was going in Uganda. Former Ugandan ambassador Thomas Melady noted that "The evolution of an authoritarian dictatorship in Uganda into a cruel, bloodthirsty, and racist tyranny escaped the full evaluation of many in the diplomatic and foreign communities."

It is speculative to consider what Uganda might be like today if the Tanzanian army had not invaded the country in 1979 and overthrown Amin. At present, while things are better, it remains one of the poorest countries in Africa. Nevertheless, the Ugandan people are united in their efforts to make things better in the country, and also to ensure "never again."

Catherine de Médicis

(1519–1589)

*Kill them all, every one of them! Do not leave a single Huguenot
to reproach me!*

> —King Charles IX, ordering the Massacre of St. Bar-
> tholomew's Eve, after his mother Catherine con-
> vinced him of the Huguenots' treachery against him

Catherine de Médicis introduced broccoli, artichokes, and cabbage to
France. She also signed the Peace of Amboise that eventually ended the hostilities between Catholics and Huguenots.

These positive acts, however, cannot erase the legacy of the Massacre of
St. Bartholomew's Eve, for which Catherine was directly responsible. In
1572, Catherine convinced her weak-willed son, King Charles IX, that the
Huguenots (French Protestants) were plotting to rise against him and his
Roman Catholic monarchy and that he needed to annihilate them. Charles
agreed (albeit reluctantly). Beginning in the early morning hours of August
24, 1572, and lasting several days, at least ten thousand French Huguenots
were massacred on Charles's (really Catherine's) orders. Some historians put
the number at several times that.

The conflict between the Catholics and the Huguenots had already caused two wars and, yet, St. Bartholomew's Massacre cannot be described as anything but wholesale slaughter and looting, with terrible atrocities and utter chaos. Atrocities occur during wartime, but the kind of rioting, killing, and mindless rampaging that took place in Paris during the Massacre *against ordinary citizens*—including housewives, children, and servants—was pure madness.

Late on August 23, 1572, while Paris slept, Charles's followers—a death squad of twelve hundred—prepared the city for the nightmares to come. They locked the gates at the city's egress points; they chained boats to their piers; they painted crosses on the houses where Huguenots lived; they set up armed guards everywhere. At 2:00 A.M. on August 24, 1572, the bells in the church opposite the east end of the Louvre began to toll. This was the signal for the slaughtering to begin.

Charles's loyalists—who were, by this time, all extremely drunk—began breaking into marked homes and dragging everyone into the streets, beating them with clubs, stabbing them with swords, and hacking them into pieces. Many were thrown from windows and crushed to death on the street below. Charles's followers threw babies into the River Seine and shot at them from the banks. The river soon became a mass of floating corpses.

After several hours, the loyalists began robbing and killing people whether they were Huguenots or not. If a Parisian seemed to have many possessions, or there were other indicators of his wealth, he was deemed by the drunken mob to be a Huguenot, and slaughtered mercilessly and robbed.

Gaspard de Châtillon, Lord of Coligny (whose assassination had been planned by Catherine) was beheaded, dismembered, dragged through the streets of Paris, and hung for public display. Charles had been very close friends with Gaspard and it had devastated him when Catherine finally convinced him that the Huguenot captain was plotting against him (which was not true). Catherine had used half-truths and comments taken out of context to paint a picture of a Huguenot overthrow of Charles's throne, led by his friend. The senseless massacre of thousands were the result of Catherine's machinations.

Several hours into the massacre, piles of naked corpses were stacked to the skies outside the royal palace. Charles was aghast and ordered the killing to stop, but it continued for hours, much to the delight of his mother.

Catherine was completely conscienceless about the slaughter and later tried to pass it off as a clerical error. She claimed that she had only intended to have a half-dozen or so French Huguenots killed and that somehow her orders were misconstrued. It is said that Philip of Spain, who rarely (if ever) smiled, broke out in hysterical laughter when he read Catherine's official announcement in which she tried to pass off her ludicrous story as true.

Charles IX was tormented his entire life by his mother's duplicity and the devastation of the massacre. On his deathbed, his last words were "So much blood!"

26

Augusto Pinochet

(1915–)

The respondent to this appeal is alleged to have committed or to have been responsible for the commission of the most serious of crimes—genocide, murder on a large scale, torture, the taking of hostages.

—the opening statement of the British indictment of
Pinochet in November 1998

Defenders of General Augusto Pinochet, the sadistic despot who brutally tortured and killed thousands of Chileans during his 1973 to 1990 regime in that South American country, point to the positive accomplishments Pinochet achieved as dictator. He instituted free-market policies that greatly helped Chile's economy. He gave back land that the previous Socialist government had appropriated from citizens. And he succeeded in lowering Chile's inflation rate by an astonishing 65 percent. As President Harry Truman said in 1959, "Whenever you have an efficient government you have a dictatorship." But the problems that then arise were spelled out in 1937 when President Franklin Delano Roosevelt said, "The ultimate failures of dictatorship cost humanity far more than any temporary failures of democracy."

One of the most insidious manifestations of evil is the denial of human rights and civil liberties. Such abuses were unchecked during General Augusto Pinochet's reign. Add to that the physical abuse of torture, plus his policy of detention with no accountability, plus widespread government-sanctioned murders and out-of-control corruption, you end up with one of the most amoral and, yes, evil governments in world history.

Augusto Pinochet's military police employed horrific tortures on Chileans suspected of being involved in any anti-government activities. And "suspected" is the key word. In many cases, no evidence was needed for soldiers to rout someone out of their home, take them away, and torture them until they died.

In January 1974, the body of a seventeen-year-old resister was found dumped in a small town south of the capital city of Santiago. His stomach had been cut open and some of his internal organs had been removed—while the boy had been alive. Each of his legs were smashed and broken in several places; he was "tattooed" with countless cigarette burn marks covering his body; and his testicles had been sliced off, again, while he was alive. The Chilean coroner who examined the boy's body (and who worked for Pinochet) declared the boy's official cause of death as acute anemia, which suggests the boy might have lived had he been given an iron supplement.

Pinochet seized power in September 1973 by overthrowing Communist leader Salvatore Allende. His first act as leader was to disband the Chilean congress. Dictators do not need lawmakers. (The United States CIA helped fund Pinochet's overthrow of the Allende government. The specifics—amounts, activities, and so forth—are on the record. Hortensia Bussi, widow of overthrown President Salvador Allende, said, "The participation of the United States in the coup was decisive, and its cooperation with the military junta was very close.")

According to Amnesty International, Pinochet's nascent government tortured 180,000 people in his first year as dictator. Many Chileans were tortured to death and their bodies were disfigured beyond recognition—all done on Pinochet's orders and with his approval.

Favored tortures of the Chilean military police included raping women at will; electric cables clamped to eyelids, lips, tongues, and electrical shocks administered during pointless "interrogations"; burning with cigarettes; breaking bones; electrocution; immersion in water and sewage; blinding; forced intake of drugs; plus an array of horrendous beatings and cuttings. Torture victims were often beheaded after death to prevent identification. When headless corpses with their hands tied behind their backs were found in a river, the Chilean military police repeatedly told the people who saw them, "You saw nothing. If you say anything, we will arrest you and cut your throats, just like those corpses."

Throughout Pinochet's regime, no matter how many people were missing, the Pinochet government consistently denied any knowledge or participation in the disappearances.

Although Chile's long-term economic situation improved under Pinochet's dictatorship, the country experienced an economic crisis from 1980 to 1983. During this period, Pinochet gave his military and police unprecedented powers. They were allowed to occupy entire neighborhoods—detain, arrest, question, and torture people with no cause. Whatever meager civil rights still survived, were, for all purposes, abolished during this period. Pinochet issued a State of Emergency decree that gave him, and, by extension, his police force, the power to arrest with no cause, torture people during questioning, and "erase" Chileans from their homes and towns. Thousands were reported missing and later, presumed dead.

It was later learned that Pinochet apparently had plans to go beyond the traditional third-world torture and execution tactics. During his regime, and with his authority, Chile experimented with sarin, the deadly nerve gas, for use as a biological weapon.

When Augusto Pinochet was eighteen, he joined the Chilean National Military Academy and seemed initially to have had a strong sense of duty to country. In his youth, he wrote that a soldier must denounce life and material possessions, as the fatherland requires. This noble creed was perverted in 1973 when he seized power in Chile, the needs of the fatherland were superseded by his megalomaniacal hunger for power and the decimation of his enemies.

In 1998, Pinochet was arrested in Great Britain and charged with terrorism and murder when he visited that country for medical treatment. He was extradited to Chile and charged with multiple counts of murder and other crimes. In November 2000, Pinochet issued a statement stating that since he was in power at the time, he must accept some responsibility for what his military and police did during his regime, but fell short of accepting full blame for issuing the orders. Pinochet lives in Chile under house arrest; his court cases are pending.

The Taliban

(1994–2001)

The Taliban is the fundamentalist Islamic religious dictatorship that ruled Afghanistan from late 1994 through November 2001.

The Taliban was decimated by U.S. military forces after the World Trade Center terrorist attacks, but it still warrants its own special ranking here as an organization of evil.

The members of the Taliban claim to be religious students ("Taliban" means students of the Koran) and yet they are reportedly the world's biggest suppliers of the opium used to make heroin; they are pathological liars (which President Bush and Secretary of Defense Donald Rumsfeld remind the world regularly); they enthusiastically support terrorist organizations; they are responsible for abominable atrocities against the Afghan people; and they have relegated Afghan women to sub-human status.

In October 2001, the United Nations released a report detailing alleged Taliban atrocities, including rampant rape; mass executions; the skinning alive of a young boy; burning people alive; and beatings, whippings, and mutilations. Taliban soldiers also burned eight hundred shops, five hundred houses, a high school, a hospital, and a mosque.

On Thanksgiving Day 2001, the White House released its own list of Taliban atrocities, which included the torture and killing of children, and the burning of whole families alive.

Before the coup that gave power to the Taliban, women were a vibrant part of Afghan's society and economy. They were doctors, teachers, lawyers, and scientists. They worked, shopped, and lived lives very close to a Western ideal of a free and open society. After the Taliban took over, they imposed strict new laws restricting women's activities, and they claimed that they were fulfilling a mandate issued in the Koran (which is another blatant lie).

Women could not leave their homes without a male relative. Women could not work. Women could not receive an education. Women had to wear a *burka,* a long all-concealing garment, if they did go out in public. If their veil slipped or they accidentally showed an ankle or an arm, they were subject to being beaten with sticks by any male Afghan who witnessed their infraction. Women without male relatives to support them and their children were forced to beg. Women were not allowed to seek or receive medical care from male doctors, resulting in many women dying from simple conditions easily cured in a civilized society, since there were no women doctors in Afghanistan under the control of the Taliban. If a woman committed adultery and was caught, she could be executed with a rifle shot to the head in a public stadium. If a woman walked too fast, she could be beaten with bicycle chains.

In addition to their mistreatment of women, the Taliban also maintained a police force charged with enforcing Taliban rules and torturing people suspected of subversion or of violations against the Koran.

Hafiz Hassani, a defector from the Taliban now living in Pakistan, told western journalist Christina Lamb in a September 30, 2001 interview in the UK *Telegraph* of the horrors he inflicted on Afghans for three years while working as a soldier for the Taliban. He spoke of beatings that left people so pulpy and bloody that it could not be told if they were wearing clothes; of crucifying people alive; of conceiving horribly inventive tortures to win the favor and approval of the Taliban; of rubbing salt in wounds if people passed out from the pain. He was given a license to rape at will and was told that if he died in the service of the Taliban, he and his family would go to paradise.

One of the more interesting comments from Hassani was his mockery of U.S. demands to the Taliban to turn over Osama bin Laden. "The Americans are crazy," he told Lamb. "It is Osama bin Laden who can hand over Mullah Omar—not the other way round."

In early November 2001, a twenty-six-year-old Mujahidin man named Karimullah told western journalists the story of being tried in a Taliban military tribunal after being captured in a Pashtun village. First, he was tortured, then imprisoned. Three months after his capture, he was taken in a Datsun pickup to the notorious Ghazi stadium, once the site of soccer games, but commandeered for public executions by the Taliban. He was laid on the ground and injected with some type of general anesthetic that did not cause unconsciousness. Seven doctors then put surgical clamps on his right hand and left foot and amputated them with surgical saws.

Karimullah watched everything.

He was taken to a hospital, ultimately released, and relegated to being a beggar. He told the journalists, "I dream only of having my hand again so I could carry a gun and go to the front line and kill and kill. I'd kill them all, every Taleb and every mullah."

The Taliban is singled out here because of their denial of basic human rights; their mistreatment of men, women, and children; their culpability as drug dealers, their endorsement of terrorism—because they did it all, ostensibly, in the name of religion, but, in truth, for money, power, and conquest.

As the French philosopher Blaise Pascal noted, "Men never do evil so completely and cheerfully as when they do it from religious conviction."

28

Jim Jones

(1931–1978)

We're going to die in revolutionary suicide—with dignity and honor. . . . Everyone has to die. If you love me as much as I love you, we must all die or be destroyed from the outside.

—Jim Jones

I damned near thought I must have been talking to the devil . . .
—Jonestown survivor Odell Rhodes

Megalomania is defined as a psychopathological condition in which delusional fantasies of omnipotence predominate.

"Megalomaniacal" is a flawless appraisal of Jim Jones, a man arrogant and delusional enough to not only proclaim himself Christ incarnate, but also to demand that his followers die for him—and to take upon himself the "holy" task of killing them if they disobeyed.

On Reverend Jim Jones's orders, 913 members of his "People's Temple"—637 adults and 276 children—died in a mass suicide, or were murdered in cold blood, in Guyana on November 18, 1978. Resisters were shot or reportedly injected with cyanide. Mothers had to kill their children.

Jim Jones convinced his followers, through an insidious combination of charisma, brainwashing, and deprivation, that dying by suicide was a noble and dignified end and that the alternative was to fall into the hands of "the enemy." Jones's enemies included the U.S. government, other religions, civic groups who were against the People's Temple, and especially a group called the Concerned Relatives, which was an organized, proactive group of family members of People's Temple members who worked to get their loved ones back from Jones.

Leaving the People's Temple, however, was almost impossible. Part of the problems the Concerned Relatives faced was that many of Jones's followers were afraid to leave because they would then be treated as traitors and hated by their friends and family who remained with the church. Adding to the problem was that they would be impoverished, because they had surrendered all their assets to Jones and the church as part of the requirement for joining.

Jerrold Post, a psychiatrist and expert on religious cults, in an interview with Al Hinman for CNN.com explained the type of person who typically gets involved in a cult and who will commit suicide at the prompting of the leader:

> It is often alienated youth who have found their way to these groups and subordinate their own psychology to the messianic, charismatic attraction of a very powerful leader. For many of the cults who have participated in group suicides, it isn't suicide in the traditional sense of coming out of despair and ending a miserable existence. Rather, it is passing to a higher state of being, of making a transition.

Jim Jones started preaching when he was sixteen and initially he believed in the brotherhood of man. Even at an early age, Jones saw himself as a leader and would react violently if anyone contradicted him. He saw this as "betrayal"; even at an early age he had a God complex and a twisted ego. Revealingly, in his teenage years, Jones was especially interested in the lives of Adolf Hitler and Joseph Stalin.

Jones would recruit followers by claiming to be able to cure cancer, make the blind see, and predict the future. Jones also performed magic surgery on acolytes. He would use only his hands and no incisions would be visible. He would pull tumors from people's bodies using only the power of God, and then assure the desperate and gullible "patients" that they were cured. The tumors were usually one-week-old rotting chicken giblets that were secreted in his hand or in a basin filled with blood, a common ruse still practiced today.

The People's Temple was officially founded by Jones in 1963 when he was thirty-two, but he had been using the name "People's Temple" since the mid-1950s. Jones taught that the highest level of commitment to the ideals of the church was to live at the People's Temple and hand over all personal property, savings, and Social Security checks to Jones.

Jones believed that Communism could be fought by communalism (which is nothing but the ideology of communism applied to a church instead of a central government), and he repeatedly cited biblical passages to defend his idea that people should give everything they had to his church.

Jones exercised total control over his congregation. Husbands and wives were encouraged to report each other for infractions against Jones's rules; parents were encouraged (although it was more a command than a suggestion) to beat their children. Couples had to reveal their spouse's sexual fantasies and habits before the entire congregation.

Similar to the worst punishments and indoctrinations prisoners of war had to endure, People's Temple members who violated the rules were placed in "The Box," a 6-by-4-foot enclosure, and left in the sweltering sun. In addition, recalcitrant children were awakened in the middle of the night, dragged off, then dangled upside down inside a well in the pitch dark as punishment. Loudspeakers blasted Jones's voice throughout the camp around the clock. In a classic example of religious hypocrisy, Jones claimed that all the rules and punishments and brutality were mandated by Scripture and they would help everyone in the church achieve a higher spirituality.

In 1974, Jones began building his Jonestown compound in Guyana. He saw it as a sanctuary away from not only the secular evils of modern America, but also away from the spying eyes of the government, other churches, and, perhaps most important, the family members of his church's members.

Life at Jonestown consisted of the harsh restrictions and mind control Jones exercised in America, compounded by the isolation of the Guyana jungle and the members' total dependence on Jones and his staff for every need.

Jones had to have ultimate control of everyone and everything, and death was the penalty for those who defied him.

In 1978, Jim Jones said of Jonestown: "It's the only U.S. communist society alive, and we sure as hell don't want to let that down."

In response to desperate pleas from the families of Jones's followers, U.S. Representative Leo Ryan visited Jonestown on November 17, 1978. Ryan and his group were ambushed the following day when they tried to leave. Ryan and four others were killed. Jones then ordered the mass suicide of everyone remaining in the compound. A few people managed to escape, one of whom was Deborah Layton, Jones's financial adviser. She later reported that Jones's congregation regularly rehearsed mass suicide drills.

The majority of the dead drank a cyanide-laced fruit punch. Jones's guards shot and killed people who refused. Jones was one of the last to die.

29

Hideki Tojo

(1884–1948)

We have our own ideology concerning prisoners of war which
should naturally make their treatment more or less different
from that in Europe and America.
                    —Hideki Tojo, blatantly dissembling

When the military police came to arrest Hideki Tojo for war crimes and crimes against humanity, he asked them to wait a moment; then he shot himself in the chest in a failed suicide attempt. Perhaps the gravity of the consequences he faced for being responsible for four million deaths between 1937 and 1945 took away all of Tojo's hope and made him look to death as the easier alternative.

Winston Churchill described the Japanese troops under Tojo as "barbarous" and it is now known that Tojo permitted, as well as encouraged, terrible atrocities against prisoners of war captured by the Japanese.

Tojo was a Japanese army officer and politician who ruled as dictator of Japan (1941–1944) during World War II. He ordered, sanctioned, and encouraged a range of abominations including sadistic killings, live vivisection, torture, rape, and cannibalism.

After the entry of the United States into World War II, U.S. and Philippine troops fought ultimately futile battles to defend the Bataan Peninsula, which is situated between Manila Bay and the South China Sea. They surrendered because of a loss of air power after Japanese air raids destroyed more than half of the U.S. planes, followed by dire shortages of food, ammunition, and medicine.

General MacArthur fled to Australia, where he subsequently gave his famous "I will return" speech. (MacArthur was obeying the orders of his Commander-in-Chief, President Franklin Delano Roosevelt, when he left the peninsula.)

All these factors combined to force U.S. and supporting troops to surrender to the Japanese.

The Bataan Death March was a walking horror show. After surrendering, seventy-five thousand U.S., Philippine, Australian, and British troops were marched to Japanese prisoner of war camps. The walked as much as seventy-five miles a day in stifling heat, with little food or water, and the Japanese soldiers brutally beat them to keep them walking. Many were sick or wounded and if a soldier fell to the ground in pain or from exhaustion, he was executed on the spot. Military experts estimate that close to one thousand soldiers of all four nationalities died each day, with close to ten thousand men dead by the time they reached the camps.

Although Tojo did not directly order the March, he had full knowledge of it, and he did not step in to prevent the mistreatment of the soldiers, or do anything to improve the conditions of the marching POWs. His rationale? He insisted that Japanese commanders were "their own bosses," so to speak, and it was not his place to step in and countermand any of his subordinates' commands.

Tojo's argument that field commanders were on their own was contradicted by his own words when in May 1942, while discussing prisoners of war, he said: "The present condition of affairs in this country does not permit anyone to lie idle, doing nothing, but eating freely. . . . In dealing with prisoners, I hope you will see that they are usefully employed."

His commanders interpreted this to mean "no work, no food," so if prisoners were sick or wounded and could not work, they were not fed.

In addition to the Bataan atrocities, that same year Tojo sanctioned the use of forty-six thousand Allied prisoners of war as slave labor to build a 250-mile railroad from Thailand to Burma. The men were fed sparingly, beaten, and housed in wretched, concentration camp–type quarters. More than fifteen thousand men died while building what became known as the "Railroad of Death."

Unbelievably, Tojo never thought he or his country would ever have to answer for the atrocities committed during the war.

Following Japan's surrender, some horrifying statistics became known. The vast majority of American and British prisoners of war held by Germany and Italy survived their incarceration. The death toll of POWs in those countries was 4 percent. In Japan, the death rate for prisoners of war was 27 percent. Causes of death included disease, malnutrition, and execution.

In the late 1990s, Tojo's granddaughter published a memoir of her grandfather, which attempted to revise his historical image and paint him as a patriot. He was only acting in self-defense, she professed, and he was the victim, not the aggressor. This argument had previously been rejected by the War Tribunals trial that had convicted Tojo and sentenced him to death. Hideki Tojo was executed by hanging as a war criminal for his crimes.

Whether or not the Japanese people will accept Tojo's granddaughter's impassioned revisionism remains to be seen, but the facts of Tojo's evil crimes are part of the war record and can never be expunged.

30

Albert Fish
"THE BROOKLYN VAMPIRE"

(1870–1936)

And I will cause them to eat the flesh of their sons and the flesh of their daughters, and they shall eat every one the flesh of his friend in the siege and straitness, wherewith their enemies, and they that seek their lives, shall straiten them.
　　—Jeremiah 19:9, Albert Fish's favorite biblical passage

What a thrill that will be if I have to die in the electric chair! It will be the supreme thrill. The only one I haven't tried.
　　　　　　　　　　　　　　　　　—Albert Fish

Two of the most evil admissions of guilt ever offered are Albert Fish's non-chalant account to the police of how he killed, butchered, cooked, and ate four-year-old Billy Gaffney, and Fish's letter to the mother of a twelve-year-old girl he also cannibalized.

Albert Fish enjoyed sticking needles into his body, inserting them at the spot between his scrotum and rectum. He also stuck needles under his finger-nails, something he would do in front of his children. When Fish was executed by electrocution, they had to jolt him twice. The first time they hit the switch, the equipment short-circuited from all the steel pins still lodged inside his body.

Albert Fish was born in Washington, D.C., in 1870. He spent much of his childhood in an orphanage. To most people who knew him, the adult Fish was a quiet man who seemed to be a good Christian and a good father to his six children. Fish married when he was twenty-eight and adored his wife, but she left him when he was forty-seven. Fish then began carrying out some of the sickest and most perverted crimes in the annals of the criminal justice system.

In 1928, a teenage boy named Edward Budd ran a classified ad as part of a job-hunting effort. Albert Fish, fifty-eight, responded to the ad and told the boy and his family that he had a position for Edward on his farm on Long Island. Fish played—with Academy Award–caliber finesse—the role of a kindly, grandfatherly farmer needing help, and he immediately enchanted the boy. There was no job on the farm, of course, and before long, Fish had managed to kidnap Edward's little sister Grace. Following is a letter Fish wrote to the little girl's mother, detailing his crime. Before you read it, though, take heed: Fish's statement could be extremely disturbing for highly sensitive people, or for the easily queasy.

The spelling and grammatical errors have been retained.

My dear Mrs. Budd,

In 1894 a friend of mine shipped as a deck hand on the Steamer Tacoma, Capt. John Davis. They sailed from San Francisco for Hong Kong China. On arriving there he and two others went ashore and got drunk. When they returned the boat was gone.

At that time there was a famine in China. Meat of any kind was from $1 to 3 Dollars a pound. So great was the suffering among the very poor that all children under 12 were sold to the Butchers to be cut up and sold for food in order to keep others from starving. A boy or girl under 14 was not safe in the street. You could go to any shop and ask for steak—chops—or stew meat. Part of the naked body of a boy or girl would be brought out and just what you wanted cut from it. A boy or girls behind which is the sweetest part of the body and sold as veal cutlet brought the highest price.

John staid there so long he acquired a taste for human flesh. On his return to N.Y. he stole two boys one 7 and one 11. Took them to his home stripped them naked tied them in a closet. Then burned everything they had on. Several times every day and night he spanked them—tortured them—to make their meat good and tender.

First he killed the 11 yr old boy, because he had the fattest ass and of course the most meat on it. Every part of his body was cooked and eaten except the head—bones and guts. He was Roasted in the oven (all of his ass), boiled, broiled, fried, stewed. The little boy was next, went the same way. At that time, I was living at 409 E 100 St., near—right side. He told me so often how good Human flesh was I made up my mind to taste it.

On Sunday June the 3—1928 I called on you at 406 W 15 St. Brought you pot cheese—strawberries. We had lunch. Grace sat in my lap and kissed me. I made up my mind to eat her.

On the pretense of taking her to a party. You said Yes she could go. I took her to an empty house in Westchester I had already picked out. When we got there, I told her to remain outside. She picked wildflowers. I went upstairs and stripped all my clothes off. I knew if I did not I would get her blood on them.

When all was ready I went to the window and Called her. Then I hid in a closet until she was in the room. When she saw me all naked she began to cry and tried to run down stairs. I grabbed her and she said she would tell her mamma.

First I stripped her naked. How she did kick—bite and scratch. I choked her to death, then cut her in small pieces so I could take my meat to my rooms, Cook and eat it. How sweet and tender her little ass was roasted in the oven. It took me 9 days to eat her entire body. I did not fuck her tho I could of had I wished. She died a virgin.

Gracie Budd was not Fish's first child victim, however. A year earlier, he had kidnapped a four-year-old named Billy Gaffney. After he was caught, he told the police everything. The following is Albert Fish's mind-boggling, on-the-record confession of what he did to Billy Gaffney. Be warned: the following confession is as graphic as the letter Fish wrote to Mrs. Budd.

I brought him to the Riker Avenue dumps. There is a house that stands alone, not far from where I took him. . . . I took the boy there. Stripped him naked and tied his hands and feet and gagged him with a piece of dirty rag I picked out of the dump. Then I burned his clothes. Threw his shoes in the dump. Then I walked back and took the trolley to 59 St. at 2 A.M. and walked from there home.

Next day about 2 P.M., I took tools, a good heavy cat-of-nine tails. Home made. Short handle. Cut one of my belts in half, slit these halves in six strips about 8 inches long. I whipped his bare behind till the blood ran from his legs. I cut off his ears, nose, slit his mouth from ear to ear. Gouged out his eyes. He was dead then. I stuck the knife in his belly and held my mouth to his body and drank his blood.

I picked up four old potato sacks and gathered a pile of stones. Then I cut him up. I had a grip [suitcase] with me. I put his nose, ears and a few slices of his belly in the grip. Then I cut him through the middle of his body. Just below the belly button. Then through his legs about two inches below his behind. I put this in my grip with a lot of paper. I cut off the head, feet, arms, hands, and the legs below the knee. This I put in sacks weighed with stones, tied the ends and threw them into the pools of slimy water you will see all along the road going to North Beach.

I came home with my meat. I had the front of his body I liked best. His monkey and pee wees and a nice little fat behind to roast in the oven and eat. I made a stew out of his ears, nose, pieces of his face and belly. I put onions, carrots, turnips, celery, salt and pepper. It was good.

Then I split the cheeks of his behind open, cut off his monkey and pee wees and washed them first. I put strips of bacon on each cheek of his behind and put them in the oven. Then I picked four onions and when the meat had roasted about one-quarter hour, I poured about a pint of water over it for gravy and put in the onions. At frequent intervals I basted his behind with a wooden spoon. So the meat would be nice and juicy.

In about two hours, it was nice and brown, cooked through. I never ate any roast turkey that tasted half as good as his sweet fat little behind did. I ate every bit of the meat in about four days. His little monkey was a sweet as a nut, but his pee-wees I could not chew. Threw them in the toilet.

Albert Fish was suspected of raping and torturing more than one hundred children and of murdering (and worse) at least a dozen of them. Although his court-appointed attorney did his best to convince the jury that Fish was insane, he was convicted of the murder of Grace Budd and was electrocuted in 1936.

31

Pedro Lopez
"THE MONSTER OF THE ANDES"

(1951–)

I am the man of the century. No one will ever forget me.
> —Pedro Lopez, in a January 1999 interview with the
> *National Examiner*

Pedro Armando Lopez Monsalve, known as the "Monster of the Andes," raped and murdered at least fifty-seven children, and it is believed he was responsible for more than three hundred murders during his "career." He was a tri-country killer, diligently building up his horrific body count in Colombia, Peru, and Ecuador.

After interviewing and examining the killer, psychiatrists concluded that Lopez the Monster was created from a series of traumatic experiences that befell him when he was young (although some who have studied him and his deeds are not convinced that he would have turned out any different if what happened to him during his youth had never occurred).

When Lopez was eight years old and living in Ecuador (he was the seventh son of a Colombian prostitute who had thirteen sons and several daughters), he was caught sexually molesting one of his female siblings. His mother threw him out of the house and left him to fend for himself on the street. Lopez was immediately picked up by a pedophile who kidnapped him and repeatedly sodomized and abused him.

Lopez managed to escape from the child molester and spent the next decade wandering around Colombia and doing anything he could simply to survive. He was often raped, and he practiced both heterosexual and homosexual sex. At the age of eighteen, Lopez was arrested for stealing a car and sentenced to prison. The prison environment brought out the killer in Lopez: it all began when he was brutally gang-raped by four fellow inmates shortly after he arrived.

Lopez sought vengeance. He somehow fashioned a crude knife and, within two weeks, brutally stabbed to death three of his four assailants.

After Lopez was released from prison, he began his three-country rape and murder spree and, in 1999, from his jail cell in Ecuador, Lopez described his deadly "technique" to journalist Ron Laytner for the January 12, 1999 issue of the *National Examiner:*

> I went after my victims by walking among the markets, searching for a girl with a certain look on her face—a look of innocence and beauty. She would be a good girl, working with her mother. I followed them, sometimes for two or three days, waiting for when she was left alone. I would give her a trinket like a hand mirror, then take her to the edge of town where I would promise a trinket for her mother. I would take her to a secret hideaway where prepared graves waited. Sometimes there were bodies of earlier victims there. I cuddled them and then raped them at sunrise. At the first sign of light, I would get excited. I forced the girl into sex and put my hands around her throat. When the sun rose, I would strangle her. It was only good if I could see her eyes. It would have been wasted in the dark—I had to watch them by daylight. There is a divine moment when I have my hands around a young girl's throat. I look into her eyes and see a certain light, a spark, suddenly go out. . . . The moment of death is enthralling and exciting. Only those who actually kill know what I mean.

Lopez also described his delight in "partying" with his victims—after they were dead. He painted a picture that would not be out of place in the most macabre horror movie: three or four dead little girls, none older then ten, propped up in chairs around a table, guests at a tea party for the dead, with Pedro Lopez as the grinning guest of honor.

One time in Peru, Lopez was caught by a Peruvian tribe while attempting to abduct a nine-year-old native girl. The little girl was rescued and Pedro Lopez experienced firsthand the consequences of attacking peoples who knew nothing about written laws, but who knew a great deal about justice and vengeance.

As part of his punishment, Lopez was first horribly tortured. He probably was subjected to whipping, burning, and beating, but spared dismemberment, mutilation, and drawing and quartering, since the method of execution the Peruvian Indians decided on for Lopez was for him to be buried alive.

Lopez was saved by a good-hearted Christian missionary—an American—who convinced the Indians that God did not want them to hurt or kill Lopez. The Indians reluctantly agreed to let Lopez go and he was deported to Ecuador, where he picked up where he left off, abducting, raping, and murdering young girls.

In 1980, a flash flood uncovered some of the bodies Lopez had buried, and he was arrested. Once in custody, he did what many serial killers have done once they were caught: he confessed to many more murders than the police knew about, and he even took the authorities to more than fifty graves where he had buried some of his victims.

Lopez was ultimately convicted of murder in Ecuador and sentenced to life in prison.

The most prolific serial killer in world history, the man responsible for brutally raping and killing more people than anyone else, was fortunate enough to be caught, tried, and convicted in a country that did not have the death penalty.

32

Henri Desiré Landru
"THE REAL BLUEBEARD"

(1869–1922)

*Widower with two children, aged forty-three, with comfortable
income, affectionate, serious and moving in good society,
desires to meet widow with a view to matrimony.*

—one of Henri Landru's classified ads

A "bluebeard" is a man who marries and murders one wife after another. The word comes from the title character in the 1697 Charles Perrault short story "La Barbe Bleue." In the story, the main character is a wealthy, monstrously ugly man with a blue beard who marries seven women and indulges their every whim with his riches, but tells each of them not to open a certain door in the basement of his castle.

Bluebeard's eighth wife was likewise told that she could go anywhere in his castle and do anything she wished, but she was not to open the door to the basement room. As a test of her obedience, her husband gave her the key to the forbidden room when he went away on business.

The wife did not obey her husband and was horrified when she saw what was inside the room. There were the bloody corpses of his previous wives.

The floor was covered with clotted blood and his ex-wives were hanging on the walls.

She also knew that she was destined to meet the same fate as his earlier wives.

Her husband returned early from his business trip and asked for all his keys back. When he saw blood on the key to the forbidden room, he knew that she had opened the door and dropped the key in the blood in shock. He was enraged and proclaimed that she must die for her transgression.

She pleaded with him to allow her a few minutes to pray to prepare herself for death, hoping to delay her execution until help in the form of her two brothers arrived.

Her stalwart brothers did arrive on horseback just as the husband raised his cutlass to chop off his wife's head. One of the brothers was a dragoon[1] and one was a musketeer,[2] so they knew how to vanquish an enemy. Although he tried to flee, they slew Bluebeard with their swords and saved their sister's life.

The young wife inherited her husband's fortune and everyone shared in it and lived happily ever after.

Henri Desiré Landru was born in France in 1869. His father was an ironworker; his mother was a homemaker.

Young Henri went to a Catholic school, was ordained a sub-deacon, then went on to study mechanical engineering. He was drafted into the French military at eighteen; he was discharged at twenty-two with the rank of sergeant. That same year, Henri seduced his cousin, and she had his child. He did not marry his cousin, and two years later, when he was twenty-four, he married the quartermaster of his military regiment.

Landru was short, bald, and had a big bushy beard and wild, unkempt eyebrows. There was something about him, however, that women found irresistible. He had a charisma and a suave manner that instantly endeared him to lonely widows and seduced them into giving him whatever he desired, which was usually continual sex and all their money.

Henri Landru was amoral and conscienceless and regularly swindled widows out of their life savings before abandoning them. He was repeatedly caught, however, and served several terms in prison. In fact, he was such a repeat offender that his father committed suicide because of his anguish over his no-good son.

Landru might have faded into oblivion if he had simply stayed the course as a conniving swindler who was in and out of French jails in the nine-

---

[1] A dragoon is a heavily armed trooper in European armies of the seventeenth and eighteenth centuries.

[2] A musketeer is a soldier armed with a musket, often a member of the French royal household bodyguard in the seventeenth and eighteenth centuries.

teenth century. However, Landru made the history books as one of the worst serial murderers in French history. His death toll rivaled the fictional Bluebeard whose nickname he bore: He killed ten women and one teenage boy (one of the women's sons). He was convicted of all eleven murders and was executed in the guillotine.

Landru killed with absolutely no remorse, and for one of two reasons: for money, or to eliminate a nuisance mistress. (And sometimes he killed one woman for both reasons.)

Landru found his victims by running classified ads, and his ads would always be answered. He would get involved with the women, and sometimes even marry them. Then they would mysteriously disappear, leaving him with all their money and possessions. (Interestingly, a professional astrologer once cast Landru's horoscope and it reportedly showed death, violence, love and romance, cold efficiency, destructive energies, and heartlessness.)

Landru went so far as to install a stove in his home to burn the remains of his victims. He also kept a notebook in which he would record the profits he scored from each death.

Acting on inquiries and information from the family and friends of some of Landru's victims, the police investigated and ultimately arrested Landru. His "death notebook" was also found.

Landru's trial began in November 1921 and lasted almost a month. Landru was sarcastic and arrogant during the trial, believing that the fact that he had been declared sane was incontrovertible evidence of his innocence. He was also convinced that he could not be convicted without evidence of a body.

The jury took two hours to find him guilty of eleven counts of murder and sentence him to death.

Landru refused the final glass of brandy offered him before his execution, and he refused to make a statement. He never expressed remorse.

Before his execution, he gave some artwork to his attorneys. Allegedly, on the reverse of one of the drawings was a written confession, but it was not found for forty-six years. Rumor has it that the message read "I did it. I burned their bodies in my kitchen stove."

33

Herman Webster Mudgett
"H.H. HOLMES"
(1861–1896)

I committed this and other crimes for the pleasure of killing my fellow beings, to hear their cries for mercy.

—H.H. Holmes

I was born with the devil in me. I couldn't help the fact that I was a murderer, no more than a poet can help the inspiration to sing. And I was born with the Evil One standing as my sponsor beside the bed where I was ushered into the world. He has been with me ever since. . . . I have commenced to assume the form and features of the Evil One himself.

—H.H. Holmes

Herman Webster Mudgett was the first identified serial killer in the United States. He was related to American outlaw Jesse James, and he was committing his horrible crimes in America at the same time that Jack the Ripper was terrorizing London.

Mudgett's personal bearing and style was suave, sophisticated, intelligent, and persuasive, and he used his talents relentlessly to seduce hundreds of gullible young women into having sex with him whenever he wanted it, and then, signing over to him insurance policies, bank accounts, land deeds, and wills.

Mudgett, better known as his most famous alias, Dr. H.H. Holmes, is the kind of criminal that has been romanticized in popular culture over the years, specifically because of his charming ways. However, Mudgett's appealing traits were a facade that concealed the face and deeds of a truly evil American monster.

Herman Mudgett was born in 1861 in Gilmantown, New Hampshire. He had an abusive father who beat him on a regular basis and was disliked by the neighborhood children, who also beat him up on an equally regular basis.

Mudgett wanted to be a doctor from an early age (he enjoyed performing a variety of "surgeries" on living animals), and he attended the University of Michigan Medical School. Many sources state that Mudgett was kicked out of the school for "unusual activities," which included dragging a female corpse across campus one night; other sources (including the University of Michigan's student magazine *Michigan Today*) state that Mudgett graduated from the school's medical program.

After he left Michigan, he moved to Chicago to be a pharmacist and it wasn't long before he was involved in an array of phony business deals as Dr. H.H. Holmes. Across the street from the pharmacy where he worked was a vacant lot. This lot would be the site of what would come to be called "Holmes's Castle," a bizarre building with rooms for sex, for killing, for dismembering, and for body disposal.

Crime writer David Lohr, in an article titled "The Terminator," on the Holmes Castle:

> Most of the rooms had gas vents that could let off lethal or sleep-inducing gases; the vents could only be controlled from a closet in Holmes's bedroom. Many of the rooms were soundproof and could not be unlocked from inside. It was a three-story building with shops on the first floor and a bizarre labyrinth of windowless rooms, false floors, secret passages, trapdoors, a well-equipped surgery area as well as several instruments of torture, such as an "elasticity determinator," a contraption he claimed could stretch experimental subjects to twice their normal length. Those who viewed it said it appeared to be a medieval torture rack. A few rooms were lined with asbestos, and the place was filled with doors

that opened to brick walls, stairways to nowhere, an elevator without a shaft and a shaft without an elevator. There was an airtight and soundproof vault, human-sized greased chutes leading from the living quarters to the cellar. The bedrooms had peepholes and were equipped with asphyxiating gas pipes connected to a control panel in Dr. Holmes's closet.

The World's Fair was held in 1893 in Chicago and, for Holmes, the multitude of naive visitors to his town made for easy pickings for his macabre endeavors.

Holmes would lure women to his Castle, seduce them, and then while they were asleep gas them and drop them into a room with no doors. Once they awakened, he would pump lethal nerve gas into the room and watch and listen to their screams as they died, often masturbating to orgasm as he did. Then he would dissect them, saving the parts that especially "interested" him.

Holmes's murder career began when he killed a business partner in an insurance scam that went bad. Holmes made a deal with Ben Pitezel that Pitezel would "die," Holmes would produce a phony corpse, and they would split the $10,000 life insurance proceeds. Instead of using a disfigured stolen corpse, Holmes killed Pitezel and ran away with his wife and kids. When Pitezel's body was discovered, all trails led to Holmes and he was charged with murder.

Police decided to investigate the "Holmes Castle" and seasoned police veterans passed out when they discovered what was in the basement. Holmes had a huge acid vat filled with body parts, a furnace for on-the-spot cremations, tanks filled with human bones, and the remains of more than two hundred bodies.

Holmes was tried and convicted and his legacy is that of someone who loved killing and torturing and stealing and lying—a classic example of the utterly conscienceless personality that embraces pure evil.

Holmes was hanged on May 7, 1896. His final statement was used to deny his crimes. In fact, he was still talking when they opened the trap door and dropped him.

Holmes was afraid of grave robbers so he left instructions that his coffin be filled with cement, which was honored. But as his pallbearers were carrying the extremely heavy casket to the grave, they dropped it. It ended up falling upside down in the grave, and they left it that way. One writer noted that Holmes spent eternity facing hell instead of heaven, which is, considering Holmes's history, only fitting.

34

Donald Gaskins
"PEE WEE"

(1933–1991)

Not many men is privileged to live a life as free and pleasured as mine has been. Once you decide to kill—and I don't mean killing some piss-ant in a bar or two old farts in a hold-up—I'm talking about deciding to kill anybody you want, anytime you want, anywhere you want, any way you want—once you get to that point, you set yourself free to live the best kind of life there is. . . . By taking lives and making others afraid of me, I become God's equal. Through killing others, I become my own Master. . . . When they put me to death . . . I'll die peaceful because my name is going to live as long as men have memories . . . as long as they talk about good and evil. . . .

—Donald Gaskins, *Final Truth*

The definition of evil was ratcheted up a notch when Donald "Pee Wee" Gaskins was alive and committing his crimes. Gaskins's misdeeds were so horrible, and his lack of remorse so inhuman, his biographer Wilton Earle came close to a psychotic break after listening to Gaskins during the fifteen months of Death Row interviews he conducted for Gaskins's posthumously published autobiography, *Final Truth* (1992).

As Colin Wilson (who calls Gaskins the "worst Serial Killer of all time") astutely notes in the Introduction to *Final Truth*, "The kinds of things that the Marquis de Sade fantasized, Gaskins actually did."

Space does not allow even a brief summary of the 110 murders Gaskins claimed credit for, but two of his murders will serve as compelling illustrations of just what this five-foot-tall, uneducated degenerate was capable of.

Of all the terrible things Gaskins admitted to doing to children, teenage boys and girls, young mothers, and college hitchhikers in his autobiography, he was actually executed for the murder of a Death Row prisoner named Rudolph Tyner. Gaskins accomplished the impossible: he murdered someone being held in a Death Row maximum-security cell. He snuck a bomb in a radio into Tyner's cell and saved the state the execution expenses.

The first murder we will look at is, appropriately, Gaskins's first serial murder.

In September 1969, Gaskins picked up an eighteen- or nineteen-year-old hitchhiker in North Carolina. He knocked her unconscious with his fist, stripped her, tied her up, and when she came to, forced her to perform oral sex on him. He then straddled her chest and asked her, "Do you mind if I suck your tittie?" Terrified, she said, "Okay." He pinched her nipple, pulled it away from her chest as "hard and far as I could" and then sliced off her nipple along with an inch of her breast. He then put the nipple in her mouth, made her suck it, and forced her to swallow it. She immediately vomited and, enraged, Gaskins turned her over on her back, and stomped on her pelvis as hard as he could with his foot. He then flipped her over and raped her anally. As he thrust, he continually tightened a belt around her neck.

After his orgasm, he made her lick his penis clean. He then put her in the trunk of his car and told her that, if she kept quiet, he would let her live (a trick he said he learned from a book about the Nazi Death Camps). This poor young girl actually believed him and said, "Thank you." As promised, she kept quiet, locked in a trunk with a bleeding, gored breast and, most likely, a broken pelvis.

After driving for a time, Gaskins stopped for gas and to buy a length of clothesline rope. He then drove to a marshy area, then gagged her with her own panties.

In Gaskins's own words:

> I tied her knees together and looped the rope around her neck and
> drew her knees up to her chin. I made two more turns around her
> neck, tightened the rope, and knotted it. She was doubled over,
> trussed for butchering, her head and legs on one end, her cunt and
> ass on the other. Her eyes bulged. I slid the point of the knife a full
> inch into her ass. Her eyes got even wider—like she knew what
> was coming. Then, real slow, I pushed all eleven inches of

Toothpick blade [a knife] inside her, all the way up to the hilt, and I sliced upward as I pulled it out. Where she had had two little holes, now she had one big one. (1992)

He then wrapped the girl in a logging chain and pulley, dragged her to the water, draped her over a log, floated it out onto the water, and dumped her in. She was still alive when he put her in the water. He waited until the bubbles stopped.

Gaskins claims he was genuinely exhilarated by what he had done and, after, went out for a big steak.

This horrific murder, his first outside of prison, was abominable in its savagery. But, incredibly, Gaskins was capable of much worse. His rape and murder of a pregnant mother and her *two-year-old* daughter may be the worst thing he ever did.

Doreen Dempsey was a twenty-three-year-old acquaintance of Gaskins. She had a two-year-old daughter named Robin, and she was seven months' pregnant when Gaskins made a deal with her that he would let her stay in a trailer he owned and give her a little money now and then if she would sexually service him whenever he asked. Doreen agreed, but on the way to the trailer, Gaskins stopped the car and forced Doreen to perform oral sex on him while her daughter watched.

As Doreen was fellating him, Gaskins began undressing the little girl. When Doreen asked him what he was doing, he hit her in the head with a ball-peen hammer and knocked her out.

He then finished undressing the toddler, performed oral sex on her, and then slid her down on top of his penis. When she screamed, he gagged her with panties and duct tape. He then raped her vaginally and anally and choked her to death as he was climaxing. He told his biographer that it was the best orgasm he had ever experienced.

He then dragged the pregnant mother out of his car, dug a grave, put her in it, cut her throat, and filled in the grave. He buried the two-year-old beneath a tree.

Gaskins never told this story until he began writing *Final Truth*, and only did so then with the agreement that his words would not be published until after his execution. In prison, he would have been considered the lowest of the low if what he had done to a child was revealed.

Gaskins likewise withheld until after his death the fact that he had raped and killed his own fifteen-year-old niece. He said he delayed telling the story because he did not want to hurt his family while he was still alive. Gaskins was executed in 1991.

35

Timothy McVeigh

(1968–2001)

I am the master of my fate.
　　　　　　　　—from "Invictus," by William Ernest Henley

Timothy James McVeigh, thirty-three, was executed by lethal injection at 7:14 A.M. Central Daylight Time on Monday, June 11, 2001, at the Federal Penitentiary in Terra Haute, Indiana.

The U.S. government, in its first execution in thirty-eight years, carried out the sentence imposed on McVeigh for the April 19, 1995, bombing of the Alfred P. Murrah Federal Building in Oklahoma City, Oklahoma, which claimed 168 lives, including nineteen children. McVeigh was found guilty of a conspiracy to use a weapon of mass destruction (Count 1); the use of a weapon of mass destruction (Count 2); destruction by explosive (Count 3); and first-degree murder (counts 4–11).

McVeigh made eye contact with the media witnesses and his lawyers as he lay strapped to the gurney, but did not make a final statement, choosing instead to release a handwritten statement consisting entirely of the nineteenth century poem "Invictus," which was written in 1875 by William Ernest Henley:

Out of the night that covers me,
Black as the Pit from pole to pole,
I thank whatever gods may be
For my unconquerable soul.

In the fell clutch of circumstance
I have not winced nor cried aloud.
Under the bludgeonings of chance
My head is bloody, but unbowed.

Beyond this place of wrath and tears
Looms but the Horror of the shade,
And yet the menace of the years
Finds, and shall find, me unafraid.

It matters not how strait the gate,
How charged with punishments the scroll,
I am the master of my fate:
I am the captain of my soul.

The message of this poem, combined with the stoic and grave mien McVeigh exhibited on his death table, added up to one dark truth: Timothy McVeigh was defiant and unrepentant to the end.

McVeigh's motive in carrying out the Oklahoma City bombing was to send the federal government a message, a warning that they should be—and will be—held accountable for "fascist" (McVeigh's word) acts such as the conflagrations at Waco and Ruby Ridge, and the Constitution-attacking efforts to impose gun control on American citizens.

McVeigh was a delusional, self-aggrandizing political zealot who researched the Second Amendment (the "right to bear arms" amendment) as a hobby when he was a child, and who modeled himself on the main character in the venomous, racist, anti-government novel *The Turner Diaries,* in which the "hero" blows up a Federal building with a truck bomb.

At McVeigh's sentencing hearing, before the judge imposed the death penalty, McVeigh was told that he could make a statement, and was asked if he had anything to say.

McVeigh said the following:

If the Court please, I wish to use the words of Justice Brandeis dissenting in Olmstead to speak for me. He wrote, "Our government is the potent, the omnipresent teacher. For good or for ill, it teaches the whole people by its example." That's all I have.

Ironically, McVeigh made the point before the court that the government would be setting a bad example for the American people if they killed *him,* and yet here was a man who thought nothing of using mass murder as a tool to make his own twisted, anti-government statement.

Tim McVeigh was born in Pendleton, New York, on April 23, 1968, the middle child of Mickey and Bill McVeigh.

From all accounts, Tim was an intelligent, curious, good-natured, and fun-loving child. Journalists have been hard-pressed to find someone in McVeigh's hometown who had a bad word to say about him. Shortly after McVeigh's execution, neighbor Bob Rooney was quoted in *USA Today* on June 20, 2001, as saying, "We just don't view him as a monster. Because we never saw that here. We never got a bad impression of him. He left with nothing but good impressions. . . . It's still a puzzle as to why it happened."

Why it happened: The agonizing, perhaps unanswerable question.

One possible answer can be found in the fact that Tim McVeigh saw *pure evil* in the actions of the U.S. government during the April 19, 1993, storming of David Koresh's Branch Davidian compound at Waco, Texas. McVeigh's sister Jennifer (who changed her name after her brother's conviction and teaches somewhere in the Carolinas) testified during her brother's trial that "He was very angry. I think he believed that the government murdered the people there, basically gassed and burned them."

In McVeigh's deranged worldview, the deaths at Waco, combined with the disregard and perceived disrespect he felt military personnel received from Americans and the U.S. government upon returning from the Gulf War (in which McVeigh himself served admirably and to great acclaim), were ominous signs that the government-punishing "something big" he wrote about in a letter to his sister needed to happen, and it needed to happen soon.

Thus, on the two-year anniversary of Waco, McVeigh parked a yellow Ryder truck loaded with four thousand pounds of explosives in front of the Murrah Federal Building, got out, and walked away. At 9:02 A.M., the bomb went off, and the death toll rose hour by hour, day by day, until all the 168 killed were accounted for. McVeigh was picked up for a traffic violation seventy-five miles from Oklahoma City a couple of hours after the blast, and was minutes away from being released two days later when the FBI made the firm link to McVeigh from a serial number on the rear axle of the bomb truck.

McVeigh admitted his guilt in a 2001 authorized biography called *American Terrorist,* and yet we still do not understand how the perpetrator of the worst act of domestic terrorism in American history could rationalize and negate the sheer evil of his deed, the blatant amorality of his actions. If McVeigh truly believed that what the government did at Waco was wrong, then it was a clear-cut contradiction for him to commit a deed of similar (to him) proportions.

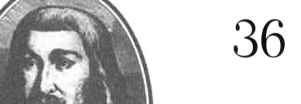

36

Gilles de Rais

(1406–1440)

. . . according to the lamentable outcries, tears and wailings coming from many people . . . Gilles de Rais has taken innocent boys and girls, and inhumanely butchered, killed, dismembered, burned and otherwise tortured them, and the said Gilles has im-molated the bodies . . . to the devils . . . and has foully committed the sin of sodomy with young boys and . . . lusted against nature after young girls . . . while the innocent boys and girls were alive, or sometimes dead, or sometimes even during their death throes . . .

—an excerpt from Charge 15 levied against Gilles de Rais

What drove the fifteenth-century French aristocrat Gilles de Rais to rape, torture, and kill young boys and girls?

A theory: After he watched his father die from being gored to death by a boar on a hunting trip, Gilles was raised by his grandfather, Jean, an amoral, greedy, cruel, conscienceless schemer who early on taught Gilles that the laws of the land were for the peons, not the royals—that elite caste that Gilles had been born into. And even though Jean dé Craon renounced his evil ways on his deathbed and apologized for "creating" Gilles de Rais (whom he described as a "monster"), the damage had been done. In 1432 or 1433, when Gilles was in his mid-twenties, the atrocities and murders began.

Gilles's routine was usually to have his lackeys (two of his cousins and a steward in particular) kidnap a poor peasant child from the surrounding hills and bring the child to his castle where he had secured a chamber for his perverse pleasures.

Gilles would first hang the child from a rope or a hook through the neck, and use a sword to inflict deadly injuries. He would then rape and sodomize the child as it died, and sometimes he would have sex with the child's corpse. He decapitated some of his victims; others he disemboweled, and then played with their internal organs and intestines. He would often dismember the bodies before cremating them, and the fires would burn constantly and at low flames to minimize the smell of cooking human flesh. During his trial, Gilles confessed to all of this, and even admitted that he would sometimes be filled with glee and masturbate as he watched the death throes and final moments of his helpless victims—all while sitting on their stomachs.

In addition to his carnal perversities, Gilles also was interested in magic, conjuring, and especially alchemy, the medieval "chemical philosophy" that had as its goal the transmutation of base metals into gold; the discovery of the panacea, the elusive single substance that would cure all illness and disease; and the compounding of the elixir that would guarantee eternal life. And even though he was ostensibly a man of great religious faith (he fought with Joan of Arc as her bodyguard during the Hundred Years War and endowed many church buildings), Gilles paid magicians to conjure up the Devil himself, although these sessions usually ended up with Gilles losing sight of his money and the magician—without even getting so much as a glimpse of the Prince of Darkness. During one particular conjuring, Gilles provided as a sacrifice to Lucifer the heart, eyes, and sex organs of a young boy. Still apparently unsatisfied, Satan declined the invitation.

In 1440, when Gilles was thirty-six, he was arrested and charged with heresy, and the kidnapping, sodomizing, and murdering of more than 140 young boys. At first, Gilles refused to accept the authority of the court, but after a dark night of the soul during which he contemplated the fate of his immortal spirit, he again appeared before the court and confessed to many of the crimes with which he was charged. This did not satisfy the court prosecutor and the judge agreed to allow Gilles to be tortured to elicit more confessions.

This threat did the trick (along with a tour of the "official" torture chamber). Gilles finally agreed to confess to everything. He was convicted and hung for his crimes on October 26, 1440. His body was thrown onto a burning funeral pyre but it was removed before it turned to ashes and given a proper Catholic burial.

There is some question today about the true culpability and guilt of Gilles De Rais. Some historians assert that because Gilles's confession was elicited under threat of torture and excommunication (at the time often considered a fate worse than torture or death), that Gilles de Rais's words must be dismissed as unreliable, if not completely false. This is easily refutable when one considers the specifics of Gilles's confession. He provided details that no one but the killer could have known and, combined with the testimony of his co-conspirators—his cousins and others—it seems clear that the number of victims Gilles admitted to murdering could actually have been closer to two hundred or even more.

37

Bruno Ludke

(1909–1944)

*Adult "wild euthanasia" involved more radical changes for psy-
chiatrists. No longer operators of gas chambers, they returned
to the familiar terrain of syringes, oral medications, and dietary
prescriptions for achieving the same end. From the regime's
medical bureaucracy came the continuing message that mental
patients were "useless eaters," burdens on the state and its war
effort, "life unworthy of life." Permission to kill was clear
enough, even if a little indirect. As one psychiatrist later testified, "In conversation with other participants in the program I
learned that there would be no fuss if some physician or other
in an institution stood ready to kill a patient by injection or
overdose, if he was convinced that the patient's extinction was
desirable."*

—Robert Jay Lifton, *The Nazi Doctors*

The nineteen-year-old, mentally retarded rapist and sex offender lay strapped
to a table in an operating room. A doctor clad in a bloody white coat busied
himself preparing his instruments. The patient was naked from the waist
down and his penis had been taped to his groin, pointing toward his head. His
scrotum had been shaved and washed with an alcohol solution. Bruno Ludke,

which was the young man's name, was soon to undergo an orchiectomy—the surgical removal of his testicles—a surgery that was intended to be corrective, and which had been ordered by none other than Reich SS leader Heinrich Himmler himself. (See page 70.) Ludke's castration was his punishment for sex crimes he had committed, and it was hoped that the loss of his testicles and the testosterone they produced would reduce or eliminate Ludke's libido, thereby putting German women out of harm's way.

The operation was a simple one. Two small incisions in the scrotum, two snips of the vas deferens, and the testicles were removed. Today, prosthetic testes are inserted into the scrotum for cosmetic reasons following the surgery; during World War II, achieving a pleasing appearance of a convicted sex offender's scrotum was not on the top of the list of Nazi priorities.

Their main concern was preventing Bruno Ludke from molesting and raping women. Himmler and his doctors believed that surgical castration would accomplish that goal.

They were wrong.

After his castration, during the years 1928 to 1943, Bruno Ludke went on to kill eighty-six women, raping many of them before he killed them, and sometimes having intercourse with many of them after they were dead.

A 1991 Czechoslovakian study of eighty-four castrated sex offenders revealed "only 3 men (out of 84) committed another sex offense after castration, and none were of an aggressive character." A similar study in Denmark found that the repeat offender rate was slightly over 2 percent in castrated offenders. Ludke was obviously one of those in these tiny percentages.

Ludke usually strangled and stabbed his victims, and would often stalk women that aroused him before attacking them. He was a callous killer, indifferent to the pain and fear of his victims. This disregard for others extended even to those he did not sexually attack. One time, Ludke was driving a horse-drawn carriage in a German city when he ran over a woman crossing the street, the full weight of the horse and the cart rolling over her. Ludke looked back, and then kept driving, leaving the broken and bleeding woman to die in the street.

Bruno Ludke was judged to be mentally retarded, and yet there was a native shrewdness to his thinking that makes this diagnosis somewhat specious. He regularly used his alleged disability as a manipulation tool, delighting in reminding people that he was retarded and, perhaps, he should not be held responsible for his actions. This is a fairly well thought out strategy and shows a level of calculation in his reasoning that belies his supposed mental inferiority.

As a child, there were signs that Ludke might eventually become a problem for German society. As has been seen in many other sociopathic serial killers, Ludke loved to torture animals when he was a young boy. He started killing at the age of eighteen and, shortly thereafter, became a chronic sexual abuser, resulting in his ineffective castration.

Ludke was eventually arrested in January 1943 for the murder of one woman and, as soon as he was in custody, he immediately confessed to eighty-five other murders. But again, Ludke may have outsmarted the authorities. Because Ludke had been certified as mentally retarded or insane, he was deemed incapable of standing trial and thus, by German law, Ludke could not be prosecuted nor sentenced to either prison or death.

Instead, he was taken into the Nazi medical experimentation system (see page 58) and used for a wide range of experiments.

This strategy may have backfired on the brutal serial killer and rapist, however. Bruno Ludke died at the age of thirty-five from an injection of some experimental chemical that the Nazis tried on him. In a sense, Ludke received an inadvertent lethal injection, thereby exacting justice for crimes for which he was never held accountable.

38

Andrei Chikatilo

"THE RED RIPPER"
"THE ROSTOV RIPPER"
"THE MAD BEAST"
"THE FOREST STRIP KILLER"
"CITIZEN X"

(1936–1994)

The purpose of life is to leave your mark on this earth.
—Andrei Chikatilo

What I did was not for sexual pleasure. Rather it brought me some peace of mind.
—Andrei Chikatilo

Andrei Romanovich Chikatilo was one of the worst serial killers of all time. During his 1992 trial, he sat in a Russian courtroom inside a cage with thick steel bars on all four sides. The cage was not to protect the people in the courtroom from Chikatilo; it was to protect Andrei Chikatilo from being torn to pieces by the families of his many victims.

Chikatilo could wear many labels, including sadist, pedophile, torturer, rapist, cannibal, mutilator, and murderer. He ultimately confessed to fifty-five rape-torture murders but, to this day, there is a pervasive belief that he was actually responsible for many more deaths than that.

During questioning after his capture, Chikatilo horrified even hard-boiled Soviet police interrogators by some of his confessions. He spoke of biting off the penises and scrotums of young boys, and the nipples and tongues of young girls. He reminisced wistfully of disemboweling his female victims so he could remove their uteruses and chew on them. "I did not want to bite them so much as chew them," he told police. "They were so beautiful and elastic." What is perhaps most horrifying about these perverted disclosures is that his later victims showed evidence of their genitals and internal organs having been removed *while they were still alive.*

Andrei Chikatilo was born in 1936 in Yablochnoye, a Ukrainian farming village. In what may be an apocryphal story, it is said that at the age of five, Chikatilo was told the story of how his younger brother, Stephan, had been kidnapped, killed, and eaten by the family's neighbors during the terrible Ukrainian famine caused by Stalin's collectivization programs. (See page 70.) Who knows what this story might have done to his immature psyche.

As an adolescent and a teenager, Chikatilo was a social pariah. There were many reasons for Chikatilo's ostracization and isolation: He had a high, effeminate voice; he reportedly suffered from gynecomastia, the enlargement of the male breasts; his penile foreskin was oddly shaped; he was obsessed with masturbation (which would play an enormous role later in carrying out his torture-murders); and he was a chronic bed-wetter.

After Chikatilo was arrested, Aleksandr Bukhanovsky, a Russian psychiatrist now commonly known as a "profiler," described to Chikatilo the characteristics he had ascribed to the ostensibly still-at-large killer: He would be a sexually impotent male who was unable to have a normal relationship with a woman. He would have no friends and would completely keep to himself. He was, however, undoubtedly a very intelligent man, and he had had a very painful adolescence marked by agonizing humiliations. He did not drink or take drugs. He was a bit of a prude and would probably gravitate toward a "power" job such as teacher, cop, or supply clerk.

This hypothetical man *was* Chikatilo, and The Red Ripper immediately confessed to everything after hearing Bukhanovsky's description.

Comrade Chikatilo's "regular" life bore the facade of normalcy. He married Fayina in 1963, and they had two children, a girl, Lyudmilla, born in 1965, and a boy, Yuri, born in 1969. (After Chikatilo's arrest, his children changed their names, packed their bags, and moved away to parts unknown, never to have contact with or even acknowledge the existence of their father again.)

Chikatilo took positions as a teacher and a headmaster of a boys' dormitory. Both allowed him access to children and he could not stop himself from sexually molesting young boys and girls. He was fired from both.

His next job was as a supply clerk. This job put him on the road, and that was when he was able to indulge his sickest fantasies for quite some time before being caught.

Chikatilo would spend hours stalking prey at bus and train stations. He always lured his victims away with charm and a gentle mien. He appeared to be nothing more than a harmless, kindly grandfatherly type, and even the youngest of children had no qualms about going off with him into the woods.

When he succeeded in snaring a child, Chikatilo was frenzied in the horrors he would commit. A quintessential example of Citizen X's rampages was his violence against seventeen-year-old Larisa Tkachenk in 1981. He bit off her nipples while she was still alive, and then he viciously killed her and ejaculated on her corpse—routine behavior for the typical cannibalistic, pedophiliac sex killer. But Chikatilo later admitted that he was so delighted with what he had done, so downright *happy,* that he "danced with joy" around her dead body, while waving her clothes in the air above him. Chikatilo also took pains to keep some of his victims alive as long as possible as he stabbed and stabbed them, performing his perverse surgery on them—amputating facial parts, internal organs—all while they were fully conscious.

Another of Chikatilo's trademarks was to stab his victims repeatedly in the eyes, and sometimes he would gouge the eyes out with his knife. Some psychologists theorized that Chikatilo believed the old superstition that the retina of a murder victim retained the last image it saw before the moment of death.

During his trial, Chikatilo tried desperately to prove he was insane so that he would not be executed. In the courtroom, in his protective cage, he would undress and waggle his penis at the spectators, shout obscenities, sing, and swear at the judge.

It did not work. Chikatilo was convicted, sentenced to death, and was executed in 1994 by a single bullet to the back of the head.

39

Anatoly Onoprienko
"THE TERMINATOR"

(1959–)

*To me, killing people is like ripping up a duvet. . . . I'm not a
maniac. I have been taken over by a higher force, something
telegraphic or cosmic which drove me. For example, I wanted
to kill my brother's first wife, because I hated her. I really
wanted to kill her, but I couldn't, because I had to receive the
order first. I waited for it, but it did not come. . . . If I am not
executed, I will escape and start killing again. I am being
groomed to serve Satan.*

—Anatoly Onoprienko

April it may be, but the nights are still cold in this part of the Ukraine, near
the border of Poland. Especially at three in the morning.

The Dubchak family sleeps soundly. Father and mother in the big bed;
son and daughter in small, separate beds in another room. The house sits dark
in farmland, far enough away from other houses and roads that no one would
hear if someone screamed. Or if someone fired a shotgun.

Suddenly the front door of the house bursts open with a terrifying
boom. A small, bald man with a compact build rushes into the house and, be-

fore the Dubchaks can react, he is standing over them in their bed with the muzzle of a sawed-off shotgun pointed in their faces.

"Up!" the man shouts in Ukrainian.

In seconds, the man has herded the four Dubchaks into the living room of the small house and he is standing in front of them, pointing his gun at them. The front door is still open; the Dubchaks are in their nightclothes.

The man looks at the father and son for a moment and then pulls the trigger of his shotgun.

Twice.

The father and son fall dead to the floor.

The mother and daughter are screaming now; hysterical, high-pitched shrieks that stab the small man in the brain and further enrage him.

The killer puts down his shotgun, reaches into his pocket, and pulls out a heavy, wooden-handled hammer.

He approaches the mother and daughter huddling together and starts swinging. He hits them both many, many times with his hammer, in the head, the face, the arms, the back, the stomach, the breasts. The small bald man keeps hitting and hitting until the screaming stops.

And then he hits them some more until he is exhausted and out of breath.

The killer stops, and bends at the waist to catch his breath.

He then looks around at the carnage, picks up his shotgun, pockets his hammer, and turns to leave. He grabs some trifles before he goes, a ring, a silver box, a watch.

There is blood everywhere. Before he leaves, he sets fire to the house. As he walks away from the blazing house into the still-dark night, he smiles.

Anatoly Onoprienko would visit other families in the cold Ukraine over the next several nights. But not tonight. The Terminator was finished for the evening.

Anatoly Onoprienko was born in 1959 in Laski, Ukraine. His father chose not to take care of him. Onoprienko had an older brother and their father decided that he could only raise one child, so Onoprienko was placed in an orphanage when he was a year old. Some of the psychiatrists who worked on the Onoprienko case claim that this de facto abandonment as a child by his biological father explains why Onoprienko slaughtered complete, intact families. He could not stand to see unbroken families continue to exist after he had been ripped from his own family, or so the psychological explanation goes. And yet, Onoprienko personally claimed that he did what he did because he was in the service of Satan and that he heard voices (that may have been space aliens, he admitted) telling him what to do.

Whatever the cause for Onoprienko's murderous impulses, fifty-two people died horrible deaths at the hands of the man who called himself the Terminator, after the Arnold Schwarzenegger movie and character.

✦   ✦   ✦

Onoprienko killed his first victim in 1989 and, over the next six years, killed eleven more times. He was never caught, and a murder every six months seemed to satisfy his lust for blood. Then he was suddenly not satisfied.

On Christmas Eve, 1995, in the small village of Garmarnia, Onoprienko began the series of home invasions, slaughters, and burnings for which he is now known, and which ultimately resulted in his capture and trial.

He started with the family of a forester, killing the parents and their two sons.

Over the next five months, Onoprienko killed forty people. He only raped one woman, but, horrifyingly, he raped her *after* he shot her in the face with his shotgun. Some of the people he killed were people who just happened to be in the wrong place at the wrong time—potential witnesses. Onoprienko was cold and clinical and simply executed anyone he came upon as he was fleeing a murder scene.

Onoprienko was staying with his cousin during his six-month rampage and, one day, his cousin found Anatoly's weapons stash. He was livid that Anatoly would bring such things into his house and he threw Onoprienko out. Onoprienko was equally angry and he threatened retaliation. He told his cousin that he would take care of him and his family at Easter time.

Onoprienko's cousin was justifiably afraid, and he called the police. The authorities found Onoprienko at his girlfriend's house, along with many items stolen from the homes of the murdered.

Onoprienko was arrested and, once in custody, he insisted on talking only to a military general. They dutifully brought him a general (or a cop dressed up as a general) and Onoprienko confessed to fifty-two murders from 1989 to 1995. He told the general that voices told him to kill and this was when he acknowledged that the voices might have actually belonged to aliens.

Onoprienko's trial began in November 1998. Just like Andrei Chikatilo (see page 119), Onoprienko was kept in a cage in the courtroom during his trial. He was convicted and sentenced to death in April 1999. There is currently a moratorium on executions in Russia so Onoprienko remains in prison. He either could serve out his life behind bars or be immediately executed if the government lifts the moratorium.

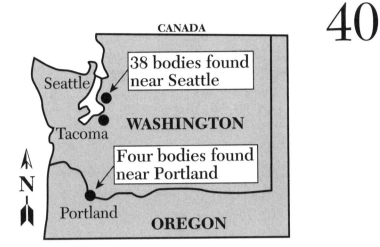

40

The Green River Killer

*I am not the Green River Killer. They have made me out to be a
very bad person, and I am not.*

—William Stevens

*I'm the adopted brother of William Stevens. I'm writing a book
exposing how he managed to commit this crime and still evade
police capture [and] conviction.*

—Robert Stevens, on his Web site, soliciting help in his
mission to prove his brother was the Green River Killer

W ho is, or was, the Green River Killer? Is he still alive? Is he in prison?
Has he left the Seattle/Portland area to continue his massacre of young
women elsewhere in America?

The serial killer dubbed the Green River Killer, named after the river
where he dumped the bodies of some of his victims, has never been caught.
The Green River Killer is believed to be responsible for at least forty-nine
murders between 1982 and 1984, and many of those involved in the Green
River case believe that that number will climb higher as more skeletons of
young women are eventually found. (Harold Schechter and David Everitt's
[1996] *The A to Z Encyclopedia of Serial Killers* suggest the Green River
Killer's body count may be as high as sixty-six.)

It is easy to get caught up in the massive mountain of details surrounding the investigation into the Green River killings. Thousands of files were compiled; thousands of people were listed as possible witnesses or suspects; thousands of individual pieces of evidence were collected; thousands of vehicles were noted for investigation; thousands of hours of police work were racked up; millions of dollars were spent on the investigatory efforts; and all of this resulted in . . . *nothing*.

The frustration of this sixteen-year dead end can easily distract from the reality of the Green River Killings: at least forty-nine daughters, sisters, friends, and lovers were abducted and murdered, and their bodies were dumped like garbage all over the Seattle/Portland area. Many were found in the woods; some were found in the Green River; many, *many* were nothing but skeletons by the time they were discovered.

It is true that the majority of the Green River Killer's victims were prostitutes. Some were as young as sixteen. Many were found naked with an article of clothing tied around their neck; some were found with rocks in their vaginas. Police found one young girl's skeleton lying in the woods with another tiny skeleton inside her abdominal region.

The FBI did come up with a profile of the killer. Pioneering FBI profiler John Douglas examined the evidence and determined that the Green River Killer was both disorganized—impulsive and hasty—and organized—deliberate and confident. He seemed to pick victims at random and, in many instances, used their own clothing to kill them: disorganized. But then some bodies were found weighted down with rocks and several were located in the same area, which suggested a high confidence level and a certain amount of preparation. Douglas also concluded that the killer had had problems with women in his past and that he targeted prostitutes because he considered them the lowest form of womanhood. There is also the possibility that the killer slayed hookers because he perceived them as the most powerful of all women: They knew what men wanted, they provided it, and they controlled access to sex. Controlling what someone wants is a power, and power over someone unavoidably assigns vulnerability to that person. The Green River Killer may have been trying, in his evil, twisted way, to take away the power that women may have had over him at some point in his life. The profile also suggested that the man was white, between twenty and forty, a heavy smoker and a heavy drinker, and may have had a history of sexual assault in his past.

During the course of the wide-ranging police investigation, the authorities were offered assistance from someone who knew what it was like to be inside the mind of a serial killer. Ted Bundy (see page 134) had been following the case and contacted the police with an offer to consult and provide information he assured they would find useful. Detectives traveled to Florida many times, where Bundy sat on Death Row, interviewed him at length, and one detective even wrote a book about his experiences with Bundy. However, it was eventually decided that all Bundy was doing was trying to delay his own execution by being indispensable in an active case. (It did not work.)

All told, five men were investigated for the Green River Killer slayings. Police long believed that the killer posed as a cop to lure prostitutes into his car and, of the five suspects, only one man seemed to fit the description and fulfill the Green River Task Force's theory of his modus operandi: William J. Stevens II.

When Stevens was finally arrested in 1989, he had in his possession a fully equipped police car, one hundred police badges, twenty-nine firearms of all types, and twenty-six license plates. Stevens did, however, manage to provide alibis for most of the killings, and he was eventually released. He died of cancer in 1991.

Stevens's adopted brother, Robert Stevens, presently works to prove that William Stevens was the Green River Killer. He has successfully shot holes in most of William Stevens's alibis, and he is now writing a book explaining his theory as to how his brother evaded the police for over two years.

There has been talk of reopening the case of the Green River Killer. New technologies and DNA tests may provide concrete evidence as to the identity of the elusive killer. Budgetary constraints, however, may hinder the progress.

One thing we *can* know for sure about the Green River Killer is that he is (or was) a heartless, conscienceless murder who preyed on young girls and who, based on the total of murders attributed to him, averaged at least one murder every two weeks, for two years straight.

Evil is never satisfied.

Late-breaking News:

On Friday, November 30, 2001, Seattle police arrested Gary Ridgeway in connection with the Green River Killer murders. As of this writing, Ridgeway has been linked to three of the Green River Killer murders through DNA evidence. His case is pending.

41

Jake Bird
"The Takoma Axe Killer"

(1901–1949)

All you guys who had anything to do with this case are going to die before I do.

— Jake Bird, to several men involved
in prosecuting him for murder

If fifty-two-year-old Bertha Kludt of Takoma, Washington, had not been hacked to death with an axe by Jake Bird, she might very well have died of a heart attack from shock after she suddenly came upon the killer in her house.

Jake Bird had entered the house through the open back door after picking up an axe from the yard and then taking off all his clothes. A naked black man coming at you swinging an axe can be a somewhat disconcerting experience, and Bertha responded by screaming at the top of her lungs. Her teenage daughter, Beverly, who was also home at the time, joined in, and the two women's screams were loud enough to alert neighbors who, wisely, immediately called the police.

By the time the police arrived, however, it was too late. The Kludt residence resembled an abattoir. Jake Bird had slaughtered both mother and daughter. They found Bird outside the house, now dressed, walking across the backyard carrying his shoes. Instead of surrendering quietly, however (which, in the face of clearly superior firepower, would have been the smart thing to do), Bird charged at the police with a knife.

The police did not shoot Bird but they did literally beat him senseless. He was finally handcuffed and arrested while unconscious and reportedly needed several days of hospitalization before he recovered enough to be questioned.

When Jake was out of the hospital, he was interviewed by police detectives and his initial stance was that he was innocent and that they had the wrong man. That was until the police produced evidence in the form of a piece of Bertha Kludt's brain, which was found in Bird's pants.

Jake knew he had been caught after that and he willingly began telling the police about many other murders he had committed. Ultimately, he was convicted of eleven murders, but suspected of forty-four. The truth about Jake Bird is that he loved to kill, and he specialized in white women.

Jake Bird was an anomaly: he was an African-American serial killer. FBI profilers have determined that an overwhelming 85 percent of all serial killers are white males. Female and black serial killers are a rarity.

Jake Bird claimed responsibility for more than forty brutal axe murders in seven states—Florida, Illinois, Kansas, Kentucky, Nebraska, Ohio, South Dakota, and Wisconsin—after he was arrested in 1947.

In addition to killing indiscriminately, Jake Bird also embraced the dark arts, specifically the malevolent practice of putting curses—he called them his "hexes"—on people he hated, or whom he felt had done him wrong.

Six men Jake Bird put hexes on died of heart attacks within a short time following his conviction and death sentence:

- Judge Hodge, the judge who presided over the case, died one month after the sentencing.
- A month after that, Joe Karpach, a cop involved in the case, died suddenly.
- The following month, Ray Scott, the chief court clerk at Jake's trial, had a massive heart attack and died.
- Six months later, Lieutenant Sherman Lyons, the police officer who had obtained Jake's confession, died suddenly.
- Shortly thereafter, J.W. Selden, one of Jake's attorneys (who had not been able to save Jake from the death penalty), died—on the one-year anniversary of Jake's sentencing.
- Soon after, Arthur A. Seward, one of Jake's prison guards at Walla Walla State Prison in Washington State, died suddenly of heart failure.

Only two people of the eight that Jake cursed survived the hex: Dr. Charles Larson and his assistant Pat Steele.

Dr. Larson was not a believer in Jake Bird's alleged demonic powers. In *Crime Doctor* by John Dennis McCallum, he recalled the first time he heard about being cursed:

> Jake didn't put his so-called hex on me personally. The way I found out about it was from Pat Steele. Pat walked into my lab one day and said that he and I, among others, were hexed; that Jake had predicted we were going to die within the year. We both laughed and went out and had a drink on it. The fact that Pat and I were the only two out of eight who survived is a matter of pure coincidence. Those six men who did die didn't die of Jake Bird, they died of coronary occlusions.

Jake Bird was able to delay his execution for two years through various appeals and legal strategies. He was hanged at Walla Walla State Prison on July 15, 1949.

42

Gerald Stano

(1951–1998)

I hate a bitchy chick.
—Gerald Stano

Gerald Stano was a textbook misogynist—and he coldly actualized his animosity and hostility, in forty-one (or more) *all female* murder victims, ranging in age from preteen—one girl was twelve years old—to midthirties.

Gerald Stano was a happy killer. The act of torturing and killing women made him so happy that, although he forced some of his victims to perform oral sex on him, stabbing them and murdering them was what truly got him off. Stano also admitted to having had sex with at least one of his victims' dead bodies, but necrophilia was not one of his primary goals.

Stano was sadistic. One of his victims, a twenty-six-year-old streetwalker named Toni Van Haddocks, got into Stano's car hoping for a quick sex act, equally quick payment, and a return to the streets of her neighborhood. Stano drove out of the area, setting off alarm bells for the prostitute. Stano forced Haddocks to perform oral sex on him and then stabbed her forty times (thirty-eight times in the head), before he left her body by the side of the road. Stano later admitted to the police that when he saw that Haddocks was wearing a cast on her right arm from a recent break, he deliberately beat her on her injured arm, taking great delight in her agony.

When Stano picked up seventeen-year-old Cathy Lee Scharf as she was hitchhiking on Route 1 outside Port Orange, Florida, he was planning on demanding sex in exchange for a ride. Cathy had been out all night partying and all she wanted to do was get home, have breakfast, and clean up.

The trouble for Cathy started immediately.

When Stano grabbed her and tried to kiss her, she told him to take his hands off her and called him "gross." This was like throwing a lit match into a pool of gasoline. Stano reflexively hit her and then laughed when she tried to get out of the car. "Those locks are burglar proof," he told her. "You can't get them open."

Stano then started driving away from Port Orange, which was where Cathy lived. Cathy lashed out and struck Stano, cutting his face with one of her sterling silver rings.

Stano was furious.

He stopped the car and choked her unconscious. He then drove to a deserted beach road. When she awakened he told her, "This is the end of the line."

Stano then enjoyed himself for hours before finally killing Cathy Scharf and putting her out of her misery.

Did he rape her or torture her sexually? No. Stano found his pleasure in stabbing Scharf repeatedly, but making sure that none of her wounds were fatal; as well as strangling her over and over, always to the point of her passing out, but never to the point of death. Stano would wait for her to wake up, then stab and strangle her again.

He did this for hours.

When Stano had had his fill of torturing Cathy Scharf, he choked her one last time, but this time not stopping until she was dead. He dumped her body on the bank of a canal and covered it with branches. He stopped at a gas station where he cleaned himself up, and then he went roller-skating.

Cathy Scharf's body would not be found for more than a month.

Stano was ultimately arrested for assault when a prostitute he beat up, but who miraculously managed to survive, identified him. After three hours of questioning, Stano began confessing to a grisly spree of murder.

Gerald Stano committed his murders in Pennsylvania, Florida, and New Jersey. He admitted to forty-one murders (all women), was convicted of nine, and given eight life sentences and the death penalty on his ninth conviction. As if Stano's grisly track record was not enough for society and the courts to deal with, the police have strong suspicions that Stano might actually have killed *twice* as many women—eighty or more.

Stano was adopted as a child and grew up as an outsider. He was short, chubby, and not popular. In fact, psychologists believe that Stano's social ostracization during his developmental years played a large role in the fierce misogyny that was the engine that powered his murderous impulses.

The fact that Stano was humiliated, taunted, and rejected by girls and young women is seen as the catalyst for an unleashing of his most primal hatreds toward women, and a justification in his mind for the evils he perpetrated against his victims. It is not a coincidence that the majority of Stano's victims were prostitutes, hitchhikers, runaways, and other females of society who were, first and foremost (due to their station), *prey*—mostly helpless and vulnerable targets to the heinous "hunters" like Stano.

In addition, Stano's victims were part of the vile "anti-Stano" contingent whose sole purpose (again, in his mind) was to snub him and his advances and further contribute to his social banishment. *All* women were bitches to Stano. He would show them, and show them he did by forcing his victims into degrading sex acts and then viciously killing them with a gun, a knife, or sometimes his own bare hands.

Evidence of Stano's truly black-hearted nature can be found in the "overkill" he employed in his murders. Anyone who stabs a victim thirty-eight times in the head is no longer stabbing to kill, he is stabbing for pleasure.

Gerald Stano was executed in Florida's electric chair in March 1998.

43

Ted Bundy

(1947–1989)

I'm the most cold-blooded sonofabitch you'll ever meet.

—Ted Bundy

Lynda Ann Healy lived in a house with three other girls, attended Washington State University, and worked as a ski forecaster for Northwest Ski Reports. She was a beautiful brunette who was kidnapped from her room on the night of January 31, 1974, beaten, raped, and finally murdered by having her skull crushed. She was the first of Ted Bundy's victims to die, transforming him from a kidnapper, abuser, and rapist to a murderer.

The next day, Lynda's roommates found her bed made, but no sign of Lynda. Her parents arrived for a planned dinner and when the seriousness of the situation was acknowledged, they called the police. In front of her parents, the police pulled back the covers of Lynda's bed and found a blood-soaked pillowcase and sheets. Lynda's bloody nightgown was found in the closet. This confirmed that Lynda had been beaten severely, if not killed, in her room, and then taken from the premises. A year later, Lynda's bashed-in skull was found.

Lynda Healy was one of countless victims of Ted Bundy, and one of the murders he confessed to before his execution. Janice Ott was another unfortunate victim of Bundy's.

There is a tragic irony in the death of Janice Ott at the hands of psychopath Ted Bundy. Why? Because Janice Ott was a caseworker for a Seattle Youth Services group and she was highly trained in the psychology of the antisocial personality.

Janice, twenty-three years old, barely five feet tall and one hundred pounds, was a newlywed and had recently moved to Lake Sammanish, Washington, for her job. Her new husband stayed behind in California and Janice lived with a roommate.

On the day of her disappearance, July 14, 1974, Janice left her roommate a note telling her that she was going bike riding in Lake Sammanish State Park and that she would be back later that afternoon. That was the last anyone heard of Janice Ott.

Her remains were found two months later on September 6, 1974, two miles from the park. Bundy had used a fake arm cast to persuade Ott to help him and, all her training aside, she had been happy to assist the poor man with the broken arm.

Bundy raped and murdered her and left her remains in the woods, uncovered—resulting in her dead body being torn to pieces by wild animals before it was found.

Ted Bundy was correct when he described himself as the most cold-blooded criminal: one would have to dig deep in the annals of crime to find someone as cruel and heartless as Theodore Robert Bundy. Bundy experienced genuine pleasure in the acts of torture-rape, physical mutilation, and murder. He beat young women with logs and crowbars and his hands. He strangled them, bit them, and ripped them to shreds, and some of his victims did not even receive the welcome blessing of death: he left one of his victims in bloody agony with a shattered skull and a bed railing rammed up her vagina. She ultimately survived but with brain damage, permanent hearing loss, and balance problems. Not to mention the nightmares.

From an early age, Ted Bundy, born illegitimately, was an anomaly. He had developed a fascination with knives when he was three, and he was singled out by his teachers for having a ferocious temper when he was five.

How Bundy's psyche developed and how it became the perverse source of his abominable crimes has been debated and discussed for years, and it was a hot topic during the ten-year period between Bundy's convictions and his execution. Bundy himself thrived on the attention and loved the idea that journalists from all over the world wanted to interview him. He rarely turned down an interview request.

In the beginning, Bundy's modus operandi was slick. He used his charm and good looks and intelligence to persuade young women to go with him: he needed help putting something in his car because he wore a (fake) cast; he was a cop trying to make sure a young lady's car had not been stolen; he was having car trouble. For many of his victims, agreeing to go with the nice, handsome young man was the last decision they would ever make. One young woman, Carla DaRonch, was convinced that Bundy was a cop. She *finally* got suspicious when he tried to handcuff her in his car and she managed to flee to safety. This encounter traumatized her terribly, though, and it was a long time before she would go anywhere unescorted. After Bundy's execution, she expressed the wish to have thrown the switch herself.

Bundy's trials were a joke. He acted as his own lawyer and, at one point, the jury had to sit through the bizarre spectacle of Bundy being the defendant, the defense counsel, and a defense witness.

None of his theatrics mattered, though; the evidence against him—which included hair, bite marks, handcuffs, and other physical evidence linking him to his murders and assaults—was overwhelming. Bundy was electrocuted on January 24, 1989.

Ted Bundy eventually confessed to thirty murders: eleven in Washington, eight in Utah, three in Colorado, three in Florida, two in Oregon, two in Idaho, and one in California. Some law enforcement officials linked him to six other unsolved homicides, bringing his body count to thirty-six. When Bundy was told of the last number, he laughed and told the FBI to add a digit. To this day, no one is certain what he meant. Was he saying his total should have been 37? Or 136? Bundy took the truth to the electric chair with him.

Ted Bundy's Known Victims

1974

February 1	Lynda Ann Healy (21)
March 12	Donna Gail Manson (19)
April 17	Susan Rancourt (18)
May 6	Roberta Parks (22)
June 1	Brenda Ball (22)
June 11	Georgeann Hawkins (18)
July 14	Janice Ott (23)
July 14	Denise Naslund (19)
August 2	Carol Valenzuela (20)
October 2	Nancy Wilcox (16)
October 18	Melissa Smith (17)
November 8	Debbie Kent (17)

1975

January 12	Caryn Campbell (23)

March 15	Julie Cunningham (26)
April 6	Denise Oliverson (25)

1978

January 15	Lisa Levy (20)
January 15	Margaret Bowman (21)
February 9	Kimberly Leach (12)

44

Fritz Haarmann

"THE BUTCHER OF HANNOVER"
"THE VAMPIRE OF HANNOVER"

(1879–1925)

*I'd make two cuts in the abdomen and put the intestines in a
bucket, then soak up the blood and crush the bones until the
shoulders broke. Now I could get the heart, lungs, and kidneys
and chop them up and put them in my bucket. I'd take the flesh
off the bones and put it in my waxcloth bag. It would take me
five or six trips to take everything and throw it down the toilet
or into the river. I always hated doing this, but I couldn't help
it—my passion was so much stronger than the horror of the
cutting and chopping.*

> —Fritz Haarmann, detailing his job description

*Keep it short. I want to spend Christmas in heaven with
Mother.*

> —Fritz Haarmann, addressing his jury regarding
> his sentencing

Fritz Haarmann holds the notoriety of being Germany's most prolific killer and yet, unlike many serial killers and mass murderers, who get their start at an early age (sometimes even during adolescence), Haarmann did not start his murder rampage until September 1918, at the relatively advanced age of thirty-nine (although he was unquestionably a hard-core criminal and had served almost two decades in prison by this time).

Haarmann was a smuggler, a thief, a pedophile, a kidnapper, a murderer, a cannibal, and a necrophiliac.

Friedrich Heinrich Karl Haarmann was born on October 25, 1879, the youngest of six children in a family for whom the term "dysfunctional" was coined.

His father was an abusive alcoholic who spent more time in bars than at home and who may have, at one point, murdered a train engineer.

His mother was a psychotic who apparently refused to accept that Fritz was a male and treated him like a girl his entire childhood, including dressing him in girl's clothes.

One of his brothers was a sexual abuser who ended up serving time in prison for molestation.

All of Haarmann's three sisters chose the same career path: prostitution.

Haarmann himself was a pedophile and frequently sexually molested neighborhood children after he flunked out of both locksmith school and a military academy and went to work for his father. Haarmann even spent time in a mental institution when he was eighteen and many experts on Haarmann's life believe that something traumatic happened to him while he was a resident in the institution.

After Haarmann was released from the asylum, he married a twenty-year-old woman and immediately left her to join the military. He was quickly discharged and ended up back home with his father.

It was around this time that Haarmann began seriously committing himself to a life of crime. He got involved in smuggling, burglary, and rape, but seemed to always get caught and, from the time he was in his early twenties through his late thirties, he spent more time in prison than on the streets.

After his release from prison in 1918, Haarmann began committing the abominable crimes for which he is best known. For almost five years, he got away with the sickest of crimes, although at one point the police questioned him about a missing young boy. The missing boy's head was hidden behind Haarmann's stove, but the police never found it. Haarmann did end up in jail for nine months, but not for the boy's murder. He was convicted of sexual abuse of a minor because the police had found him in bed with a different young boy. Haarmann's being questioned may have saved the life of his young sex partner.

Over a period of nine months in 1923, Haarmann sweet-talked a dozen young boys back to his apartment (which is the M.O. also used by American serial killer Jeffrey Dahmer—see page 183). He would have sex with the boys and then kill them with his teeth: he would bite through their trachea and then chew all the way through their neck, ravenously tearing the young flesh to bloody shreds.

As if this was not bad enough, Haarmann then took his atrocities to an almost unimaginable level: after the murder, he would carve up his victims' bodies and sell cuts of their flesh as roasts and steaks and chops on the black market. He knowingly turned his unwitting "customers" into cannibals. (One woman who bought meat from Haarmann took the roast to the police because she was certain it was human flesh. Not to worry, the police told her. It was pork.) Haarmann also regularly gave the bones of his victims to his neighbors, which they used to make soup.

Haarmann's final victim was murdered in 1924, after which he was arrested, tried, charged with twenty-seven murders, and convicted of an array of monstrous, unspeakable crimes, including twenty-four murders. Haarmann defended himself and behaved terribly in court, which may have inspired future "court clowns" like Andrei Chikatilo and Ted Bundy.

As part of his defense, Haarmann told the court, "Believe me, I'm not ill. It's only that I occasionally have funny turns."

His defense arguments didn't work and Fritz Haarmann was given twenty-four death sentences and beheaded *by sword* in the Hannover Town Square in 1925. In a letter found after his death, Haarmann asserted that he could not be killed and that he would be back. Throughout his life, and even after his death, Haarmann was consistent in admitting that he experienced profound pleasure for his acts.

An autopsy of Haarmann's brain was inconclusive.

Richard Kuklinski
"The Iceman"
(1935–)

I'm a hard-working expediter. I'd do something that someone wanted done and would pay a price.

—Richard Kuklinski

Richard "The Iceman" Kuklinski is ranked in *The Evil 100* because he killed for money. Or convenience. Or for the heck of it.

He started killing at an early age, loved his work, and was utterly amoral when it came to taking another human life for profit. Kuklinski claims that he has no feelings or compunctions about killing people because he was viciously abused by his father when he was a child. As a result, he has deliberately "distanced" himself from other people and trained himself to turn his feelings on and off at will. He admitted weakness and emotional vulnerability when it came to his own wife and children, but any other human being was a cipher to The Iceman: live or die, the only difference was whether or not he got paid.

Killing someone was strictly business.

Kuklinski once shot a complete stranger in the forehead with a crossbow just to see if it worked as an effective murder weapon. (It did.) He also once nonchalantly shot a man who was stopped at a traffic light for no reason at all: he just felt like killing someone.

Kuklinski is currently serving multiple life sentences with no chance of release at the Trenton Maximum Security Prison in New Jersey. His notoriety and body count have made him a star: There have been two HBO documentaries about Kuklinski, both of which were made with his full cooperation and participation. There has also been a book written about the contract killer.

Kuklinski started killing when he was fourteen years old. Throughout his career, he was involved in auto theft, drug dealing, the porn business, illicit weapons trafficking and, of course, killing for hire.

One of his favorite methods of murder was to use cyanide because it was an especially painful and gruesome way to die. But it was difficult to kill with cyanide because it had to be ingested.

In the early 1980s, Kuklinski's problem with cyanide was solved when The Iceman hooked up with Mr. Softee. Mr. Softee was really Robert Prongay, a hit man who drove an ice cream truck and was not averse to storing a corpse in the freezer of his vehicle as he made the rounds selling ice cream to the neighborhood kids.

Mr. Softee taught The Iceman how to convert solid cyanide into a liquid and put it in a spray bottle. It seems that once cyanide spray enters the body through the nose, the person is doomed, and death is fast and inevitable. Prongay explained to Kuklinski that all he had to do was walk up to a target, spray him in the face with a blast of the liquid cyanide, and walk away.

Kuklinski found this quite efficient as it usually resulted in a corpse within fifteen seconds. "You spray it on someone's face," he once said, "and they go to sleep."

Kuklinski, who was a master of disguises, also used the usual methods of murder, including shooting, stabbing, strangling, bombing, and poisoning by injection, and his standard operating procedures were meticulous. He would first shoot his victim, usually in the head, and next wrap the body in a large towel. Afterwards, he would stab the body in the heart and drain the corpse of all its blood. Kuklinski would then cut the body up into small pieces and throw the pieces in a dump. He was also known to stuff bodies in 55-gallon steel drums and bury them. (Sometimes a limb would have to broken or cut off to make it fit.)

Interestingly, Kuklinski was not called The Iceman because he was cold-hearted (which he most assuredly was). He acquired that nickname because he would sometimes freeze his victims for a long time and then dump them in a field somewhere and let them defrost. He believed that the freezing hampered police identification of the body and eliminated evidence.

An undercover team effort of the Bureau of Alcohol, Tobacco, and Firearms, the New Jersey Attorney General's Office, and the New Jersey

State Police Organized Crime Task Force finally nailed Kuklinski in 1986 and he was found guilty of murder in 1988.

When Kuklinski was on his way to prison, he asked the guards if they would take off his shackles and handcuffs, promising them that he would run away and they could then shoot him in the back. He would rather have died than be in prison under someone else's control.

Needless to say, the guards did not agree to Kuklinski's escape plan and he is behind bars with no chance of release.

Moses Sithole
"THE ABC MURDERER"
(1965–)

There is nothing I can say to lessen the hurt of the mothers and relatives of the young women who were so brutally raped and murdered. . . .

— Judge David Curlewis, at Moses Sithole's sentencing

He bears the name of the great leader, lawgiver, and prophet of the ancient Israelites, and his biblical name means "deliverer." In a horrible perversion of the legacy of his ancient name, Moses Sithole was, indeed, a deliverer. He delivered forty women to the darkness; he delivered forty women to a nightmare from which death was a salvation from pain and fear. Moses Sithole delivered the AIDS virus to these same women, who, if they had lived, would have carried with them an irrevocable death sentence.

The jury sat silently as the prosecutor walked across the courtroom carrying a videotape. He slid it into the VCR and the TV suddenly showed Moses Sithole, eating an apple. He did not seem tense or worried and, for the following hour, he calmly recounted his abduction, rape, and murder of thirty-seven women.

He hated women because a woman had lied about him, he told the interviewer. A woman had said Moses had raped her, and another jury had believed her, and Moses Sithole had spent seven years in a South African prison because of her lies.

When he was released from prison, he explained, he decided to get even. But did he go after the woman who put him away? No. He slaughtered women who *reminded* him of her. This was why, he continued, he sometimes wrote the word "bitch" on the corpses of some of his victims before he buried them in the foothills of the Skurweberg Mountains near Germiston and Boksburg (which happened to be a popular place for body disposal by the burgeoning roster of post-apartheid South African serial killers).

During his hour-long "homily," Sithole did not once express remorse for his actions, crimes that gave him the despicable title of South Africa's worst serial killer.

In a stunning example of unconscionable hypocrisy, Moses Sithole formed a charitable organization called Youth Against Human Abuse when he left prison at the age of thirty. This group's mission was to work for the complete elimination of the horrible crime of child abuse, and Moses Sithole was valiantly leading the charge. The reality of Moses Sithole's motives and the purpose of his group were much different.

Moses would approach women and introduce himself as the founder of Youth Against Human Abuse. He always dressed nicely, always was very polite, and he always made a point of mentioning that he was married.

Women were immediately disarmed by his seeming harmlessness and many agreed to help with his noble cause.

Sithole would then take them to an utterly deserted area and, by the time the woman realized that she had made what could be generously described as an error in judgment, it was too late.

Trustworthy Moses Sithole would undress her, rape her, then strangle her with her own underwear. This routine went on for eighteen months and gave Sithole an average of a murder and a rape every two weeks for a solid year and a half.

Sithole was finally arrested and, after a trial in which his own words on the videotape were the strongest evidence against him, he was found guilty of thirty-seven counts of the murder of women; one count of the murder of a child; forty counts of rape; and six counts of robbery. He was sentenced to 2,410 years in prison, believed to be the longest prison sentence ever imposed.

Sithole's defense attorney had pleaded for a shorter sentence because Sithole had AIDS. Judge David Curlewis was stony: he said that the fact that Sithole had AIDS and a life expectancy of between five and eight years did not make "the slightest difference" to him. The judge also admitted that he would have given Sithole the death penalty if the government had not recently outlawed executions. (Judge Curlewis is on record as believing that that decision to abolish the death penalty by the South African legislature was a *big* mistake.)

Sithole is still alive and currently serving his sentences (which run concurrently) in a maximum-security prison in Pretoria.

How did South Africa end up with a Moses Sithole?

One theory is that, after the end of apartheid, many blacks found themselves in poverty and unable to afford to care for their children. Moses Sithole's mother was one of these poor women, and she decided to put Moses in an orphanage. Thus, Moses Sithole was deprived of a family life when growing up, and this could have been the catalyst that transformed him into a serial killer. (There are, of course, opponents of this argument.) Irma Labuschagne, a criminologist based in Pretoria, South Africa, talking about the Sithole case and other South African serial killers with similar backgrounds, in an October 2000 *Maxim* article, explains, "The family is the only possible way any person can grow up remotely human: That's where you learn everything about self-worth. If you miss that, you have no norms, values, nothing to teach you the value of human life."

If any of this theory applies to Moses Sithole, it is the last sentence. Blaming the abolishment of apartheid for the creation of Moses Sithole, however, muddies the water and does not mitigate his actions in the least.

Martin Bryant

(1966–)

I can't talk now, I'm having too much fun. I want to have a
shower and if you ring me back again I will shoot the hostage.
　　—Martin Bryant, talking to a reporter while holed up in
　　the Seaside Cottage

Australia has one of the lowest homicide rates among industrialized nations in the world, and yet it is also the country that must live with the reality that it is the homeland of the man responsible for the worst spree killing of all time.

On Sunday, April 28, 1996, twenty-eight-year-old Martin Bryant visited the Broad Arrow Cafe at the Port Arthur Historic Site on the Australian Island of Tasmania. He carried with him a blue sports bag, in which there were two guns—a self-loading AR-15 rifle and an SKS assault rifle, both of which were powerful military weapons.

After ordering a meal, Bryant sat down at a table on the outside balcony area, muttered a couple of comments about how there were a lot of white tourists but not too many Japanese, and ate his meal.

Around 1:30, Bryant walked back inside the cafe, unzipped his bag, withdrew a rifle, and began shooting people. He killed twenty and wounded fifteen in the cafe; then he proceeded outside. First he killed a bus driver, then a mother and her two daughters, aged three and five.

One young man in the cafe watched as Martin Bryant shot his fiancée in the back of the head. Outside, Bryant chased down a five-year-old girl who ran to hide behind a tree after he had killed her mother—and then he shot the child at point-blank range. A mother screamed at the emergency workers to treat her little daughter—who was already dead. One man who was hiding under a table mistakenly said, "He's gone." Bryant heard him, backed up, and shot him in the head. Bryant was so close and the force of the bullet was so powerful, the man's head literally exploded.

On his way to his car, Bryant shot at anyone he saw, killing some, wounding others. He then drove to a gas station where he carjacked a young couple, shot the woman three times, killing her, and put the man in the trunk of the car. Next, Bryant drove the man to the Seaside Cottage, about four miles from the Port Arthur site, where he held him hostage. The man was killed when Bryant set fire to the cottage. Two other people in the cottage (the owners) were also killed by Bryant, either before his shooting spree at Port Arthur, or sometime during the sixteen-hour hostage standoff.

When Bryant set fire to the cottage, he himself caught fire, ran outside in flames, ripped off his burning clothes, and was arrested and taken to a hospital for treatment of second-degree burns.

Bryant's total body count was thirty-five dead, eighteen wounded. His victims ranged in age from three to seventy-two. Bryant was charged with sixty-nine counts, including thirty-four counts of murder, nineteen counts of attempted murder, plus charges of aggravated assault, wounding, causing grievous bodily harm, arson, and unlawfully setting fire to property. He was sentenced to life in prison.

Bryant has made four suicide attempts while in prison. He cut the femoral artery in his groin; took an overdose of sleeping pills; tried to strangle himself with bandages; and tried to choke himself to death by swallowing a tube of toothpaste. None of his attempts were successful.

Martin Bryant has a tested I.Q. of 66, but was determined to be functional, not mentally ill, and be declared fit to stand trial. The psychiatric report on Bryant stated, "Mr. Bryant's limited intellectual capacities and, equally importantly, his limited capacity for empathy or imaging [sic] the feelings and responses of others, left a terrible gap in his sensibilities which enabled him not only to contemplate mass destruction, but to carry it through. There also has to be acknowledged that Mr. Bryant took delight and gained excitement from tormenting others."

Bryant's former girlfriend, Jenetta Hoani, had nothing good to say about the gunman. She told police that he was obsessed with bestiality, loved violent movies, and obsessively collected, of all things, teddy bears. His neighbors painted a portrait of an irrational, cold, and isolated loner who may have even murdered his own father: shortly after Bryant's father was found drowned (with Bryant's weight belt around his neck), Bryant was reportedly seen outside working with a weed whacker.

Authorities believe that several elements contributed to the creation of the monster that would kill so many without the tiniest shred of moral compunction or empathy. First, he was mentally disabled, which isolated him from others. Second, he felt persecuted and believed that the world was against him. He had a severe insecurity complex, which he compensated for by buying guns. Third, he had an almost unlimited supply of money. Bryant inherited a half-million dollars from an older woman he had once lived with.

These combined to create a heartless killer who, it was determined, knew what he was doing, but simply did not care. He cunningly targeted his victims and shot them, one by one. He also shot at the helicopters that were bringing his wounded to the hospital. During his trial, he laughed when the names of the dead were read aloud in court.

Martin Bryant is currently serving a life sentence in a maximum-security cell in Hobart, Tasmania. His record as being responsible for the worst massacre by a lone gunman still stands.

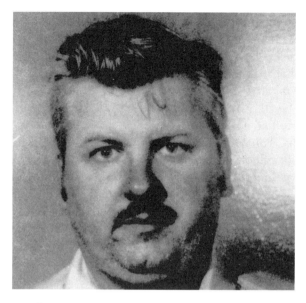

John Wayne Gacy
"THE KILLER KLOWN"

(1942–1994)

You know, clowns can get away with murder.

—John Wayne Gacy

All the police are going to get me for is running a funeral par-lor without a license.[1]

—John Wayne Gacy

Duplicity, thy name is Gacy.

John Wayne Gacy was named for an American hero and, like the rest of his vile life, that was a lie, too. Heroic is the least likely word that might be used to describe the terrible deeds committed by Gacy. A pederast, child abuser, rapist, kidnapper, and murderer, John Wayne Gacy wore a mask, both literally—a clown's—and figuratively—upstanding citizen, husband, and fa-

---

[1] This quote has also been reported as *"All the cops are going to get me for is running a cemetery without a license."* Most sources give the "funeral parlor" version more credibility but we wanted to acknowledge the alternative version for the record.

ther. It seems the only thing he did not lie about was his crimes: When finally captured, Gacy confessed to thirty-three murders and even led police to spots where he had dumped the bodies of some of his victims.

Gacy was the son of an alcoholic abuser who treated his son—a junior, proudly named for his father—with contempt, hostility, rejection, and criticism. Gacy's father died while Gacy was in prison and Gacy was emotionally distraught that they had never had a better relationship. Even though his father was hostile and abusive, Gacy still loved him and had hoped to resolve some issues between them at some point in his adult life.

Unlike many other serial killers, John Wayne Gacy was never a loner, never someone who kept a low profile and lived a secluded, quiet life—the kind of person that neighbors might have described as someone who "kept to himself" after his evil deeds were discovered. He was quite the contrary, actually.

Gacy was active in the Boy Scouts as a youth, worked in a number of civic and charitable organizations throughout his adolescence and adult years, and was known in his community as a hard-working, affable fellow who was always ready to lend a hand—or throw a party, many of which boasted a guest list comprised of some of the area's most respected political, business, and civic leaders. Little did they know.

In Springfield, Illinois, Gacy met and married his first wife, Marlynn Myers; was membership chairman for the Chi Rho Club; a member of the board of the Catholic Inter-Club Council (he was raised Catholic); a volunteer with the Illinois Federal Civil Defense; a commanding captain for the Chicago Civil Defense; an officer for the Holy Name Society; and vice president and Man of the Year of the local Jaycees. Later, when he lived in Chicago, he was a Democratic Party volunteer and, most disturbingly, entertained children at hospitals and parties dressed as the loveable "Pogo the Clown."

During the seven-year period from 1972 until his arrest in 1978, John Wayne Gacy kidnapped, drugged, raped, tortured, and killed thirty-three young men and buried most of their bodies on the grounds beneath and around his own home. A few he threw in the river.

Gacy's lack of remorse, combined with his confessions and the overwhelming evidence against him, made it easy for the jury. On March 11, 1980, he was found guilty of all thirty-three murders; two days later was sentenced to death. It would be another fourteen years before the state of Illinois would carry out Gacy's sentence. On May 10, 1994, Gacy was executed by lethal injection.

In 1968, at the age of twenty-four, Gacy was convicted of sexually assaulting a teenage boy and sentenced to ten years in prison. A model prisoner, Gacy was released for good behavior in only eighteen months.

Gacy started over, with financial help from his mother and, again, became the kind of model citizen many communities would love to have in their neighborhoods.

Gacy started a painting and remodeling company but had an ulterior motive: he planned to transform his young teenage workers—all boys—into his sex partners. Suspicions grew when many of the boys who worked for Gacy suddenly disappeared.

Many of the young boys were ultimately found buried in the crawlspace beneath Gacy's house. Ironically, many people who attended Gacy's parties often remarked about the foul stench permeating his house. One neighbor was certain a rat had died somewhere in his walls. Gacy simply nodded sympathetically when people complained about the smell and told them a story about a mold and moisture problem.

Eventually, the truth about Gacy and his deviant and murderous impulses surfaced and the law took over. Gacy's defense attorneys tried an insanity defense but there was too much conflicting evidence about just how intelligent Gacy actually was. One of his neighbors, called as a witness for the prosecution, called him a "brilliant man."

Dean Allen Corll
"THE CANDYMAN"

(1939–1973)

Listen, yah better come over. Ah killed a guy here.
  —Wayne Henley, to the police after fatally shooting
  the Candyman

Parents routinely instruct their children in the ways of the world, and try to teach them how to protect themselves.

"Never tell a caller you're home alone."

"Look both ways before crossing the street."

"Don't run with scissors."

"If you get lost, find a policeman."

And one of the most important, "Don't take candy from strangers."

In the case of the twenty-seven victims of Dean Corll, though, this warning might have worked, except for one fatal flaw: Dean Corll was not a stranger to the young boys he drugged, sodomized, tortured, murdered, and buried. In fact, Corll was a thirty-year-old bachelor who was still very close to his mother; who worked as the plant manager of the candy company his mother had started; and who was also an electrician who worked as a relay tester for Houston Lighting & Power Company. Dean Corll was, at first glance, a nice boy.

Corll regularly took teenage kids in his neighborhood for rides in his van, always keeping his hands to himself, and he regularly gave them candy from his mother's company. Locally, Corll was known in the neighborhood as "a real good neighbor and a real good guy."

Little did anyone know.

Dean Corll served briefly in the army, and upon his discharge, returned to Pasadena.

Corll began hanging out with teenagers and started throwing parties at his house, a place that soon became a popular hangout. What added to the attraction of Corll's place was his willingness to allow the kids to get high when they visited. Glue, sometimes paint, marijuana, and beer were the drugs of choice at the Corll parties.

After lulling neighbors and neighborhood kids into thinking he was harmless, Corll began a rape, torture, and murder rampage that would last three years and result in twenty-seven bodies buried around town.

Using drugs and money, Corll enlisted the services of a local boy, Wayne Henley, the accomplice who would eventually kill Corll.

Corll paid Henley $200 for each boy he brought to Corll's house. Once at the house, Corll would overload the kid with glue and beer and, as soon as he passed out, he would bring him into his special "torture room," strip him naked, and handcuff his hands and feet to a large plywood board. He would then sodomize the boy, usually torture him, and strangle or shoot him.

Corll sometimes left his victim handcuffed to the torture board for days before killing him.

At Henley's trial, Corll's tortures were described. In addition to violent anal rape, Corll would pluck out the boys' pubic hairs one at a time, insert thin glass rods into their urethras, and jam large butt-plugs up their rectums. He would play a radio on top volume to mask the boys' screams.

He would bring the bodies to one of three or four locations for burial. Corll buried seventeen of his bodies under the floor of a boat shed he rented at Southeast Boat Storage. After Henley led police to the shed, detectives brought in four convicts to dig.

The seventeen corpses unearthed beneath the shed were in varying stages of decomposition. Some were relatively fresh; some were skeletons. Corll had covered the corpses with limestone powder to hasten their decomposition. The convicts dug up body after body until body parts and personal effects began surfacing. One convict then had an emotional breakdown and could not go on; another began violently vomiting. The smell was unbearable, and perhaps the single worst moment of the dig occurred when the convicts pulled up the tenth body: it was the body of the missing nephew of one of the detectives.

The Candyman's rapes, tortures, and killings came to an end in August 1973, when Wayne Henley shot Corll six times with a .22-caliber pistol.

That month, Henley had brought his girlfriend to one of Corll's parties, in addition to the requisite young boy for Corll. Henley eventually passed out from the glue and beer and when he woke up, he was naked and handcuffed to Corll's plywood torture board. Corll was likewise naked and began screaming at Henley that he had to be punished for bringing a girl to one of their parties.

Henley begged for his life. Corll told him he was going to shoot him, but Henley offered him a deal. He would personally rape and murder his girlfriend, and Corll could do likewise to the boy Henley had brought, if Corll let him live. Corll loved the idea and agreed to Henley's plan. Corll then unshackled Henley, and Henley seized the opportunity to grab a gun and empty six shots into Corll's chest. Corll died instantly, and Henley then called the police. When the police arrived, Henley spilled his guts and told the police everything.

Eventually, twenty-seven bodies were found, including four at Lake Sam Rayburn and six at High Island.

Henley was tried for murder and, during his trial, there were many questions as to how so many boys could end up missing over a three-year-period and no one thought to investigate if there was a connection. The missing children had been reported to the police by their parents, but the Houston Police Department had 2,200 cops for a city of two million, and they did not have the time or manpower to look for links connecting all the missing boys.

If they had been able to investigate similarities in some of the missing boys' cases, Corll might have been caught earlier and lived to stand trial.

Wayne Henley was sentenced to six 99-year prison sentences. Dean Corll now ranks as one of the worst serial killers of all time.

Jane Toppan

(1854–1938)

That is my ambition, to have killed more people—more helpless people—than any man or woman who has ever lived.

—Jane Toppan

The hospital corridor was quiet at this time of night and the nurse's rubber-soled shoes made a soft sucking sound as she walked toward room 109. The nurse carried a metal tray with a small white towel draped over it, covering a syringe filled with morphine. It was time for Henry Williams's injection. Henry was in a great deal of pain, and the nurse did not like to see her patients in pain. When the nurse arrived at room 109, she stopped and looked back down the length of the dark hall. No one. The nurse entered Henry's room and closed the door behind her. She walked to the side of Henry's bed and placed the tray on the table next to the bed. She looked down at Henry's sleeping face and she could hear the labored breathing and see the grimaces that came and went as waves of pain washed over the elderly man. The nurse removed the towel from the tray and picked up the syringe. She held it up to the light. "One-fifty ought to do it," the nurse thought to herself. "He's thin." Satisfied that her reasoning was correct, the nurse squirted a tiny amount of the clear liquid into the air to remove air bubbles, and with her free hand, swabbed a cotton ball soaked with alcohol on Henry Williams's emaciated forearm. These two steps—the squirting and the swabbing—always made the nurse smile. Both were for the safety of the patient, but after the shot, the patient's safety was irrelevant. The nurse placed the tip of the syringe against Henry's skin, pressed gently, and once the needle was inserted, she squeezed the plunger all the way to the bottom of the barrel. She removed the syringe and then, very quickly, pulled a second syringe out of the pocket of her uniform and immediately injected it into Henry's arm, close to where she had injected the morphine. Atropine enhances the effects of the morphine and would also prevent any death spasms that could get noisy and messy. The nurse put both empty syringes into her pocket, stared down at Henry for a moment, and then turned and left the room. She smiled as she walked back to the nurse's station. By the time she sat down at her desk, Henry Williams was dead.

Morphine, a derivative of opium, is a powerful narcotic pain reliever. It is addictive, and it has been used in medicine for centuries. In high doses, morphine causes central nervous system depression, cardiac or respiratory collapse, coma, and death. The usual dose of morphine for analgesia is between 5 and 30 milligrams injected intravenously; morphine is lethal in doses of between 120 and 250 milligrams.

Jane Toppan was a nurse and was fully aware of the uses—and abuses—of morphine. From 1880 through 1901, it is believed she killed at least thirty-one of her patients, and there is a strong likelihood that she actually did away with more than one hundred of the people in her care. After she was arrested, she claimed dozens of "morphine murders," but she could only provide specific details for thirty-one.

"Yes, I killed all of them," Toppan told police. "I fooled them all—I fooled the stupid doctors and the ignorant relatives; I have been fooling them for years and years. . . . I could not bear to see then suffer. When I kill anyone, they go to sleep and never wake up. I use morphia and atropia, the latter to hide the effects of the former."

Jane Toppan was born "Nora Kelley" in Boston in 1854. She had three sisters and, after her mother died when they were all young, her father was left with the responsibility of taking care of his four daughters. This was not something Pete Kelley handled very well. He was soon placed in a mental institution after he was discovered in his tailor shop trying to sew his eyelids together.

The girls ended up in the care of their grandmother but this was short-lived and they were all eventually placed in an orphanage.

The Toppans of Lowell, Massachusetts, adopted Nora and they changed her name to Jane. The rest of Jane's childhood was relatively normal until she was dumped by her fiancé for another woman. She then became very withdrawn, depressed, rarely left her room, and attempted suicide twice.

Sometime before her twenty-sixth birthday, the idea occurred to Jane to become a nurse and start killing people. What better way to commit murder without getting messy than to work in a hospital and do away with people who are sick and could die anyway?

Jane enrolled in the nursing program in a local hospital, graduated, and it was not long before patients began dying.

After a brief meeting with the hospital's chief surgeon, Jane was fired and began working as a private duty nurse for well-to-do families with someone at home who was sick and needed regular, professional care.

As before, it wasn't long before Jane's patients started dying. She also began killing her patients' family members.

When one suspicious husband demanded an autopsy, the truth was discovered and Jane Toppan was arrested and questioned about the deaths of her patients. "I have a clear conscience," she told the police. "I wouldn't kill a chicken, and if there is any justice in Massachusetts [you] will let me go." Instead of letting her go, however, the police began exhuming bodies all over New England. They found evidence of murder by morphine in every one of Nurse Toppan's patients.

While this was going on, Toppan was confessing.

She went on trial in June 1902, was judged to be insane, and was ordered locked up in the Taunton State Asylum for the Criminally Insane. She died of natural causes in 1938 at the age of eighty-four.

Jane Toppan did not inject her patients with lethal doses of morphine to put them out of their misery. She did it because she loved to kill. Her purely evil acts were not mitigated by the finding that she was insane.

Louis "Lepke" Buchalter

(1897–1944)

If I would talk a lot of big people would get hurt. When I say
big, I mean big. The names would surprise you.
                                        —Louis Lepke Buchalter

His reprieve had run out and Louis Lepke's execution by electrocution would proceed as planned.

His last meal was roasted chicken, shoestring potatoes, and salad.

When a person dies, his or her bladder and bowels release their contents. To prevent an even *more* unpleasant scene in the death chamber (for the witnesses and executioners, that is) the condemned are now put into adult diapers. Years ago, either a rubber band was wound around the penis, or a blocked catheter was inserted into the urethra; and cotton wadding was inserted into the rectum. This is probably the procedure used when Louis Lepke Buchalter was electrocuted, and, in all likelihood, would probably have been more acceptable to Lepke than diapers. After all, the man responsible for creating a "corporation" of murder and for ordering a thousand deaths—a man considered one of the deadliest organized crime figures of all time—would probably not want to go to his final reward (which was probably his final *punishment*) dressed like an infant.

Those who work in organized crime accept killing and the possibility of being killed as a given "job duty" of their chosen line of work.

Mob justice is often "executed" by execution: instead of a judge's gavel, the judicatory instrument of choice is often a gun, a knife, an ice pick (in the ear, eye, or base of the skull), a fire axe, or other more exotic means of dispatchment, including live cremation, live burial, live dismemberment, and death by torture.

Brutal? That word doesn't come close to describing the Mob's methods, but there is a cold logic to the implementation of such a system. In an episode of the hit HBO mob series *The Sopranos*, mob boss Tony Soprano talked about this dynamic with his psychiatrist, explaining that "family members" consider themselves soldiers and that soldiers know that dying is a real possibility when they go forth into battle. They also specifically draw a line between "civilians" and enemy soldiers, avoiding civilian casualties if possible.

Louis Lepke Buchalter, the subject of this chapter, changed all that (if only for a decade or so) when he created Murder, Inc. in 1930. For the first time, "murder for profit" became a division (a lucrative one) of the Syndicate's roster of financial interests. For a price, ranging from $1,000 to $5,000, anyone could have anyone, anywhere, killed. The murder was called a *hit,* the victim was referred to as the *bum,* and the deal between Murder, Inc. and the "customer" was called a *contract.*

Jay Robert Nash (1995), author of the comprehensive crime encyclopedia *Bloodletters and Badmen,* writes that there is no "other single man [more] responsible for the establishment of the national crime syndicate," and describes Lepke's Murder, Inc., as the "deadliest organization ever known in America." Validating Lepke's ignoble legacy was none other than FBI Director J. Edgar Hoover who, during Lepke's heyday, described him as "the most dangerous criminal in the United States."

Louis Buchalter was born Louis Bookhouse in Manhattan on February 6, 1897, and he died in the electric chair at Sing Sing on March 4, 1944.

As a child, he was given the nickname "Lepke," which is short for the Yiddish word "Lepkeleh," which means "Little Louis." It became the name by which he was known during his criminal life. Lepke had very little education and began robbing pushcart owners before he even became a teenager. By the age of twenty-two, he had already served two prison terms and, when he got out, he hooked up with a group of career criminals in New York, consisting of Jewish, Irish, and Italian gangsters.

Lepke rose quickly through the ranks until he became the CEO of Murder, Inc., the murder branch of the powerful crime syndicate. A minimum of one hundred corpses can be attributed to Lepke himself, and several hundred more people were killed on his orders. Lepke was commander-in-chief of an execution task force that was ultimately responsible for over a thousand murders all over the United States.

Lepke was ruthless in extorting money from labor unions and businesses. Moreover, he was incredibly powerful. Judges, politicians, and even cops were afraid of Lepke because he knew a great deal about their corruption and he could easily incriminate them if they crossed him.

Lepke also had his own death squad on the payroll. He used killers from Brooklyn almost exclusively, and he paid them a flat $12,000-a-year retainer for murders as needed. At his peak, he had a killing army of two hundred very efficient assassins, all of whom were on call twenty-four hours a day, seven days a week, no questions asked.

In the thirties and forties, Lepke was one of the most wanted men in America. The FBI initially offered a $25,000 reward for any information that would lead to Lepke's arrest and conviction. The FBI eventually doubled the reward offer to $50,000.

Lepke was ultimately taken into custody, but not through a raid, or some undercover operation. Lepke surrendered to J. Edgar Hoover himself (using Walter Winchell as an intermediary), believing he had a deal in which he would not be turned over to New Jersey district attorney Thomas Dewey, who was Lepke's nemesis.

There was no deal, though, and, in due course, Lepke was convicted and sentenced to, first, fourteen years; then, thirty more years to begin after he had served the fourteen-year sentence; and then, finally, death by electrocution.

52

Dr. Marcel Petiot

(1897–1946)

This is serious. My head may be at stake.
          —Dr. Marcel Petiot, after being charged
          with a multitude of crimes

Marcel Petiot was born in Villeneuve, Paris, and was elected Mayor of that town in 1928 at the age of thirty-one. Shortly after assuming office, he began stealing money from the city coffers.

Petiot had earlier been convicted of black marketeering in World War I (1914–1918) and had also been convicted of drug trafficking while in the military. He had stolen drugs to sell on the black market and the army had determined that he was mentally unstable. Petiot then earned his doctor of medicine at the University of Paris in 1921 at the age of twenty-four and apparently took great delight in the fact that he had graduated from medical school shortly after being certified mentally unbalanced by the military. His official certification as mentally ill also had not prevented him from being elected mayor.

Sixteen years later, Petiot would begin killing Jews for profit and, for three years, would betray every moral code indigenous to being a physician.

* * *

Dr. Marcel Petiot cold-heartedly exploited the nightmarish fears of French Jews during World War II, and then cold-bloodedly robbed and killed them when they put their trust in him.

During the Nazi occupation of France during World War II, Dr. Petiot put out the word to French Jews that he was a member of the French Resistance, and that he could get them safely out of France, but for a price. Reportedly, Petiot's fee was extremely high, but to Jews fearful of the Nazi death camps, gas chambers, and ovens, it was well worth paying.

The good doctor emphasized to his clients that they should bring with them whatever valuables they wanted to keep with them on their trip to freedom. With complete trust, the desperate Jews stuffed suitcases and bags with jewelry, clothing, furs, and anything else precious to them.

When Petiot's "escapees" arrived at his Paris house, the first thing the doctor did was give them an injection that he said was an immunization against typhoid. What it actually was, was the extremely toxic poison strychnine. He would then lock them into a triangular-shaped cement chamber and watch through a peephole as they died agonizing deaths.

Petiot kept their money and valuables and even sent some things to his brother a few towns away.

After his victims died, Petiot would dismember some of their bodies and burn them in a furnace in his basement. It takes quite a long time to burn a human corpse, so he would stack up the backlog like firewood in his cellar until he could get around to disposing of it.

In March 1944, Petiot was caught when the furnace in which he was burning the bodies set fire to his chimney and sent a horrific stench throughout the area. The police and fire department arrived and found twenty-seven bodies in his basement.

Petiot claimed he was a Resistance fighter and that the bodies were those of Nazis that he had discovered, captured, and killed. The police believed him and did not arrest him. Shortly thereafter, Petiot fled Paris.

After the Nazis were thrown out of France, Petiot resurfaced as a Captain Henri Valery and began writing letters to the magazine *Résistance* as Valery. In the letters, he defended Petiot as being innocent. Apparently, some Parisians were suspicious after he abruptly left Paris and many did not believe that the bodies in his basement were Nazis or pro-Nazi sympathizers.

Petiot was eventually arrested in November 1944 and, while in custody, he took responsibility for sixty-three murders, but he claimed that they were all Nazis or sympathizers.

There were pieces of burnt bone and pools of cooked human fat in his furnace, and there were corpses decomposing in pits of lime in his stable. They also found forty-seven suitcases stuffed with valuables.

Petiot was charged with twenty-seven murders, and found guilty of twenty-four in a three-week trial, during which Petiot put on a show for the spectators. He was arrogant, violent, funny, and disrespectful and no one seemed to catch the irony of the situation: Petiot burned Jews in a stove as the Nazis were burning Jews in their ovens.

Petiot was guillotined on May 26, 1946.

Charles Ng and Leonard Lake

(1960–)(1945–1985)

What kind of idiots actually tape themselves committing a crime? I suspect only evil, crazy ones.

—Juror Nancy McEwan

You should hear the screams; sometimes I have to gag them because they scream so hard I can't hear myself.

—Charles Ng

The victims ranged in age from two to forty. When authorities began digging around the house where Charles Ng and Leonard Lake committed multiple murders and atrocities, one of the first things they found was part of a human spinal column covered with maggots. Further excavation would uncover decomposed bodies, cremated and dismembered body parts, a range of human organs, and forty-five pounds of human bones.

Charles Ng (pronounced "Ing") and Leonard Lake were a serial-killer-and-torture-rape team that, in the mid-1980s, kidnapped two infants, three women, and seven men, brought them to a torture chamber that Lake de-

165

signed and built himself in the northern California hills, and then raped the women and tortured them all before killing them and then dismembering and burning their bodies.

For added "fun," Ng and Lake recorded their heinous deeds with a video camera, kept a diary of their acts, and took still photographs. Ng and Lake *enjoyed* torturing their victims. Moreover, they did not limit their actions to physical torture. They also used psychological torture to make their victims' ordeals as horrible as possible. On one of the videotapes shown at Ng's trial, Ng can be heard saying to O'Connor (whose child they had likely already killed by this time), "Your baby is sound asleep, like a rock . . ." and "You can cry and stuff like the rest of them, but it won't do you no good. We are pretty, ha, cold-hearted . . ." (The "rest of them" remark by Ng contributed to the jury's conviction that Ng and Lake were responsible for multiple victims, even if all of the torture and deaths were not videotaped.) Evidence was presented at Ng's trial that he had amputated Paul Cosner's penis with a chain saw and hammered nails into the man's hands; and that he had forced Brenda O'Connor to perform oral sex on him while her boyfriend watched; among other sexual and physical tortures.

Ng and Lake's crimes were sickening and repulsive in their range of perversity. They kidnapped, enslaved, tortured, raped, killed, dismembered, cremated, and buried their victims. During Ng's trial—a $20 million trial which was the most expensive court proceeding in the history of California's judicial system—some of the victims' families actually had to watch the tapes of their loved ones' final hours. And as for the cost of prosecuting Ng, his trial ultimately cost California's taxpayers more than O.J. Simpson's criminal trial, which previously had been the most expensive trial to date.

Although they were a team, and their crimes took place in a house owned by Leonard Lake's in-laws, Lake never lived to stand trial. After being arrested in 1985 on an unrelated shoplifting charge, Lake swallowed two cyanide capsules that he had cached under his shirt lapel. Within seconds, he began having seizures and, even with immediate medical attention, he ended up brain dead and on a respirator. Four days after his arrest, Lake's relatives had him removed from the respirator and he died within seconds.

Lake's death gave the cunning Charles Ng the perfect defense: *I participated in some of the deeds shown on the videotapes, but they were all Lake's idea and I myself didn't kill anybody.*

No one—including the jury—bought this blatant lie, and on June 30, 1999, Ng was found guilty of eleven counts of felony murder and sentenced to death.

The Victims of Charles Ng and Leonard Lake

- Sean Dubs
- Deborah Dubs

- Harvey Dubs
- Clifford Peranteau
- Jeffrey Gerald
- Michael Carroll
- Kathleen Allen
- Lonnie Bond Sr.
- Robin Scott Stapley
- Lonnie Bond Jr.
- Brenda O'Connor
- Paul Cosner (Ng was not found guilty of Cosner's death due to a lack of evidence, but most involved in the case believe Ng did kill Cosner.)

54

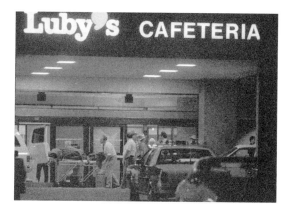

George Hennard

(1956–1991)

*I want you to tell everybody if they don't quit messing around
my house something awful is going to happen.*

—George Hennard

The most ordinary of places can quickly become an extraordinary landmark and, in many cases, this occurs when the place is the site of an unspeakable crime.

Luby's Cafeteria is a well-known, family-style restaurant chain that offers reasonably priced food with more than two hundred locations in ten states in the South and Southwest. The company was founded by Bob Luby in San Antonio, Texas, in April 1948. Around 150 of Luby's restaurants are in Texas.

In October 1991, the Luby's in Killeen, Texas, became known for being the site of the worst mass murder (until then) in American history.

Prior to George Hennard's rampage, the mass murder at a McDonald's in California by James Huberty in 1984 had been the record holder with twenty-one dead (see page 174). George Hennard killed twenty-four in Luby's (counting himself) and injured twenty more.

❖   ❖   ❖

George Hennard was a bitter, angry, misogynist malcontent from Belton, Texas, who never had a smile on his face and who professed a hatred for women and a raging persecution complex that he made no attempt at hiding.

Following his mass murder rampage, two sisters who lived near Hennard in Belton, but whom had never met him, told reporters that Hennard had written them a rambling, delusional four-page letter in which he told them that all the other women in Belton were evil and bitches, and that they were the only good women in town. The girls' mother (a relative of then–Texas Governor Ann Richards) was extremely worried about the letter and took it to the police. Nothing was done however, because no specific threat had been made. The girls' father, a Tennessee hospital administrator, showed the letter to one of his staff psychiatrists, who said that the letter was an indication of "obsessive infatuation with the two young women." The psychiatrist also said that Hennard "could be dangerous."

The doctor was right, and on October 16, 1991, George Hennard drove his light blue Ford pickup truck through the front window of the Killeen Luby's, got out of the truck, and started killing people. Hennard was careful and deliberate and, in most cases, walked right up to people, held the gun to their heads and fired.

Hennard shot an old man in the head as his wife, daughter, and grandchild watched. The wife stayed with her husband and Hennard then shot her in the forehead, killing her instantly. In an out-of-character gesture, Hennard then told the daughter and granddaughter to get out of the restaurant.

The scene in Luby's was utter madness. Hennard had two pistols, a Glock 17 semiautomatic and a Ruger P89, and he reloaded as he emptied them.

Some people did manage to survive. An autoworker threw himself through a plate glass window, allowing twenty or thirty people to escape, and ending up with deep gash wounds in his shoulder. One worker hid in a dishwasher for most of the day; another hid in the freezer. Both lived.

As he was massacring innocent people, Hennard shouted nonsense about payback for what Belton had done to him. "This is what Bell County has done to me!" he screamed. "I hope all this is worth it, Texas!"

Fourteen minutes after Hennard crashed through the front window, retired undercover narcotics investigator Ken Olsen shot at Hennard and managed to hit him twice, once in the shoulder, and once in the upper body. Hennard then crawled into a bathroom and killed himself with one shot to the temple.

The Luby's massacre was over.

Police later discovered that Hennard had two fully loaded clips of ammunition when he killed himself. He had clearly come prepared for an enormous slaughtering, and it is a certainty that perhaps dozens more could have been killed if Ken Olsen had not hit Hennard when he did.

George Hennard had been a Merchant Marine from 1981 to 1989, and in February 1991, a few months before his killing spree, he had been rejected for reinstatement in the service. Investigators learned that Hennard took this rejection especially hard and that he had always told people that his years in the Merchant Marine had been the best years of his life. His superiors recalled otherwise. Hennard was unruly, arrogant, and, with his personality, did not last on one ship for too long a period. A maritime agent who knew Hennard recalled, "He would come in with a very cold look and be very argumentative, loud, boisterous, sometimes cursing and swearing."

A seventy-one-year-old survivor of the Luby's shooting summed up most people in Texas's feelings about native son George Hennard: "I'm glad he's dead. I tend to think people get what they deserve, and he got what he deserved."

Earle Leonard Nelson

"THE GORILLA MURDERER"
"THE DARK STRANGLER"

(1897–1928)

"Room to Let"
> —The sign Earle Nelson would look for
> to find his next victim

I only do my lady killin' on Saturday night, fellas.
> —Earle Nelson

I forgive those who have wronged me.
> —Earle Nelson's last words before being hanged

Earle Leonard Nelson was a rapist, murderer, pedophile, and necrophiliac, who strangled and raped twenty-two women in the United States and Canada in less than two years. Leonard killed women in San Francisco, San Jose, Oakland, and Santa Barbara, California; Portland and Oregon City, Oregon; Seattle, Washington; Council Bluffs, Iowa; Kansas City, Kansas; Philadelphia,

Pennsylvania; Buffalo, New York; Detroit, Michigan; Chicago, Illinois; and Winnipeg, Manitoba, Canada.

Nelson was known as the "Gorilla Murderer," and the nickname was insultingly literal. Nelson had a high, receding forehead, thick, protruding lips, and big, hairy hands; his appearance was quite simian.

Also contributing to his nickname was the animalistic savagery of his crimes.

When Nelson was a child, he suffered a serious head injury when a moving streetcar hit him. This accident caused him lifelong pain and may have contributed to the sudden change in his personality, a change towards a sex-crazed, violent persona that raped and murdered at will.

Nelson was born in Philadelphia in 1897 and his mother died of syphilis when he was a year old. He was then sent off to be raised by his Aunt Lillian. Nelson was a weird child. He would head off to school impeccably dressed and clean, but would return home wearing filthy rags. It is believed he switched clothes with homeless beggars on the way home. Why? Charity? Mental illness? No one really knows.

Nelson's Aunt Lillian was a devoutly religious woman who believed in literal interpretation of the Bible and who saw as her duty the teaching of the Bible to her orphaned nephew. It worked. Even during the height of his killing rampage, Earle Nelson preached and read the Bible, almost to the point of religious hysteria.

Knowing and loving the Good Book did not, however, temper Earle Nelson's carnal lusts or his blood lusts. After he married a sixty-year-old spinster in 1919 (he was twenty-two), he forced her to have sex with him at least twice a day. She later testified that he would also masturbate all day long. The marriage lasted six months and did nothing to prevent Earle Nelson's soon-to-follow cross-country odyssey of rape and slaughter.

When Nelson was twenty-six, he was institutionalized in a mental asylum for sexually assaulting a little girl. He managed to escape from the institution three times.

Nelson committed his first murder on February 20, 1926. He was on the hunt in San Francisco and came upon a boarding house with a "Rooms to Let" sign in its front window. Nelson knocked on the door and persuaded the woman to let him in to see the room. Once inside, he strangled the woman to death, raped her corpse, and then hid her body in the attic of the boarding house.

Over the next several months, Nelson traveled the United States, leaving a trail of victims in his wake. He would use the same strategy in each town and, once he was inside a private room or boarding house, he would turn into a violent beast and strangle and rape the innocent woman who simply thought she was showing a room to a potential tenant.

Nelson's victims ranged in age from fourteen to sixty-three and, in Kansas City, Nelson also strangled the eight-month-old daughter of his twenty-eight-year-old victim, Germania Harpin.

One characteristic of the Gorilla Murderer's crime scenes was the hiding of the body. Nelson never left his victims' corpses out in the open. He always hid them in a closet or under a bed when he was finished.

Nelson was eventually caught when the police traced him to some of Emily Paterson's stolen clothing he had sold to a secondhand store. He was arrested four miles from the U.S. border and tried in Winnipeg, Manitoba, Canada, in November 1927 for the murder of his final victim, Emily Paterson. (Even after his death, police suspected that Nelson had been responsible for a triple murder in New Jersey in 1926. All three women had been landladies who had been killed during the day, raped, and then stuffed under beds. It was known that Nelson was in the New Jersey area at the time of the killings but he was never charged or credited with those murders.)

Nelson was convicted and sentenced to death. He was hanged on January 13, 1928. His final words were, "I have never committed murder; never, never, never. I forgive those who have wronged me."

It is understood that no one believed him then, and nothing has been learned since his death to make anyone believe him now. The truth is, Nelson had twenty-two known victims; there could have been several more.

56

James Oliver Huberty

(1942–1983)

Society had its chance. I'm going hunting. Hunting humans. . . .
I killed thousands in Vietnam, and I want to kill more!

—James Oliver Huberty

When James Oliver Huberty walked into a McDonald's restaurant on July 18, 1984, in San Ysidro, California, and began slaughtering innocent people, he devastated lives, but he also attacked and debased an American icon. Huberty was a self-professed hater of "children, Mexicans, and the United States," and sadly, the McDonald's where he unleashed his vile hatred was a place where all three could easily be found.

James Huberty was born in 1942 in Canton, Ohio. When he was three he contracted polio, from which he recovered, but the viral disease did enough damage to leave him with a limp. When he started school, he was taunted mercilessly by classmates for the way he walked.

When Huberty was seven, his father bought a farm and moved him and his brother there, but his mother refused to go with her family. She, instead, embraced religious fanaticism and became a missionary preacher.

The Huberty family farm was in Amish country in Pennsylvania and most of their neighbors were staunch advocates of the strict Amish code of conduct. Apparently, the only acceptable single-parent household in Amish territory would be those in which one of the parents had died. Thus, the Huberty's broken home did not sit well with many of their neighbors, and young James Huberty was once again tormented by his classmates.

It was around this time that Huberty became interested in guns.

He learned the technique of "hot loading," which is overloading ammunition shells with more gunpowder than they are rated to hold. Huberty's grandmother (who had moved into the household to help her son raise his boys after the boys' mother left) once found a pile of dust in a room where Huberty had been working. She swept it up and threw it into the fire in the fireplace. The dust was gunpowder, it exploded, and Grandma was scorched from the blast.

Huberty made it through high school and enrolled in college, but soon dropped out to attend mortuary school. In 1965, while studying the mortuarial arts, Huberty married a woman named Etna. After Huberty's killing spree in 1983, the minister who had married Huberty and Etna came forward and told authorities that he remembered Huberty as being someone who was "ready to explode."

Shortly thereafter, Huberty embraced atheism, and yet, his understanding of the doctrine seems to have been skewed. He said he did not believe in God because he blamed God for taking his mother away from him. Yet, if there is no God, how can he be blamed for anything? This subtle theological point did not seem to matter to Huberty.

Huberty was able to find work at a funeral parlor in his hometown of Canton, but did not last long at the job. He was a good embalmer and loved the work, but he was such a misogynist that he refused to offer sympathy or counsel to the bereaved, a necessary part of the profession. His ongoing hatred for people manifested itself in his interactions with those who had lost a loved one, so he left the funeral business and became a welder.

Huberty scored a job working at a public utility plant, began making a good income, and bought a house, but he was always angry and was, again, the subject of taunts. His plant coworkers deliberately called him "Puberty" instead of Huberty, knowing how much it angered him.

So Huberty began collecting a great many guns. He became an expert on all kinds of weapons and specifically enjoyed talking about the kinds of damage different bullets could do to human flesh. He was rapidly reaching the point of no return and this was extremely evident in his paranoid ravings about the U.S. government, foreign enemies, foreigners in America, the failings of American presidents, and anything else on which he could fixate. In addition, he kept a fully loaded gun within arm's reach no matter where he was seated in the house. He also made sure that none of the guns in his domestic arsenal had on their safeties.

Huberty was keeping German shepherds during this time and one of his dogs once jumped up on top of a visitor's car and scratched the paint. Huberty shot and killed the dog, telling his friend, "There, I took care of it."

Huberty bled hostility toward his neighbors and coworkers and he also physically abused—slapped and punched—his wife and children. He once broke his wife's jaw and held a knife to his daughter's throat. He was also unspeakably cruel to animals and, in the months before his killing spree, James Oliver Huberty was a textbook example of a malevolent personality.

On July 18, 1984, at around 4:00 P.M., Huberty walked into the San Ysidro McDonald's, shot the female manager, and then ordered everyone in the restaurant to lie down on the floor. The customers obeyed and he then began shooting as many people as he could. His arsenal that day consisted of a Browning P-35 Hi-Power 9-mm pistol; a Winchester 1200 pump-action 12-gauge shotgun; and an Israeli Military Industries 9-mm Model A Carbine (Uzi).

Only one of Huberty's murder victims lived long enough to make it to a hospital. The others in the restaurant that day were either killed instantly, wounded, or managed to escape. Huberty was impartial in choosing his victims: He killed, men, women, infants, and children at will.

At 5:10 P.M., sixty police SWAT officers surrounded the building and a SWAT team member fired one shot and severed Huberty's aorta.

Huberty's final toll was twenty-one men, women, and children killed, and nineteen injured.

McDonald's tore down the restaurant, donated money to the city, and put up a park as a memorial for the victims.

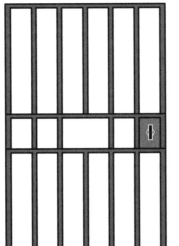

57

Carl Panzram

(1891–1930)

*In my lifetime, I have murdered 21 human beings, I have com-
mitted thousands of burglaries, robberies, larcenies, arsons and,
last but not least, I have committed sodomy on more than 1,000
male human beings. For all these things, I am not in the least
bit sorry. I have no conscience so that does not bother me.*

—Carl Panzram

Sometimes the sheer depth of evil in a person is astounding. In the case of
Carl Panzram, there is a man who exhibited nothing but contempt and defi-
ance for even the most basic laws and rules of a civilized society. Murder, robbery, arson, fraud, assault, pedophilia, necrophilia, and more, were his regular
endeavors, and he even went to his death with an arrogant hatred for the people trying to secure him a stay.

Panzram was consistent. He once proclaimed, "I don't believe in Man,
God, nor Devil. I hate the whole damned human race, including myself."
Misanthropy and self-loathing commingled in Panzram's psyche to create one
of the most malevolent human monsters of all time. Revealingly, Panzram's
persistent fantasy was mass terrorism that would result in the deaths of every-

one in a town. During his many prison stays, he plotted ways to poison water supplies or blow up passenger trains.

Panzram was repeatedly tortured during his various incarcerations. He was hung naked and blasted with a fire hose; he was given electric shocks in a bathtub; he was put in a straitjacket so tight it eventually stopped his blood circulation to some body parts. These episodes inculcated an almost unimaginable, deep-seated hatred for anyone with whom he came in contact. Society would pay the price. Panzram's philosophy after the tortures and rapes he endured was the following: If he could not hurt the people who hurt him, he would hurt others instead. And he did.

Carl Panzram was arrested for being drunk and disorderly when he was eight years old. This was the beginning of thirty-one years of evil and crime.

When Panzram was eleven, he was caught burglarizing a neighbor's house and, in 1903, was sent to a reform school. He did not like it there, and so he urinated and masturbated into beverages he served to the guards and teachers, then set fire to the institution and did $100,000 worth of damage.

Upon his release, Panzram got drunk and joined the army. Within weeks, he was court-martialed for stealing military equipment and sentenced to three years in Leavenworth.

After he was released, he traveled through the Southwest, sodomizing and robbing along the way. He was repeatedly caught for all manners of offenses and sentenced to various terms in prison.

In 1919, during one of his "out of prison" periods, he got a job working for the Sinclair Oil Company and promptly burned down an oil rig.

He then sailed to Scotland, traveled through Europe for a time (robbing and killing as he moved from place to place), and ended up in Africa where he quickly sodomized and killed a twelve-year-old boy. Of this murder he said, "I sat down to think things over a bit. While I was sitting there, a little kid about twelve or thirteen years old came bumming around. He was looking for something. He found it, too. I took him out to a gravel pit about one-quarter mile away. I left him there, but first committed sodomy on him and then killed him. His brains were coming out of his ears when I left him, and he will never be any deader."

While in Africa, he hired six black porters to take him on a crocodile-hunting trip. He killed them all, sodomized them after they were dead, and then fed their bodies to the crocodiles.

He then returned to the United States and began committing burglaries and sodomizing children. He killed a twelve-year-old in Salem, Massachusetts, and left him, too, with his brains coming out of his ears.

Traveling through New England in 1920, he robbed the New Haven, Connecticut, home of former president William Howard Taft. (This was seven years after Taft's term in office had ended.)

By this time, Panzram had built up quite a substantial cache of cash and he used some of the money to buy a yacht. He lured ten sailors onto the yacht with the promise of work, and then robbed, raped, and killed all ten men.

Panzram stood trial for the murders and at the trial that would eventually send him to Leavenworth for the rest of his days, he threatened the jury, telling them, "If I live I'll execute some more of you."

When Panzram arrived at Leavenworth, he told the warden that he would kill the first man who bothered him. That man was prison laundry foreman Robert Warnke, who apparently regularly reported Panzram's infractions to the guards. Panzram killed him by bashing in his head with an iron bar and he was given the death penalty on top of the twenty-five-years-to-life sentence he was already serving.

The Society for the Abolishment of Capital Punishment tried to get Panzram's stay commuted. Panzram wrote to them, telling them that he was looking forward to being hanged and that he would go to the gallows with a smile on his face. He also told them, "I wish you all had one neck and that I had my hands on it."

Panzram also wrote to President Hoover, telling the president, "I absolutely refuse to accept either a pardon or a commutation should either one or the other be offered to me." Panzram could have saved the stationery, for he was offered neither a stay nor a commutation.

Panzram was hung at Leavenworth on September 5, 1930. True to form, his last words were, "Hurry it up, you Hoosier bastard! I could hang a dozen men while you're fooling around!"

The hangman obliged.

58

Thomas Hamilton

(1952–1996)

All these guns have caused too much pain, this town will never be the same, so for the bairns of Dunblane, we ask—please never again.
> —the revised lyrics of Bob Dylan's "Knockin' on Heaven's Door," recorded as a tribute to the children of Dunblane lost at the hands of Thomas Hamilton

The coroner who performed the autopsy on Scottish child-slayer Thomas Hamilton was surprised to discover that Hamilton had several broken ribs. This was astounding news, since it is unlikely that Hamilton could have carried out his killing rampage with that many broken ribs. After some discrete investigation, the coroner learned that Hamilton's ribs had been broken postmortem. One of the ambulance drivers was so angry over what Hamilton had done, he repeatedly kicked the killer's dead body in the ribs before loading it into the ambulance. The driver was not charged with any wrongdoing.

Around 9:30 on the morning of March 13, 1996, Thomas Hamilton parked his car in the Dunblane School parking lot. He got out of his car carrying two 9-mm Browning pistols, two Smith & Wesson revolvers, a supply of ammunition, and other equipment.

Using wire cutters, Hamilton cut several phone lines on a telephone pole in the school parking lot. None of the lines fed the school; they all serviced the surrounding homes.

Hamilton then entered the school through a side door, fired two shots into the stage of the school's assembly hall, and then fired two shots into the girls' bathroom.

The story of the three or four minutes that followed can best be told by Scotland's official *Public Enquiry*, dated October 16, 1996, into the shooting at the Dunblane School:

> He then entered the gym. He was wearing a dark jacket, black corduroy trousers and a woolly hat. . . . He had a pistol in his hand. He advanced a couple of steps into the gym and fired indiscriminately and in rapid succession. Mrs. Harrild was hit in both forearms, the right hand and left breast. She stumbled into the . . . store area which adjoined the gym, followed by several of the children. Mrs. Mayor was also shot several times and died instantly. Mrs. Blake was then shot but also managed to reach the store, ushering some children in ahead of her.
>
> From his position near the entrance doorway of the gym Hamilton fired 29 shots in rapid succession. From that position he killed one child and injured others. During this shooting, four injured children made their way to the store. In the store, Mrs. Blake and Mrs. Harrild tried to console and calm the terrified children who had taken refuge there. The children cowered on the floor, lying helplessly in pools of blood, hearing the screams and moans of their classmates in the gym, and waiting for the end or for help. Thomas Hamilton walked up the east side of the gym, firing 6 shots. At a point midway along it he discharged 8 shots in the direction of the opposite side of the gym. He then advanced to the middle of the gym and walked in a semi-circle systematically firing 16 shots at a group of children who had either been disabled by the firing or who had been thrown to the floor. He stood over them and fired at point-blank range.
>
> It appears that Thomas Hamilton then advanced to the south end of the gym. From that position, he fired 24 rounds in various directions.
>
> He then went outside the doorway and fired 4 more shots towards the library cloakroom, striking Mrs. Grace Tweddle, a member of the staff, a glancing blow on the head. A teacher, Mrs. Catherine Gordon, and her class . . . saw and heard Thomas Hamilton firing. . . . She immediately instructed her class to get down on the floor, just in time before he discharged 9 shots into her classroom.

At this point, Hamilton seems to have decided that he had fulfilled his twisted mission, and that he had wreaked the havoc he had obviously thought about and planned for some time. The *Public Enquiry* goes on to describe Hamilton's final moments:

> Thomas Hamilton then re-entered the gym where he shot again. He then released the pistol and drew a revolver. He placed the muzzle of the revolver in his mouth, pointing upwards and pulled the trigger. His death followed quickly.

A teacher and fifteen children were dead in the gymnasium from a barrage of fifty-eight bullets. One child shot in the gym would die later at the hospital. Seventeen others were injured by gunshots, but survived.

Thomas Hamilton grew up thinking that his grandparents were his real parents and that his biological mother was his sister. He was an unremarkable student, and was remembered as being a loner. As he got older, he became increasingly paranoid and some recalled his increasing sense of self-importance and superiority.

Hamilton got involved with the Boy Scouts while in his late twenties but was kicked out for placing his charges in situations that were unsafe or that did not meet the Boy Scout's regulations. He made Scouts sleep outdoors in thin clothing, for instance. After a half-hearted attempt to fight the dismissal, Hamilton started his own boys' clubs and solicited members in the age group seven to eleven. He was remembered as not feeling comfortable around adults, especially women, and spending most of his time with the members of his clubs.

In his early thirties, Hamilton started buying and selling guns and ammunition. Records indicate purchases of a range of firearms over the two years before the Dunblane massacre, and the two pistols he used in his shooting rampage were part of own collection.

There are still no adequate explanations as to why Thomas Hamilton decided to kill sixteen five-year-old children, a teacher, and then himself.

Some may suggest mental illness, or a rage against society, or an almost incapacitating sense of alienation.

None of these reasons means anything to the parents of the dead, or to the children and teachers lucky enough to have survived.

Jeffrey Dahmer
"THE MILWAUKEE CANNIBAL"

(1960–1994)

I bite.
— Jeffrey Dahmer, to his prison guards

There is an overwhelming sense of fiction, of unbelievability, of *artifice,* in the macabre story of serial killer Jeffrey Dahmer.

The facts of his case cannot be real, we tell ourselves; they simply could not have actually happened. No human being could have done *what Jeffrey Dahmer did.*

But the facts *are* real, and Jeffrey Dahmer did, indeed, commit the unspeakable acts that made his name known around the world when the media revealed what went on, first, in his grandmother's house, and then, from 1990, in his vile charnel apartment on North 25th Street in a rundown section of Milwaukee, Wisconsin.

Dahmer's atrocities were discovered on the night of July 22, 1991, when Tracy Edwards, thirty-two, raving and wearing handcuffs, stopped police on patrol and told them that he had been in the apartment of a man who had said he was going to cut out and eat his heart.

The police followed up on these claims by paying a visit to apartment 213 at the Oxford Apartments, where they were unconcernedly welcomed in by Dahmer. Once inside, they saw Polaroids scattered around the apartment of Dahmer engaging in oral and anal sex with men, plus pictures of eviscerated corpses and body parts. Most alarming to the cops, however, was the smell in the apartment. The place reeked of what smelled like a combination of spoiled meat and backed-up sewage, but what homicide cops and battle veterans can immediately recognize as the smell of death: the stench of decomposing human flesh.

A background check revealed that he was on probation for a felony conviction for sexual assault on a twelve-year-old boy, but Dahmer was calm and cooperative, and answered the police officers' questions. It was around this time that one of the officers opened the door of Dahmer's refrigerator and found the severed head of Dahmer's victim Oliver Lacy staring back at him. The head sat in a box on the bottom shelf of the refrigerator, next to an open box of baking soda. Further investigation revealed even more stomach-churning discoveries: In the freezer were three plastic bags filled with human body parts, including Lacy's heart, lungs, intestines, kidney and liver. Dahmer told police he had frozen these parts "to eat later."

Dahmer's stinking apartment was now officially a crime scene, one of the most notorious in the history of Milwaukee, not to mention in the annals of modern crime.

In Dahmer's apartment was also a large freezer, which was found to contain three human heads and several parts of human torsos. The police also found two human skulls in a filing cabinet and three more skulls in boxes. Some of the skulls had been stripped clean of flesh and hair and painted gray. Police also found a 57-gallon drum, which contained three headless torsos, and a large kettle on Dahmer's stove contained human genitals and two decomposed hands.

For several surreal hours, neighbors watched as crime scene investigators, clad in stark yellow biohazard suits, emptied out the disgusting contents of Dahmer's apartment. The refrigerator, the freezer, the plastic barrel—all were wheeled out and taken to crime labs. Witnesses said the refrigerator could be smelled from blocks away.

Dahmer was cooperative and confessed to his crimes. On his lawyer's advice, he pleaded guilty but insane.

Jeffrey "the Cannibal" Dahmer's crimes included pedophilia, necrophilia, murder, cannibalism, dismemberment, torture, and kidnapping, and in 1992, he was convicted of sixteen counts of first-degree murder and sentenced to sixteen consecutive life sentences. During his sentencing of Dahmer, Judge Lawrence Gram stated: "The sentence is structured in such a way that the defendant will never again see freedom."

In November 1994, Dahmer was beaten to death by his fellow inmates in a prison bathroom.

Dahmer had once said the following regarding his motivation for his horrific actions:

> Am I just an extremely evil person or is it some kind of Satanic influence? I have no idea. I have no idea at all. Is it possible to be influenced by spirit beings? I know that sounds like an easy way to cop out and say that I couldn't help myself, but from all that the Bible says, there are forces that have a direct or indirect influence on people's behavior. The Bible calls him Satan. I suppose it's possible because it sure seems like some of the thoughts aren't my own, they just come blasting into my head. These thoughts are very powerful, very destructive, and they do not leave. They're not the kind of thoughts that you can just shake your head and they're gone. They do not leave.

If there is someone who manifests the essence of pure evil, it just might be the demonic Jeffrey Dahmer. Dahmer's all-encompassing, completely ego-driven goal was *satisfaction:* he would do anything necessary to satisfy his deranged appetite for human flesh, necrophiliac sex, and the torture, murder, and dismemberment of innocent young men. He exhibited absolutely no empathy for his victims or compassion for their families, instead reveling in his deeds by repeating them over and over, until he was stopped the only way possible: by being caught.

Insane or not, evil is as evil does, and the acts of Jeffrey Dahmer were the epitome of evil.

Dahmer found God in prison, and he expressed remorse for his actions and believed that Jesus would forgive him.

60

Dennis Nilsen

(1945–)

I wished I could stop but I could not. I had no other thrill or happiness.

—Dennis Nilsen

I put the head into a pot, popped the lid on and lit the stove. Later I listened to some music and had a good drink, also watching some TV as the head was simmering.
—Dennis Nilsen, from a pre-sentencing statement

Dennis Nilsen was a British serial killer who killed and dismembered a great many homosexual men in Great Britain in the late 1970s and early '80s. He admitted to all his crimes when an array of dismembered male body parts were found in his drains. He is currently serving a life sentence in England.

The first time Dennis Nilsen killed a young man he had brought home from a bar, he used a tie to strangle him. He then made coffee, smoked some cigarettes, and gave the fresh corpse a bath. He then put the corpse to bed, and went out and bought an electric knife and a large kettle. He decided, however, that the corpse of the young man was too beautiful to desecrate by cutting it into pieces, so he instead dressed it in new underwear, took a bath, and then tried to have sex with the corpse. He could not maintain his arousal, so he lay the body on the floor and took a nap. He then watched TV and decided that he needed to "bury" the body. He tried to put it under the floorboards in his apartment, but the body was already too stiff, so Nilsen propped it up against a wall and went to sleep. The next morning he massaged and bent the corpse's limbs so he could squeeze it into the space under the floor. This time it worked. Nilsen left the corpse there for a week. Then he removed it, bathed it, masturbated on it, and then put it under the floor again. Seven and a half months later Nilsen burned the then-decomposed body in a bonfire.

He began to kill in 1978, shortly after Christmas, and by 1981, Nilsen had murdered twelve men, mostly homosexuals or male prostitutes.

Nilsen was a necrophiliac and regularly had sex with his corpses. He also cooked the heads of some of his victims, but did not eat them. He boiled them to be able to more easily remove the flesh.

He washed the corpses, sat them up, and had them watch TV with him. He would have sex by rubbing his penis between the thighs of a corpse, then store the body under the floorboards. Sometimes he would keep a body in a cupboard for a couple of weeks before putting it under the floorboards. He would also make the corpse sleep with him, being sure it was dressed in fresh pajamas. Nilsen often talked to the corpses of his victims as though they were alive, and he liked to arrange mirrors around his bed so he could see himself and his victim naked in bed together.

After he had gotten good use out of the corpses, he would often burn the bodies in his garden in a big bonfire. The neighborhood kids would gather round to watch, and no one ever questioned him about what he was burning. There were times when Nilsen had so many bodies in his apartment—under the floorboards, in the cabinet under the sink, in suitcases—that he would have to spray insecticide constantly to kill the flies attracted to the decomposing bodies.

Nilsen would usually strip down to his underwear and butcher the bodies on his kitchen floor. Then he would boil the skin off the heads, put the internal organs in plastic bags, and bury body parts in his garden, hide them behind fences, as well as other select spots. After Nilsen was arrested, the police found more than a thousand individual bone fragments in his garden.

Nilsen was caught when he cut up one of his victims and flushed the body parts down his toilet. He caused a backup that clogged the other tenants' toilets. The plumber got suspicious when he found pieces of meat in the drain with hair attached to them. When the pipes were traced to Nilsen's apartment, Nilsen admitted to everything and even told the cops where to find other human remains.

Nilsen was born in 1945 in Fraserburg, Scotland, and blames several traumatic episodes in his early life for turning him into the monster that terrorized Great Britain for almost four years. He remembers being traumatized by the sight of his grandfather's corpse. He also remembers almost drowning and being rescued by an older boy who masturbated while standing over him and ejaculated all over his chest, although some authorities suspect he may have made this story up. He also revealed that during that time, he would make up his body with fake blood and masturbate while staring at himself naked and pretending to be dead.

Nilsen worked as a cop for a year and remembers loving the sight of autopsied bodies in the morgue. He learned how to butcher meat while serving as a cook in the Army Catering Corps, and made good use of this skill on his victims.

Nilsen ultimately pled not guilty to all the charges against him, but he wrote several journals detailing his crimes and insisted that he did feel remorse over his deeds.

He was determined to be judged as sane and was found guilty on all charges in 1983. He was sentenced to life in prison, and will be eligible for parole in 2008, after twenty-five years served. He has been nonviolent in prison and is now known as the "British Jeffrey Dahmer."

61

Richard Ramirez
"THE NIGHT STALKER"

(1960–)

Now wouldn't you be surprised if I turned out to be the Stalker?

—Richard Ramirez, before he was caught,
to his former landlady

You maggots make me sick. I will be avenged. Lucifer dwells within all of us! Evil . . . evil . . . evil . . . death comes with the territory . . . see you in Disneyland . . .

—Ramirez, during his sentencing in court

Richard Ramirez was a professed Satanist who chanted "evil" over and over at his trial and claimed that he murdered because he truly enjoyed killing people.

Witness accounts of Ramirez were as dark as his deeds. He was almost universally described as having rotten teeth, an ugly face, disgusting breath, and terrible body odor.

Ramirez ultimately received nineteen death sentences. Today, he is on Death Row in San Quentin Penitentiary in California, waiting for one of the nineteen to be carried out.

Ramirez's first victim was a seventy-nine-year-old woman whom he stabbed and then hacked at her neck until he almost decapitated her. Then, in a ten-week period in the summer of 1985, Ramirez went on a horrifyingly savage assault and murder rampage.

He killed a thirty-two-year-old woman in her home by slashing her throat.

He killed a seventy-five-year-old woman in her home by beating her almost to death and then cutting her throat.

He ferociously beat a sixteen-year-old girl with a tire iron in her home, but she lived.

He beat to death a sixty-one-year-old woman in her home and then mutilated her body.

He raped and sodomized a sixty-three-year-old woman in her home, but fled before he could kill her.

He shot to death a husband and wife in their midsixties in their beds and then hacked at the husband until his head almost came off.

He broke into a home in Sun Valley and killed the thirty-two-year-old husband, and then beat and raped his wife. He also forced the woman to perform oral sex on him and then he beat their eight-year-old son while his mother listened.

He broke into a house in Northridge and shot both the husband and wife in their bed. He shot the husband in the head and the wife in the face and, yet, amazingly they both survived.

As in the Sun Valley home invasion, Ramirez broke into the home of an Asian couple, shot the husband in the head and killed him, and then beat and raped his wife. He also forced her to perform oral sex on him. She lived.

He broke into a home and killed the couple that lived there. He shot the husband in the head and then butchered the wife. He gouged out her eyes, cut a huge T-shaped gash in her breast, and then stabbed her repeatedly all over her body, including her pubic region.

Shortly after these horrible crimes, Ramirez declared he was a Satanist and that all of his assaults and murders were heartfelt sacrifices to the Dark Lord.

He began to leave pentagram symbols at the scenes of his attacks. He carved a pentagram into the inner thigh of an elderly woman he murdered, and also left one on a wall. Ramirez was careful to place the top point of the five-lined star downwards. Detectives later learned this was a sign for devil worship.

Ramirez's crimes were perverse, sadistic, and he did not discriminate when it came to picking his victims. He preyed on young people, senior citizens, men, women, children, Asians, Caucasians . . . it didn't matter. His bloodlust was insatiable and whoever was in his crosshairs was a target. He even took some of his victims' eyes with him. A Los Angeles sheriff who had been on the force for many years, and had seen many crime scenes, called Ramirez's crimes the most bizarre he had ever come across.

Moreover, Ramirez was cruel for the sake of being cruel. He once kidnapped a very young child whose father he had just killed and mother he had just raped, and drove the child a great distance out of town and then abandoned him there.

Ramirez was finally arrested during a drug deal that went bad. One of the primary detectives on the case (out of a task force of over two hundred) was Frank Costello, who had previously helped nab Kenneth Bianchi and Angelo Buono.

At his arraignment, Ramirez verbally threatened the judge, gave the prosecutor the finger, and flashed pentagrams that he had drawn on his palms. Through legal wrangling, Ramirez's trial was delayed for almost three years, but he was eventually tried, convicted, and sentenced.

62

Charles Whitman

(1941–1966)

I think most men are wired up to perform acts of violence, usually defensive, but I think that we're still very primitive creatures, and that we have a real tendency toward violence. Most of us are like . . . well, most of us are like most airplanes. Remember TWA Flight 800, the one that exploded over Long Island Sound? That was an electrical problem, or at least they feel that it was probably an electrical problem, and a fire started in the wiring. And when you see a guy who suddenly snaps, a guy who goes nuts, a Charles Whitman, who goes to the top of the Texas Tower and shoots a whole bunch of people . . . that's a guy with a fire in his wires, basically.

—Stephen King, from a
1998 interview with *Salon* magazine

I don't quite understand what is compelling me to type this note. Perhaps it is to leave some vague reasons for the actions I have recently performed. . . . I have had some terrific headaches.[1]

---

[1] As requested by Whitman (and required by law), an autopsy was performed on him after his death, and a malignant tumor was discovered in his brain. Although many leaped to the conclusion that this is what caused Whitman's shooting rampage, further study later determined that the tumor was in an area of the brain that did not influence emotions.

*. . . It was after much thought that I decided to kill my wife,
Kathy . . . I love her dearly . . . I don't want her to have to face
the embarrassment my actions would surely cause her . . . I intend to kill her as painlessly as possible. . . . Similar reasons
provoked me to take my mother's life also.*
> —Charles Whitman, in a letter he wrote before going on
> his Texas Tower shooting rampage

The University of Texas Tower is open these days for visitors, and many people climb to the top each year to see for themselves the incredible panoramic
view. Many of the visitors are young people who were not even born in 1966
when Charles Whitman unleashed a nightmare of death on utterly unsuspecting students, and other hapless souls who, unfortunately, were in the wrong
place at the wrong time. Many of the Texas Tower visitors have never even
heard of Charles Whitman, but they are impacted by his deeds nonetheless;
to get to the top of the Tower, all visitors now have to pass through a metal de-
tector.

The scene is iconic in American culture. Young students carrying books,
walking on crisscrossing lanes on a college campus, surrounded by manicured
lawns, stately buildings, and, often, a statue or memorial to a renowned alum-
nus. We have seen this countless times in movies and on TV shows, and many
of us have walked those lanes in our own lives, on our way to this building or
that, eager to be on time for an American lit class or a chemistry final.

The commonplace aura of familiarity and, yes, security that pervades
the typical college campus makes what Charles Whitman did especially horrific and repellant.

Charles Joseph Whitman—former altar boy and Boy Scout—was the
sniper mass murderer who, on August 1, 1966, killed sixteen people (his first
two murders were his mother and wife the night before) and injured thirty-
one more from the University of Texas Tower in just over ninety minutes. It
was a massacre now considered the first U.S. school shooting.

On the evening of July 31, 1966, Whitman met his mother in the lobby
of her apartment building. They went upstairs together and when they were
inside her apartment, he pulled out a length of black rubber hose, wrapped it
around her neck, and then strangled her until she was unconscious. He then
took out his Bowie hunting knife and stabbed her repeatedly in the chest.

Whitman then returned to his own house and entered the bedroom
where his wife Kathy was sleeping naked in their bed. Whitman unhesitat-
ingly buried a bayonet in her chest as she slept. She never awakened, and
Whitman covered her nudity before he left. Whitman then returned to his
mother's apartment to retrieve a bottle of amphetamines he had inadvertently
left behind, went back to his house, and prepared for the next day.

✧   ✧   ✧

Whitman lugged an arsenal to the top of the Texas Tower. He brought three handguns—a 25-mm Galesi-Brescia pistol, a 9-mm Luger pistol, and a Smith & Wesson .357 magnum revolver—and four rifles—a Remington 35-mm pump-action rifle, a Remington 6-mm bolt-action deer rifle with a scope, a .30 caliber M-1 Carbine, and a sawed-off 12-gauge shotgun. He also carried a hunting knife in a leather scabbard. Whitman killed three people in the stairwells of the Tower before beginning to pick off people from the ob-servation deck.

Whitman's first victim was an unborn child.

At 11:48 A.M., Whitman put Claire Wilson, an eight-months'-pregnant eighteen-year-old, in the cross-hairs of his Remington deer rifle and fired. His bullet hit Wilson in the abdomen, fracturing the skull of her unborn child and killing it. Claire Wilson survived.

Whitman continued to shoot people from different spots on the deck until two police officers were able to sneak up on him, put two bullets in his head, and then finish him off as he lay "flopping" on the ground. Whitman was dead at 1:24 P.M., ninety-six minutes after he had fired his first shot.

It was later learned that Charles Whitman had been seeing Dr. Heatly, a part-time university psychiatrist, and that he had told the doctor that he be-lieved something was happening to him. During a press conference following the Tower massacre, Heatly read from the notes he had written following Whitman's final visit (from Gary M. Lavergne's *A Sniper in the Tower*):

> [The patient] readily admits having overwhelming periods of hos-tility with a very minimum of provocation. Repeated inquiries at-tempting to analyze his exact experiences were not too successful with the exception of his vivid reference to "thinking about going up on the tower with a deer rifle and start shooting people."

Dr. Heatly did not contact authorities to inform them that he believed that Charles Whitman was a potential threat to society.

Michael Ryan
"Rambo Ryan"
"The Maniac Next Door"

(1960–1987)

You have been one of my greatest Terran priests and as such are worthy of the power I offer. But Phodius, you have one last point to prove . . . can you kill your fellow Terrans? I offer you one last challenge. Will you accept, Phodius, to go back to Terra and slay them, to devour their souls in the name of Set the immortal god? . . . . When at last you awake you are standing in a forest, there is a throbbing in your head, a madness that is the exhilaration of the serpent god, you know what you must do, know what power is to be gained from this.

> —a message Michael Ryan received while playing the
> role-playing fantasy game, *Further Into Fantasy*

Michael Ryan's first gun was an air rifle he received as a birthday gift when he turned ten. It was a gift from his mother and, seventeen years later, Michael Ryan would use a 9-mm Beretta pistol to kill her. He would shoot her once in the leg, then once in the abdomen, and, as she was pleading with him not to shoot her any more, he would walk over to where she lay and put two bullets in her back, the muzzle of his Beretta almost touching her blouse when he fired. Ryan would then kill his dog and set fire to his own house, which would then burn to the ground.

Hungerford, England is the kind of quaint, rural English town in which one would not be a bit surprised to see a Hobbit walking about. Rolling country-sides, quiet parks, bucolic lanes, and ancient forests are all part of this tiny hamlet that sits fifty miles west of London and has a population of a mere five thousand. Hungerford is so small, you probably will not even find it on many maps of England.

Michael Ryan put Hungerford on the map, so to speak, one stifling hot day in August 1987, when he went on a killing walk through the streets of his hometown, executing a rampage that would result in sixteen people dead (seventeen, counting Ryan) and another fifteen wounded.

Michael Ryan's first victim on the 19th day of August was a young mother of two named Sue Godfrey, who was preparing a picnic lunch for her children in a park. When Ryan spotted her, he heartlessly shot her thirteen times. He pumped ten bullets into her in the park, and then shot her three more times after she fell bleeding and dying through a wire fence.

Next Ryan shot and killed Roland and Sheila Mason at their home as he passed by, then killed Ken Clements as he was walking toward the town green. He then killed Roger Brereton and Abdul Rahman Khan, and he killed George White as he passed by in a car. Ryan returned to his home and killed his own mother. Next, he killed a man walking his dog, followed by two men in cars and one man in a van. He then killed a woman in her car as she drove down Priory Road, then Jack and Myrtle Gibbs in their home on the same street. His final victim, Ian Playle, was killed in his car as he drove his wife and kids into town for a shopping trip. In addition to these innocent victims, Ryan also randomly shot sixteen others, all of whom recovered.

During Ryan's odyssey of death, he was deliberate and emotionless. Fully playing out the role of the cold and mechanical soldier, Ryan had dressed himself in army fatigues and he carried military weaponry. He had with him a World War II–vintage M-1 carbine, an AK-47 assault rifle, and the 9-mm Beretta pistol he had used to kill his mother.

After the shootings, Ryan headed for a place of sanctuary: his childhood grammar school, the John O'Gaunt School, named for John of Gaunt, Duke of Lancaster, the royal who granted residents of Hungerford perpetual rights to hunt in his forests.

After he holed up in an upstairs classroom, the school was surrounded and a police sergeant established a dialogue with Ryan:

SERGEANT: Will you come out now please, Mr. Ryan?
RYAN: I want to think about it. Why won't you tell me about my mother?

SERGEANT: I don't know. As soon as you come out, we'll find out together.

RYAN: Will I be treated OK?

SERGEANT: Of course you will, Mr. Ryan.

RYAN: Will I go to prison for a long time?

SERGEANT: I don't know, Mr. Ryan. It is not up to me.

RYAN: You must have an idea. I will get life, won't I?

SERGEANT: I don't know, Mr. Ryan. You will go to prison for a long time.

RYAN: It's funny. I killed all those people but I haven't got the guts to blow my own brains out.

SERGEANT: Mr. Ryan, just leave all your weapons in the room and do exactly as you are told. Don't do anything silly. Do you understand?

RYAN: What time is it?

SERGEANT: Six-forty-five. What do you want to know the time for?

RYAN: I want to think about it. I am not coming out until I know about my mother.

SERGEANT: Mr. Ryan, I am still trying to find out. If you come down we will be able to find out together.

The police then heard a muffled shot and when they stormed the building, they found Michael Ryan dead from a gunshot to his head.

Michael Ryan's shooting rampage was the worst mass murder in England's history.

A tabloid newspaper later reported that there was wild celebration by the people of Hungerford after hearing the news that Ryan had killed himself. According to the paper, people ran into the street shouting, "The bastard's dead, the bastard's dead." The paper also reported that kids rode their bicycles up and down the streets of Hungerford yelling "Good riddance," and that many toasts to Ryan's death were drunk in Hungerford pubs that day.

64

Henry Lee Lucas

(1936–2001)

There's no reason denying what we become. We know what we are.

> —Henry Lee Lucas, to his cannibal partner Ottis Toole

I have a sex problem. I just crave women all the time.

> —Henry Lee Lucas, to detectives

I been meaning to ask you . . . that time when I cooked some of those people. Why'd I do that?

> —Ottis Toole, to Henry Lee Lucas

"I done some pretty bad things . . ."

> —The beginning of Henry Lee Lucas's confession to the police

"Pretty bad things" is an apt, if ludicrously understated description of the crimes and atrocities committed by serial killer Henry Lee Lucas and his cannibal partner Ottis Toole.

Even if he is *not* guilty of the 360 murders he ultimately confessed to, or the six hundred crimes law enforcement authorities cleared based on Lucas's confessions, what he was *proven* to have done is despicable, and a textbook example of exquisitely evil actions.

The best way to illustrate the horrors perpetrated by Henry Lee Lucas and Ottis Toole is to hear it from Lucas himself:

> We killed them every way there is except one. I haven't poisoned anyone. We cut 'em up. We hanged 'em. We ran 'em down in cars. We stabbed 'em. We beat 'em, we drowned 'em. There's crucifixion—there's people we filleted like fish. There's people we burnt. There's people we shot in cars. We strangled them by hand. We strangled them by telephone cord. We even stabbed them when we strangled them. We even tied them so they would strangle themselves.

Ottis Toole, Lucas's partner in crime, was the cannibal of the duo. He claimed to have cut up, cooked, and eaten with barbecue sauce some of his and Lucas's victims. Lucas told police that he did not join Toole because Toole always put barbecue sauce on the human flesh as he was barbecuing it, and Lucas did not like barbecue sauce. Lucas's comment notwithstanding, it seems undeniable that Lucas did, at some point, also eat human flesh. He is on the record as saying he didn't eat with Toole because he found human flesh "too gamey." How would he know if he had not consumed human flesh in the past?

Henry Lee Lucas was born in 1936, the last of nine children, and he and his family lived in a four-room shack in Virginia with no electricity. Everyone slept in the same bedroom, and Lucas's prostitute mother would have sex with her customers in the same room, often forcing her children to watch.

Henry's home life as a child was, shall we say, less than ideal. Whether or not his childhood environment and treatment contributed to the cannibalistic, rapist, serial killer he would become as an adult, is for the criminal psychologists to determine, but it could not have helped.

An example: Henry once refused to do a chore. Angrily, his mother hit him in the head with a log, cracked open his head all the way down to the skull, and he ended up in a coma for an entire day. Henry's parents finally took him to a hospital and told the doctors he fell off a ladder. Henry confirmed the story because he was afraid of what his mother would do to him if he told the truth. Eventually, the beatings at home got so bad that Henry began having seizures and hearing voices.

Henry's mother never cooked for her children, never cleaned the house, and she beat them regularly. In desperation, Henry and his brother started stealing food at an early age. In addition, when Henry was ten, his father turned him into perhaps the world's youngest alcoholic by allowing him to drink from the still he made the boy guard.

Also, when Henry started school, his mother-of-the-year Viola curled his hair and made him wear a dress to school. As might be imagined, the other kids were *merciless* toward Henry. A kind-hearted teacher cut Henry's hair and gave him a pair of boy's pants and a shirt to wear. Henry went home dressed like a boy and his mother rushed back to school and screamed at the teacher for interfering in how she raised her children.

Not surprisingly, teachers remembered that Henry was always filthy and undernourished and had learning problems.

Alarming signs were omnipresent in young Henry: The boy had sex with a dead calf when he was ten; when he was thirteen, he trapped different kinds of animals, tortured them, had sex with them, and then killed them. Henry claimed he committed his first murder when he was fourteen. He told police that he kidnapped a seventeen-year-old-girl, beat her unconscious, began to rape her, and, that when she woke up, strangled her to death. However, no record of this crime ever having been committed exists. Also, Henry was convicted of breaking and entering when he was about fifteen and sent to a juvenile detention where he got into a homosexual relationship with a black inmate.

In 1960, Henry killed his mother and was sentenced to twenty to forty years in prison. He was paroled in 1970, but went back to prison in 1971 for four years after trying to kidnap a young girl at a bus stop at gunpoint. He was paroled in 1975 and moved into a trailer with a relative. She threw him out when she suspected he had been molesting her young children. After serving time in 1981 for car theft, Lucas moved to Florida where he met Ottis Toole and Toole's niece Becky.

Lucas and Toole went on a savage crime spree. In one instance in Texas, Lucas and Toole came upon a teenage couple walking along the side of the road. They stopped the car, and Toole got out and nonchalantly shot the boy in the head nine times. They then abducted the girl and Toole drove as Lucas raped her repeatedly in the back seat. Supposedly, Toole was jealous of Lucas having sex with the girl, so Toole stopped the car, threw the girl onto the side of the road, and shot her six times.

Another of Lucas and Toole's victims was a thirty-five-year-old woman who was found naked in a field. Her nipples had been cut off, she had been stabbed thirty-five times, and her body had been cut open.

The horrors committed by Lucas and Toole over the next few years are too many to recount in this limited space, but suffice to say that they raped, murdered, and robbed at will. Lucas was not kidding when he told the police, "Killing someone is just like walking outdoors. If I wanted a victim I'd just go and get one."

Lucas eventually killed his one true love Becky because she slapped him during an argument. He stabbed her to death, had sex with her corpse, cut her body up into pieces, and left her by the side of the road in trash bags.

Lucas was convicted of eleven murders, sentenced to death, and then had his sentence commuted to life by then–Texas governor George W. Bush. He died in prison of heart failure in March 2001. Before he died he said, "I made the police look stupid. I was out to wreck Texas law enforcement."

To this day, many believe Lucas confessed to unsolved crimes to receive privileges and benefits. Some also suggest that he knew that he would be executed if he stopped giving the police cases for which they could close the books. Lucas did come up with some ridiculous stories: At one point he claimed to have masterminded the Guyana Jim Jones mass suicide, and he also took credit for killing Jimmy Hoffa. He eventually recanted most of these stories.

However, the possibility that Lucas was lying does not remove the legacy of evil cruelty and unspeakable crimes *proven* to have been committed by the one-eyed drifter with no morals and a penchant for necrophilia.

Eric Harris and Dylan Klebold

"THE COLUMBINE SHOOTERS"
"THE TRENCH COAT MAFIA"

(1981–1999) (1981–1999)

God, I can't wait until I can kill you people.
     —Eric Harris, posting on his Web site

Mass murderers prey on the innocent, the vulnerable, the unsuspecting, the powerless, and the unlucky who happen to be in the wrong place at the wrong time.

Mass murderers are cowards and bullies who exact vengeance—for imagined slights, injuries, and injustices—on the perceived perpetrators of the abuse they have endured, as well as anyone else who gets in the way.

Seventeen-year-olds Eric Harris and Dylan Klebold were a mass murdering duo who went on a shooting rampage on April 20, 1999, at Columbine High School in Littleton, Colorado. The attack took place on the 110th anniversary of Adolf Hitler's birth. As has been the case with many serial killers and mass murderers, Harris and Klebold were followers and fans of Nazism.

The assault on Columbine—which authorities believe was one year in the planning—resulted in thirteen dead, twenty-five seriously injured, and the suicides of Harris and Klebold. The dead shooters were found in the library. They both had bombs strapped to their bodies. Almost fifty more bombs were later found in the school, in the parking lot, and in cars around the school. More than one survivor reported that Harris and Klebold laughed aloud as they killed their teachers and classmates.

As part of a school project, Harris and Klebold had filmed a video showing the two of them walking through the corridors of Columbine High, shooting and killing anyone who happened to cross their path. Their teachers refused to allow the video to be shown because of its violent nature.

Police investigators were shocked to learn that the assault on Columbine was supposed to be only the first phase of a massive reign of death and destruction by Harris and Klebold. They had originally planned on killing up to five hundred students and teachers at the high school, and, if the largest of their homemade bombs had detonated, they could very well have achieved that death toll. Following their attack on the high school, Harris and Klebold planned to walk through the neighborhood in Littleton, where the school was located, and randomly slaughter any residents they came upon. The final stage of their demented plan was to hijack an airplane, fly it across the country, and crash it into the middle of New York City.

The police investigation following the massacre revealed some alarming facts, and brought up the real possibility that the Columbine shooting might have been preventable. Harris and Klebold had previously made no attempt to hide their contempt for the fellow students and others in their lives. On Harris's Web site, they actually posted the results of pipe bomb tests they had conducted, and one student was even singled out for a personal death threat.

The depth of hatred Harris and Klebold felt for their victims is almost unimaginable. It was a free-floating loathing that seemed to have no foundation, other than that the two felt like outsiders. Trying to understand how their hatred grew, and how it manifested itself in such evil acts, seems like an exercise in futility.

Columbine High School was rebuilt and classes resumed. Several students transferred to other schools rather then walk back through school doors that opened onto a nightmare.

The following time line is from the final sheriff's department report on the tragedy:

11:14–11:17 A.M.: Eric Harris and Dylan Klebold carry bombs into the school and plant them in the cafeteria.

11:17 A.M.: The cafeteria bomb, set to go off at this time, fails.

11:19 A.M.:	With a shout of "Go! Go!" Klebold and Harris start shooting from the top of the stairs leading into the west side of the school.
11:21 A.M.:	Report comes in to Jefferson County dispatch of an explosion in a field at Elmhurst Drive and Wadsworth Boulevard. The bomb was placed there by Harris and Klebold in the hope it would divert authorities there and away from the school.
11:23 A.M.:	The first 911 call comes into sheriff's dispatch from the school.
11:24 A.M.:	School resource officer Neal Gardner responds to a report of trouble and later trades gunshots with Harris.
11:25 A.M.:	The first police car pulls up to school.
11:27 A.M.:	A pipe bomb goes off in the cafeteria, scattering students and sending smoke billowing through the room. Harris and Klebold enter the library.
11:30 A.M.:	Officers block access to the Columbine campus.
11:34 A.M.:	The gunmen fire the last shot that kills a victim.
11:36 A.M.:	Harris and Klebold leave the library.
11:44 A.M.:	Harris and Klebold go to the cafeteria and shoot at their large bombs but fail to set them off.
11:45 A.M.:	Harris stops momentarily in the cafeteria to take a sip from a left-behind drink in a Styrofoam cup. They later leave the cafeteria and go to the administration area.
11:46 A.M.:	Ten police officers put together a makeshift SWAT team and, using a fire truck as cover, attempt to enter the school.
11:47 A.M.:	Another pipe bomb goes off in the cafeteria.
11:56 A.M.:	Harris and Klebold, still carrying guns, re-enter the cafeteria.
12 P.M.:	Harris and Klebold leave the cafeteria and later return to the library, where they commit suicide.
12:06 P.M.:	A second makeshift SWAT team enters the school.
4:00 P.M.:	Sheriff's spokesman Steve Davis announces the two gunmen have been found dead of apparent suicide.
4:45 P.M.:	Sheriff John Stone arrives at Leawood Elementary School to advise parents that no other survivors remain in school.

Marc Lépine

(1964–1989)

Even if the Mad Killer label is stuck on me by the media, I regard myself as a rational and intelligent person who had been forced to take extreme acts only by the arrival of the Grim Reaper. For why continue to make efforts to exist if it is only to please the government? Being rather backward-looking by nature . . . the feminists always have a talent for enraging me. They want to keep the advantages of women . . . while grabbing those of the men. They are so opportunistic they neglect to profit from the knowledge accumulated by men through the ages. . . . Will we hear of Caesar's female legions and female galley slaves who of course took up 50% of the ranks of history, though they never existed?? A real Causus Belli.

—Marc Lépine, from his suicide note

How such a thing could happen in our society is the major question.

—Quebec Party leader Jacques Parizeau, in a statement following Lépine's shootings

School shootings do not only occur in the United States. The atrocities of Scotland's Thomas Hamilton (see page 180), and the killings carried out by the subject of this chapter, Canada's Marc Lépine, sadly prove otherwise.

Marc Lépine walked into an engineering classroom at the University of Montreal shortly after 5:00 P.M. on December 6, 1989. He was carrying a semiautomatic rifle, and when he entered the room, two students were giving presentations on heat-transfer. He did not shout and he did not move quickly. He held his rifle with two hands, walked up to the two students, and said, "Everyone stop everything."

They thought he was joking.

After all, Lépine was smiling, and college pranks have long been an honored tradition on the campuses of higher learning all over the world.

Thus, the students' and the professor's instantaneous reaction was that this was a joke.

In fact, some students actually laughed at Lépine.

But then the smile vanished from Lépine's face and he ordered the class to stand up and to separate into two groups, male and female.

At first, the students hesitated, not knowing if they should obey this guy who looked like one of them . . . just a student . . . or if he was serious and his gun was real.

Lépine took away all their doubt and hesitancy by firing a round into the classroom ceiling.

Instantly the students moved to two separate groups, men in one corner, women in another.

Lépine then told the men to get out.

The male students hurried out of the room, unaware that their lives had just been spared, and unaware that a mass slaughter was about to begin.

Nine female students huddled together in a corner of the room, terrified and uncertain about what would happen next.

Lépine walked back and forth, the muzzle of his rifle always pointing directly at the horror-stricken women.

"Do you know why you are here?" Lépine asked of no one in particular.

A twenty-three-year-old student named Nathalie Provost spoke up and said, "No."

Lépine then stated the twisted purpose of his mission and why he had taken these women as hostages.

"I am fighting feminism."

Provost again acted as spokesperson for the group and told Lépine that they were only students and just because they were women did not mean that they all subscribed to the tenets of feminism.

Provost's words fell on deaf ears. Lépine was already lost in some sick, paranoid mind realm where all women were feminists, all feminists were evil, and all feminists were his enemy.

He started to shoot.

Lépine just stood there and calmly began executing, by one-man firing squad, these nine defenseless women.

The room was a nightmare of gunfire and screams and panic and blood and moans.

Six young women died instantly; three were mortally injured and would die shortly thereafter.

Lépine, satisfied that he had done what he wanted to do in this class-room, walked out into the hall where some of the male students stood huddled in terror.

Lépine did not shoot them and said, simply, "I want the women."

He then began prowling through the university's corridors like a sniper sneaking through a forest overrun with enemies.

Lépine spotted one girl and shot and killed her.

He went to the cafeteria and shot three girls sitting eating their dinner.

He then climbed the stairs to the third floor, entered the first classroom he came to, and shot the two girls who were writing at the blackboard. One of these poor creatures did not die immediately from Lépine's bullets, so the mass murderer stabbed her three times in the chest to finish the job.

At this point, Lépine decided he was finished.

He removed his parka, and sat down at the desk at the front of the room. He then wrapped his parka around the barrel of his rifle, placed the muzzle of the gun against his forehead, said, "Ah, shit," and pulled the trigger.

Lépine was wearing a cap, which he left on when he killed himself. Eyewitnesses to Lépine's suicide reported that the cap and the top half of Lépine's skull went flying across the room when he fired. Police later learned that Lépine kept a human skull in his dining room at home.

Who was this murderous young man and what did women ever do to him that would cause him to lash out so violently out of hatred for feminism?

Police learned that Lépine was a loner and that he never had a relationship with a woman. His neighbors told police that he used to play music at high volume all night long and that the police had been called on him three times.

It was also learned that Lépine's father was Algerian and that he was violent and punched and beat his wife and kids—Marc included—regularly. In fact, Marc Lépine was on the receiving end of his father's worst physical violence. The police also learned that Lépine had been turned down when he applied to join the Canadian Army.

Of course, none of this explains why Marc Lépine went on a shooting rampage in December of 1989 that culminated in his own suicide.

Marc Lépine murdered fourteen women and seriously injured fifteen women and men in the worst mass murder in Canadian history.

Joachim Kroll
"The Ruhr Hunter"

(1933–1991)

It's clogged with guts.
> —Joachim Kroll, talking about the toilet in which he had
> flushed one of his victim's internal organs

It is probably a safe bet that the German police officer who looked into the pot on Joachim Kroll's stove one summer day in 1976 never again had an unbroken night's sleep.

That summer, the police in the Ruhr district of northwest Germany were looking for a missing four-year-old girl named Monika Kettner. This particular day they were canvassing playgrounds near where the Kettner girl lived. One of the people they questioned was an old man who told them an interesting story about one of his neighbors, a man in his forties who lived alone and kept to himself. This man had told the old man that the bathroom they shared at the end of the hallway was out of order. When the old man inquired as to the nature of the problem, his neighbor nonchalantly told him it was "clogged with guts."

The police decided to investigate, and they called in a plumber who took apart the bowl and poured its contents into a bucket. Out came six individual

208

human body parts: a liver, two lungs, two kidneys, and a heart. The police could not help but notice that the organs would fit quite neatly into the chest cavity of a four-year-old girl.

The police decided they had enough cause to check out the old man's neighbor, whose name, they soon learned was Joachim Kroll.

Kroll let the police into his apartment and was not the least bit hesitant about letting them look around.

The first thing the police did was open Kroll's refrigerator. There, on the shelves, were individual plates of small, neatly cut pieces of meat; slabs of flesh that they would soon learn were pieces of Monika Kettner.

Apparently, Kroll was not a glutton. Inside his freezer were securely wrapped pieces of meat, which, of course, were more of Monika Kettner.

The police then went to Kroll's stove. On top of the stove was a pot that Kroll told them contained a stew he was simmering. In the pot were carrots, potatoes, and other vegetables in a boiling broth. And right in the middle of the bubbling mixture was a little girl's hand. By the time the police found it, it was cooked all the way through.

In the twenty years between 1955 and 1976, Joachim Kroll abducted, raped, killed, dismembered, and ate fourteen females, ranging in age from five to sixty-one.

After Kroll was arrested, he willingly told police about as many murders as he could recall, but admitted that there may have been others he could not remember.

It is literally almost impossible to find something good to say about Joachim Kroll. He was a vile pervert who collected dolls to use as bait for his toddler victims. He was a heartless killer who deliberately varied his killing routine to confuse the police (and it seems to have worked—if Kroll had not fallen into the hands of the police by chance, he may have continued for years). He was a conscienceless cannibal who rivaled Jeffrey Dahmer and Albert Fish in his appetite for human flesh.

Kroll kept a rubber sex doll in his apartment for sex, which, in and of itself, is not an evil act, except that Kroll admitted that he would often strangle the doll as he had sex with it: first, to re-create the wonderful feeling he craved of strangling a young girl as he raped her; and, second, to rehearse his modus operandi for his next victim. Kroll also told police that he would sometimes hold one of his little victim's dolls as he masturbated, and strangle it until he reached orgasm.

Ironically (and sadly), Kroll was known in his neighborhood as kindly "Uncle Joachim." Parents never suspected anything bad about Kroll and often allowed their little daughters to go for walks with the meek man with the quiet voice. Kroll would hold their hand and walk with them through the parks, and he always brought them home safely.

Was Kroll just fulfilling a deviant lust to be around little girls? Was he trying to set the stage for an abduction?

One story told by a former neighbor of Kroll's could have served as a harbinger of Kroll's later crimes. One day, Uncle Joachim took ten-year-old Gabrielle Puettmann for a walk. When they stopped at a park bench, Kroll pulled a book out of his pocket and told Gabrielle he had something to show her. The book contained hard-core pornographic photographs and Kroll began flipping through the pages as Gabrielle sat in stunned horror. She immediately put her hands over her eyes and then, when she felt Kroll's hand on her shoulder, she leaped up and ran home. Kroll probably chuckled and went home to his rubber doll. Gabrielle never told her parents because she was mortified at the idea of them knowing that she had seen such photos.

When Gabrielle was twenty-one and the truth was known about kindly Uncle Joachim, she realized just how close she had come to becoming one of Kroll's victims—and one of his meals.

Joachim Kroll's trial began in 1979 and lasted until 1982. When it was over, Kroll was found guilty and sentenced to nine life sentences in prison in Rheinbach. He died of a heart attack in 1991.

68

Howard Unruh

(1921–)

They have been making derogatory remarks about my charac-
ter. . . . I'm no psycho. I have a good mind. . . . I'd have killed a
thousand if I'd had bullets enough.

—Howard Unruh

Howard Unruh of East Camden, New Jersey, was a tank machine-gunner in Italy and France during World War II. Unruh also qualified as a sharpshooter, and he was decorated for meritorious service in the Battle of the Bulge.

Soldiers who served with Unruh later recalled that he would keep a detailed diary of every one of his kills, including specific descriptions of what each of his German victim's dead bodies looked like after he killed him. This somewhat macabre hobby could have been perceived as a fairly significant warning sign, but no one who knew Unruh seemed to think it was all that unusual.

However, there was also something else that was odd about Howard: he never went with his comrades into town when he had the opportunity, and he did not seem to be interested in girls. What *was* he interested in? His Bible and his rifle. Howard loved nothing better than staying in his barracks, reading his Bible, and taking apart and cleaning his rifle.

Someone should have paid closer attention to Howard.

Three years after the war ended, Howard Unruh would make exceptionally good use of his sharpshooting skills, although there was actually nothing "good" about the rampage of murder that would christen him with the ignoble title of the father of modern American mass murder.

On September 6, 1949, Unruh embarked on a twelve-minute killing rampage that would result in the bloody deaths of thirteen people and end with him giving himself up to the police. After he was resigned to the fact that he had killed as many people as he could with the ammunition he had brought with him, Unruh returned to his own house and locked himself inside. More than fifty police officers soon surrounded the house and, after giving him a chance to surrender peaceably, the police lobbed tear gas grenades into the house, forcing Unruh to flee the building. He was arrested and charged with thirteen counts of murder and three counts of atrocious assault.

When Howard returned from the war, he lived in the basement of his parents' house, and he seemed reasonably normal—for the most part. What Howard's parents and neighbors did not realize, however, was that Howard was slowly deteriorating into a state the psychiatrists identified as paranoid schizophrenia. When he was arrested, the doctors wrote in their report that Unruh was suffering from "dementia praecox, mixed type, with pronounced catatonic and paranoid coloring." This was the gravest manifestation of his paranoia, and the warning signs had been there all the time.

After the war, Howard began to suspect that his neighbors were talking about him and that they were plotting against him. He became increasingly reclusive and even went so far as to build a huge wooden fence around his parents' backyard, complete with a very secure gate.

Well, the gate was not secure enough, it seems, for sometime during the evening of September 5, 1949, somebody (or some*bodies*) stole Howard's gate.

In all likelihood, the stealing of the gate was a prank specifically designed to annoy Howard since, by this time, everyone in the neighborhood knew what he was like. Howard's own paranoia left him vulnerable to taunting that would exploit his paranoia, thereby becoming a self-fulfilling prophecy.

Howard was livid when he discovered the gate had been stolen. He was so angry and out of control that he even went so far as to threaten his mother with a wrench. His mom fled the house, and as soon as she was gone, Howard grabbed his 9-mm Luger, and began his walk of death.

He walked a few blocks to a shoe store where he shot the owner.

He then went next door to the barbershop and shot the six-year-kid kid getting his hair cut for the first day of school. Then he shot the barber.

Unruh next headed to the corner drugstore, which was owned by the

Cohens, whom Howard hated. As he arrived at the drugstore, his insurance agent was coming out of the store. Howard shot him point blank and killed him. Maurice Cohen saw what Howard had done and fled upstairs to his residence above the store. Howard gave chase and first killed Mrs. Cohen, who was hiding in a closet; then he killed Maurice Cohen's mother in the kitchen as she tried to call the police. Maurice had climbed out onto the roof and Unruh shot him, but only wounded him. Cohen fell to the ground and Unruh, not one to leave a job half-done, leaned out the window and finished him off.

Unruh then started strolling the street. He killed a motorist, then three people (including a child) in a car stopped at a red light. He then took a shot at a trucker, but only wounded him. Next, he walked into the tailor's shop and killed the tailor's wife.

Unruh continued his walk and soon shot his final victim: a two-year-old boy watching what was going on from the window of his house. Twelve minutes had elapsed since Unruh had left his house at 9:20 A.M.

And then he went home. The assistant city editor of the local paper called Howard as the police were surrounding the house.

"Why are you killing people, Howard?" he asked.

"I don't know," Howard replied. "I can't answer that yet. I'm too busy. I'll have to talk to you later."

Howard Unruh never stood trial for his crimes. Criminal psychiatrists determined that Unruh was incurably insane and he was institutionalized in the Trenton Psychiatric Hospital for the Criminally Insane, where he still lives today.

69

The Boston Strangler
ALBERT DESALVO?

(1931–1973)
GEORGE NASSAR?

*I knew it was me who did it but why I did it and everything
else, I don't know. . . . I wasn't excited. I didn't think about it. I
sat down to dinner and didn't think about it at all.*

—Albert DeSalvo

In the case of Albert DeSalvo, we use the "Boston Strangler" because there
is ongoing controversy about whether or not DeSalvo truly was the sadistic
rapist and killer. DeSalvo confessed to the crimes but was never convicted of
them. At the time of his confession, he was already serving prison terms for
rape and armed robbery, so he was never tried for the Strangler crimes.
DeSalvo's brother and the daughter of one of the Strangler's last victims are
behind efforts to reopen the case and attempt to determine the identity of the
real killer. At the end of December 2001, DeSalvo's body was exhumed for
DNA testing in an attempt to determine his guilt or innocence.

DeSalvo was stabbed to death in 1973 in prison, the evening before he was scheduled to meet with his doctor and reveal something to him that DeSalvo had described as very important.

Someone committed the crimes attributed to the Boston Strangler, thus, the Strangler's ranking in this volume. This chapter looks at DeSalvo and Nassar, the two men most often associated with the crimes.

From June 14, 1962, through January 4, 1964, 13 single women in the Boston area were raped or sexually molested, then strangled with an article of clothing. Of the 11 official "Strangler" victims, 6 were between the ages of 55 and 75; 2 possible additional victims were 85 and 69; the remaining 5 victims ranged in age from 19 to 23.

Regardless of the true identity of the real Strangler, the person who committed the Boston Strangler crimes was unquestionably a sadistic and cruel person, with a horribly evil personality. The perpetrator made a deliberate effort to continue to humiliate his victims even after they were dead. The Strangler always left his victims displayed so that their spread legs and exposed vagina would be the first thing people—neighbors, family, the police—would see when the body was discovered.

In addition, there were elements of depraved torture in the Strangler's killing routine. One victim was found with a bull's-eye design on her breast from knife stabs. Another was found propped up in bed with semen dripping out of her mouth onto her breasts and a broomstick rammed almost four inches into her vagina. One victim was left with a Happy New Year's card stuck between her toes.

Albert DeSalvo confessed in detail to close to one hundred murders; yet, some experts on the case believe that DeSalvo could have been told specifics about the crimes while in a mental institution with the real Strangler, a man named George Nassar.

At one point, DeSalvo was locked up with Nassar, a highly intelligent, manipulative murderer serving time for the execution-type murder of a gas station attendant. Two of the Strangler's surviving victims identified Nassar as the man who tried to kill them, but he was never charged with any of the Strangler crimes.

Other theories regarding DeSalvo's possible innocence include DeSalvo's family making up the story and DeSalvo going along in order to sell the rights for big money, as well as suspicion that DeSalvo (who had a photographic memory) simply remembered facts and details about the crimes (that he read or heard) with such accuracy that anyone who heard him believed only the perpetrator could have known what DeSalvo reported.

Contributing to the belief in DeSalvo's guilt was his conviction for crimes committed as the "Measuring Man" and the "Green Man."

Before the Strangler murders began, DeSalvo was pulling off a scam in which he would talk his way into the homes of young women and tell them that he was with a modeling agency and that he could get them into magazines and maybe on TV. Con artists have always said that the secret to a great con is in the details, and DeSalvo had the details: The pay was $40 an hour; there was no nudity, only swimsuit and eveningwear. During his Measuring Man "career," DeSalvo was able to convince many of his model wannabes to have sex with him.

Sometime after his modeling scam, DeSalvo broke into a woman's apartment, tied her up, stuffed her underwear in her mouth, left her with legs spread open, and sexually fondled her—but left her alive. The woman's description of DeSalvo fit the description of the Measuring Man, and DeSalvo was arrested. DeSalvo admitted he committed the Measuring Man crimes and went to prison.

The Strangler murders began two months after DeSalvo was released from prison.

Albert DeSalvo was born in September 1931 in Boston, the son of an alcoholic, abusive father who taught his kids how to steal and often brought home prostitutes and allowed (forced) his children to watch him have sex with them. Young Albert was also known to prostitute himself to homosexuals to raise money, and all of these dysfunctional elements could have easily contributed to the creation of a sociopath who could commit the crimes of the Boston Strangler.

In his early twenties, DeSalvo joined the Army and married a German girl with whom he fathered a child with disabilities. DeSalvo's wife refused him sex after this on the chance they would have another defective child. Because of his upbringing, DeSalvo's libido was permanently corrupted by this time and he was a rabid sex addict. He needed to have several orgasms a day to function. Some of this need was met by successful Measuring Man seductions.

DeSalvo was eventually arrested for a series of crimes committed in New England by a man dubbed the Green Man (for his green work pants). While being held for the Green Man assaults, DeSalvo claimed to have sexually molested over three hundred women, and then confessed to cellmate George Nassar that he was the Boston Strangler. Nassar informed his lawyer, F. Lee Bailey, of what he had been told; Bailey subsequently interviewed DeSalvo and came away convinced that he was the Strangler.

DeSalvo was never charged with the Strangler crimes because the prosecution refused to allow him to plead insanity. He was, however, tried for the Green Man sexual assault and robbery crimes, and was convicted.

DeSalvo was stabbed to death in prison while serving time for the Green Man crimes in what authorities said was a prison brawl.

Update

In December 2001, Albert DeSalvo's body was exhumed for DNA testing at the request of DeSalvo's family and the family of one of his victims, neither of whom believe DeSalvo was responsible for the Boston Strangler killings. As of this writing, there have been no reported findings regarding the DNA tests.

70

Peter Sutcliffe
"THE YORKSHIRE RIPPER"

(1946–)

I see you are still having no luck catching me. . . . I reckon your boys are letting you down . . . you can't be much good, can you? . . . Well, I'll keep on going for quite a while yet. Even if you do get near, I'll probably top myself[1] first. Well it's been nice chatting to you. . . . Yours, Jack the Ripper.

> —from a tape recording sent to the British police by a
> Yorkshire Ripper hoaxer—steering police
> away from Peter Sutcliffe

In this truck is a man whose latent genius, if unleashed, would rock the nation, whose dynamic energy would overpower those around him. Better let him sleep?

> —from a note found in Peter Sutcliffe's truck

Peter Sutcliffe is in Broadmoor Mental Institution in England these days and there are reports that his mental state has deteriorated significantly, at the

---

[1] Commit suicide.

same time that his weight has ballooned. Sutcliffe has been institutionalized since 1982, when he was sentenced to thirteen life sentences for his horrific crimes.

Peter Sutcliffe was arrested on January 2, 1981, for parking his car in the wrong place. He told police his name was "Peter Williams" and asked if he could urinate before being brought in to the police station. The cop okayed it, and then took him in. The next morning the cop had a hunch and went back to where "Peter Williams" had urinated, and there, in the bushes, he found a ball peen hammer and a large knife, the weapons of choice of the Yorkshire Ripper.

After five years, 250,000 interviews, 32,000 statements, and 21,000 house searches, the police had finally nabbed their man—and all because Peter Sutcliffe had to urinate.

Peter "the Yorkshire Ripper" Sutcliffe terrorized West Yorkshire, England, from 1975 to 1980. He assaulted twenty women, thirteen of whom died. Their ages were between sixteen and forty-seven, and many were students, housewives, or prostitutes. All were bludgeoned, usually with a ball peen hammer, stabbed repeatedly, raped, and often mutilated. Sutcliffe stabbed one woman in the abdomen so violently, her intestines spilled out of the wound.

Sutcliffe used a variety of knives for his stabbing and mutilation work, particularly kitchen knives and carving knives, but on at least one occasion, he used a Phillips head screwdriver. The Ripper's third victim was a housewife who started turning tricks for extra money with her husband's blessing and management. Sutcliffe hit her on the head twice with his ball peen hammer, and then stabbed her neck, chest, and abdomen with a sharpened Phillips head screwdriver. He also left his boot print on her right thigh when he violently stomped on her after he killed her.

Most of his victims were killed in similar fashion: He would smash them in the head with his ball peen hammer and then stab them repeatedly, up to fifty times in some cases. Sometimes he would mutilate their vaginas.

Sutcliffe committed his first assault on July 4, 1975. The woman's name was Anna Rogulskyj, and Sutcliffe hit her on the head with his hammer, pulled down her panties, and stabbed her in the stomach. He fled when a neighbor investigated what all the noise was. Anna survived but needed an emergency twelve-hour operation, after which they performed Last Rites on her. To this day Anna is terrified and still suffering from terrible post-traumatic stress. She insists that she wishes she had died that night. She lives alone, and she walks in the middle of the street when she does marshal enough courage to leave her apartment, which is not very often.

Sutcliffe assaulted another woman before committing his first murder. Again he was interrupted and the woman survived. Victim number two was in the hospital for ten days, was traumatized beyond belief, and her daughter ultimately had a nervous breakdown over what had happened to her mother.

Sutcliffe's first murder victim was Wilma McCann, twenty-eight, whom he killed on October 30, 1975. He smashed in the back of her skull twice with a ball peen hammer, then stabbed her fifteen times in her neck, chest, and abdomen. Police found traces of his semen.

His second murder victim was Emily Jackson, forty-two. Sutcliffe hit her in the back of her head with a shoe and then brutally *kicked* her to death. He also had sex with her anally and vaginally (possibly post-mortem) and, again, he left semen on his victim. Examination showed that the killer was a secretor, meaning that his blood type was identifiable from other body fluids, and the Yorkshire Ripper was determined to be the rare Type B.

After the discovery of the body of his final victim, Jacqueline Hill, in 1980, a British newspaper ran the headline "Did one man really do all this?"

After his arrest, it was discovered that Peter Sutcliffe had been questioned by police an astonishing nine times without being identified, or even suspected of being the killer, except by one man. One detective wrote a report in which he voiced his opinion that Sutcliffe was the Yorkshire Ripper. The report was ignored.

It turns out that Sutcliffe was an evangelical do-gooder. He said his God-given mission was to rid the streets of prostitutes. He once told his brother Carl: "I were just cleaning up streets . . . just cleaning up streets."

Before he began killing women, Sutcliffe worked as a gravedigger at the Bingley Cemetery. That was where he claims he heard the voice of God coming from a grave, telling him to rid the world of prostitutes. It was later suspected that he claimed he heard voices to prove a "diminished responsibility" defense.

On May 22, 1981, Peter Sutcliffe was found guilty of thirteen counts of murder and sentenced to thirteen life sentences.

Yorkshire women sleep better knowing Sutcliffe is in Broadmoor for the rest of his life.

All the Yorkshire women except for his surviving victims, that is.

71

Fred West and Rosemary West

(1941–1995) (1953–)

You'd better get back home. They're going to dig up the garden, looking for Heather.
> —Rosemary West, talking to Fred West on a cell phone
> the day the police showed up with a warrant

The depravity of Fred West boggles the mind. His crimes read like an index of perversity, ranging from raping his prepubescent daughters whenever he felt like it, and prostituting his wife, to killing and dismembering young women after subjecting them to a nightmare of sadomasochistic torture and sexual deviance.

Fred's wife, Rosemary, was a willing participant in her husband's orgies, incest, torture, and murder, and is currently serving a life sentence in prison in England. Fred did not stick around to be tried or sentenced: he committed suicide on New Year's Day in 1995 by hanging himself in his cell. His brother John, who Fred allowed to have frequent sex with his daughter, John's nine-year-old niece, also committed suicide when *his* actions came to light.

* * *

After Fred West murdered the young women he and his wife had lured to their home on 25 Cromwell Street in Gloucester, England, he would dismember them and then bury them in the garden in his backyard. (The garden would later be paved over to make a cement patio.) Fred did not just cut up the bodies to make them fit; he took it further than that. During his grisly dismantling of his victims' bodies, he would also cut off each of their ten fingers, each of their ten toes, and both of their kneecaps, and keep them separate from the corpse. Was this a Satanic rite? Did removing these parts have something to do with witchcraft? Or was Fred West just a deviant psychopath who got off on this particular ritualistic dismemberment?

Fred and Rosemary West's victims ranged in age from eight to twenty-one years old. After Fred was arrested in 1994, the police began excavating the Wests' patio, pulling up cement, and digging into the ground beneath. They eventually recovered twelve bodies, including the body of the Wests' own 16-year-old daughter Heather, who had been reported as missing in 1987, but who had actually been killed by her father and mother in June of that year. Rosemary told the police that Heather had left them in 1987, that she was on drugs and a lesbian and that was why she did not want to continue to live with them. Heather joined ten other young girls under the patio, and the police found another girl buried under the cellar floor of their previous home. Fred later told police that Heather's head had made a "horrible, scrunching sound" when he cut it off and that he "re-killed" her after he killed her because he did not want to chance her "waking up" as he started to dismember her.

When Fred was twenty, he impregnated a thirteen-year-old girl. He is reported to have been surprised that everyone was upset that he had had sex with the girl as Fred did not see anything wrong with it. He also did not see anything wrong with having sex with his adolescent daughters. His argument was, since he had made them, he could do whatever he wanted to them.

In November 1962, Fred married Rena Costello. Rena was pregnant at the time and the father was Asian. When Charmaine was born, Fred told his parents that the baby had died in childbirth and that he and Rena had adopted an Asian baby. Fred eventually left Rena and met Rosemary. It was Rosemary who killed Charmaine when the little girl was eight. Fred buried Charmaine and used her murder as leverage against Rosemary for the rest of his life. Also while married to Rena, Fred impregnated one of her friends, killed her, and her remains were later found with a fetal skeleton inside her abdomen. Fred later also killed Rena, whose body was found buried in a field ten miles from their home. (It was during this period that Fred also killed a young child by accidentally backing over her with his ice cream truck. This death is usually not considered part of Fred's total kills.)

✳   ✳   ✳

Once Rena and Charmaine were out of the picture, Fred and Rose began luring young girls to their House of Horrors on Cromwell Street where they would subject them to rape, torture, bondage, and more, and then kill them and bury them in the garden.

In 1973, they tortured, raped, and killed a twenty-year-old, a fifteen-year-old, and twenty-one-year-old Lucy Partington, the niece of British novelist Kingsley Amis.

In 1974, their victims were 21 and 15, respectively.

In 1975, they killed the twenty-one-year-old daughter of a United States serviceman stationed in England.

In 1978, they killed an eighteen-year-old and her unborn child (which was Fred's).

In 1979, their victim was only sixteen.

Rosemary was an active participant in the violent sex games Fred so loved. One victim was tied up naked, and then Fred whipped her on her vagina with a belt buckle. Rosemary then performed oral sex on the girl following the beating. Rosemary and Fred both killed her.

At first, Rosemary denied everything and blamed Fred for all the murders and tortures. This defense did not stand up to scrutiny and she was sentenced to life in prison. Recently, Rosemary West revealed that she planned to marry an inmate who was in prison for indecent assault. She wrote in a letter, "Yes, it is true we are planning to marry. We are very much in love dispite [sic] everything and we need each other so very badly. I believe he loves me for the woman I am."

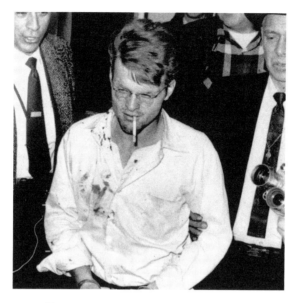

Charles Starkweather
and Caril Ann Fugate

(1938–1959) (1943–)

The more I looked at people, the more I hated them because I knowed there wasn't any place for me with the kind of people I knowed. . . . A bunch of Goddamned sons of bitches looking for somebody to make fun of . . . some poor fellow who ain't done nothin' but feed chickens.

—Charles Starkweather

Charles Starkweather killed a gas station attendant, then his girlfriend's family, and then went on a week-long rampage during which he stabbed and/or shot another seven people. One of the reasons Starkweather qualifies for a ranking on this list is because of his utter amorality and disregard for human life, and his willingness to kill anyone for sheer fun, including an infant.

After shooting Velda and Marion Bartlett to death with his hunting rifle (as their daughter, fourteen-year-old Caril, coldly and uncaringly watched), the nineteen-year-old Starkweather entered two-year-old Betty Jean Bartlett's room and jammed the barrel of his rifle down the baby's throat, choking her to death. Unbelievably, Betty Jean's half sister, and Velda's own daughter, who was also Charles's girlfriend, Caril Ann Fugate, watched all these murders and then went into the living room and put on one of her favorite TV programs. Equally unbelievable (yet all too true) Charles Starkweather then went into the Bartletts' kitchen and made sandwiches for him and Caril Ann.

Robert Colvert was a twenty-one-year-old gas station attendant who holds the distinction of being the first person Charles Starkweather ever murdered. On December 1, 1957, Starkweather drove into the gas station where Colvert was working and robbed him at gunpoint. This was not enough for Starkweather, however. He then forced Colvert into his car, drove him out to the barren empty plains outside of Lincoln, Nebraska, and murdered him by shooting him several times in the head.

Two months after Starkweather shot Robert Colvert to death, he was sitting in the Bartletts' living room, waiting for Caril to come home from school. He just so happened to have his .22-caliber hunting rifle with him, and he held the rifle lovingly in his lap and stroked it affectionately as he sat and watched TV.

Suddenly, Mrs. Bartlett snapped.

She could not stand watching this arrogant little creep, this James Dean-wannabe sit there and nonchalantly play with a rifle. She confronted Starkweather. She started shouting at him that they did not like him hanging around their house, or dating their daughter, and apparently, Velda pushed Starkweather to the point of no return.

The first thing he did was shout back at her, which prompted Mrs. Bartlett to make the mistake that would cost her her life. She slapped Starkweather in the face.

Starkweather hit her back, which resulted in Velda's husband Marion attacking him in defense of his wife.

Starkweather then blew them both away with his rifle.

Following the three murders, Starkweather and Fugate decided to stay in the Fugate home for a couple of days. They put a sign on the door telling visitors that everyone in the house had the flu and that they should leave immediately, and they spent the next two days in bed, eating junk food, watching TV, and having sex.

They left the house when the food ran low and embarked on a two-week murder, rape, and robbery spree.

First, they killed a farmer in his home. Next they carjacked two teenagers. They took them to an isolated barn where Starkweather raped the girl repeatedly as Fugate watched. Starkweather shot the two teens and Fugate, who was at that point insanely jealous over Starkweather having sex with the girl, then violently carved up the dead teen's genitals with a knife.

They continued on their journey and next broke into a businessman's house. The man of the house was at work, so Starkweather and Fugate tied up, tortured, and killed his wife and their maid. They waited around until the man came home and shot him the minute he walked in the door.

They headed out and came upon a salesman asleep in his car. Starkweather shot and killed him and decided to steal the car. Unfortunately for them, though, a police car drove by as Starkweather was trying to drag the salesman's corpse out of the car. Fugate must have realized what was next, so she betrayed Starkweather by telling the cop that he had abducted her and forced her to go along on his killing spree.

Fugate's hostage story only served to lessen the penalties levied against her. The two were each convicted of the charges against them and Starkweather was electrocuted on June 25, 1959. Fugate was sentenced to life in prison, but was paroled in 1977 at the age of thirty-two, after serving eighteen years of her sentence.

Starkweather and Fugate's story has become part of the American pop culture zeitgeist, and they inspired the movies *Badlands* (1974), *Wild At Heart* (1990), *True Romance* (1993), *Kalifornia* (1993), and *Natural Born Killers* (1994), as well the Bruce Springsteen song, "Nebraska."

Edmund Kemper III
"THE CO-ED KILLER"

(1948–)

One side of me says, "Wow, what an attractive chick, I'd like to talk to her, date her." The other side of me says, "I wonder how her head would look on a stick."
> —Edmund Kemper, when asked what he thought when he saw a pretty girl walking down the street

T he dark seed of evil can be planted and take root at an early age and, in the case of Edmund Kemper, it first blossomed when he shot his grandparents in cold blood with his hunting rifle and then repeatedly stabbed his grandmother's body, all before his sixteenth birthday. "I just wondered how it would feel to shoot Grandma," he later told the authorities.

After confessing to the murders, Kemper was sent to Atascadero State Hospital, where he was immediately diagnosed as a sociopath. He refused to take responsibility for his grandparents' death, and told his doctors that it was beyond his control.

Kemper's time in Atascadero was like a graduate level seminar in serial rape and serial murder. Kemper paid close attention to his fellow inmates (the "patients") and filed away each bit of valuable information for later use.

Even while incarcerated in a mental hospital, Kemper was planning his future crimes, while displaying the face of a Bible-reading, hopeful, troubled, yet eager-to-get-better, young man.

After his release from Atascadero, Kemper lived with his mother for a time (frequently fighting with her) and then moved into an apartment with a friend. During this period, when Kemper was twenty-two and twenty-three, he regularly picked up female hitchhikers (more than a hundred, he guessed) in a car he had outfitted to look like a police vehicle, but he did not harm them and actually drove them where they needed to go. Kemper was *rehearsing* being a kidnapper.

When Kemper was twenty-four, he stopped rehearsing and launched the main production in earnest.

Kemper's first three victims as an adult—Mary Ann Pesce, Anita Luchese, and Aiko Koo—were all picked up as hitchhikers, killed, dissected, and decapitated. He had sex with their corpses and kept their heads as souvenirs before disposing of their bodies. These three murders took place in August and September of 1972.

His next three victims—Cindy Schall, Rosalind Thorpe, and Alice Liu— were all, again, picked up as hitchhikers, and subjected to the same necrophiliac assault after they were murdered. Kemper was back living with his mother when he killed Cindy Schall, and he brought her body back to his mother's house and had sex with her corpse in his bedroom. He then buried her head in his backyard facing the house so he could imagine her looking at him. Also, on at least two occasions, Kemper cut slices of flesh from his female victims' legs and cooked and ate them in a macaroni and cheese casserole.

A month after he killed these final three hitchhikers, Kemper killed his loathed mother by hitting her in the head with a hammer as she slept. He then decapitated her, placed her head on a mantle in the living room, and threw darts at it. To cover up his matricide, he invited his mother's friend Sally Hallet over for dinner, strangled her by crushing her larynx, and then had sex with her corpse.

Following these two final murders, something in Kemper spurred him to confess. He was eventually taken into custody and began a marathon confession session, during which he admitted all eight murders, described them in grisly details that only the killer could know, and even took the police on a guided tour of his favorite body part disposal sites.

Kemper was quickly found guilty of eight counts of first-degree murder and sentenced to life in prison with no chance of parole. When asked what he felt was the appropriate punishment for his crimes, Kemper stated simply, "death by torture."

The warning signs of trouble were present at an early age in Kemper. It seems that even when he was very young, sex and violence were interwoven in one huge twisted tapestry of emotions and urges in Kemper's mind. He once told his sister that he wanted to kiss his second grade teacher, but that "If I kiss her, I would have to kill her first." This was the same sister with whom Kemper would play "gas chamber": She would pretend to be the executioner and Kemper would feign dying in excruciating agony after she pulled the imaginary cord that dropped the imaginary cyanide into the imaginary hydrochloric acid. Edmund Kemper also indulged in animal torture and killing for fun.

Kemper came from a broken family, and it was his stepfather who taught him how to hunt and handle guns. Kemper's mother, Clarnell Strandberg, treated her only son terribly. One incident believed to have been devastatingly traumatizing to Kemper occurred when he was only ten.

Because Kemper's sister found his hulking presence disturbing if she happened to come upon him wandering the halls in the middle of the night, his mother made him move out of his second floor bedroom and into the basement, a place which was like a coffin to the young Edmund. The basement had a cement floor and walls and a creaky wood ceiling, and the furnace would burst frighteningly into life in the middle of the night. In addition, Kemper had to walk halfway across the cold, dark basement before he could get to the light switch. He later admitted that the place terrified him and experts believe his having to sleep down there may have contributed to his later violent morbid impulses.

Whatever the reasons for his crimes, the bottom line is that Edmund Kemper is one of the twentieth century's most evil denizens, a truth made even more blatant by Kemper's own admission that if he were ever to be set free, he would assuredly kill again.

Kenneth Bianchi and Angelo Buono Jr.

"THE HILLSIDE STRANGLERS"

(1951–)(1934–)

Angelo Buono and Kenneth Bianchi subjected various of their murder victims to the administration of lethal gas, electrocution, strangulation by rope, and lethal hypodermic injection. Yet the two defendants are destined to spend their lives in prison, housed, fed, and clothed at taxpayer expense, better cared for than some of the destitute law-abiding members of our community.

   —An angry Judge Ronald George, upon learning that the jury had spared Bianchi and Buono the death sentence

I'm sure, Mr. Buono and Mr. Bianchi, that you will only get your thrills by reliving over and over the tortures and murders of your victims, being incapable, as I believe you to be, of ever feeling any remorse.

         —Judge Ronald George, speaking at Bianchi's and Buono's sentencing

Kenneth Bianchi and Angelo Buono earned the epithet "Hillside Stranglers" (which was created by the media) for their signature method of disposing of their victims' bodies. They would leave many of them on hillsides near Los Angeles, California, naked and with their legs spread in a sexual position. The women's bodies always showed signs of rape, both vaginal and anal; torture, including burn marks and bruises; and signs of injections, although none of them had been drug addicts. The needle holes, police would later learn, were from injections of window cleaner. (This atrocity was horrifyingly depicted in the 1996 movie *Copycat,* which starred Sigourney Weaver as a psychiatrist stalked by a copycat serial killer who used the torture and killing methods of deranged repeat murderers like Bundy and Bianchi and others to leave clues for the police. In the window cleaner scene that was inspired by Bianchi and Buono, the killer's victim is seen strapped to a table in a basement. The killer then fills an enormous syringe from a half-gallon jug of blue liquid and tells his terrified victim that, yes; this is going to hurt.)

Bianchi and Buono's first victim, twenty-one-year-old Elissa Kastin, was found in mid-October 1977 near Forest Lawn Cemetery.

Their second, nineteen-year-old Yolanda Washington, was found around ten days later in Glendale.

On November 20, 1977, the Sunday before Thanksgiving, Bianchi and Buono abducted, raped, and killed two young girls and a twenty-year-old woman. The girls were twelve-year-old Dolores Cepeda and fourteen-year-old Sonja Johnson; the woman was twenty-year-old Kristina Weckler. Weckler's body was found in Highland Park; Johnson and Cepeda's, in Elysian Park. All three were naked and showed signs of brutality.

Bianchi later described to police Kristina Weckler's death by gas asphyxiation.

> She was brought out to the kitchen and put on the floor and her head was covered with a bag and the pipe from the newly installed stove, which wasn't fully installed yet, was disconnected, put into the bag and then turned on. There may have been marks on her neck because there was a cord put around her neck with a bag and tied to make more complete sealing.

Three days later, on the day before Thanksgiving, Bianchi and Buono raped and killed twenty-eight-year-old Jane Evelyn King and dumped her naked body on an off-ramp of the Golden State Freeway.

In the week after the 1977 Thanksgiving holiday, Bianchi and Buono abducted, raped, tortured, and killed Lauren Rae Wagner and Kimberly Diane Martin, both eighteen.

Bianchi and Buono, both Italian Catholics for whom, ironically, Christmas is an important time, took the holiday season off from killing. Then on Friday, February 17, 1978, the tortured, nude body of Cindy Lee Hudspeth was found in the trunk of a car.

Bianchi and Buono made the decision to embark on their nightmare journey of rape, torture, and murder on a whim.

In 1975, Kenneth Bianchi decided to leave New York State and move to California, where he stayed with his cousin Angelo Buono. During this time, the two latent sexual psychopaths had many discussions about what it would be like to kill someone, specifically a woman, and one day they decided to actually try it and experience it firsthand. This first savage assault inflamed a blood lust that they indulged wholeheartedly.

Bianchi and Buono once left a body by the curb in a middle-class neighborhood. They admitted that this was done deliberately so that people would see it as soon as they left their houses. Their victim was around sixteen years old and had been raped and sodomized.

During the Hillside Strangler investigation, a forensic psychiatrist profiled the killer: The killer was white, late twenties, early thirties, single, separated, or divorced; average intelligence, unemployed; perhaps an ex-con; cold and manipulative personality; product of a broken family; probably abused as a child by his mother.

Bianchi was born in 1951 in Rochester, New York, and his biological mother was an alcoholic prostitute. She gave him up for adoption at birth and the Bianchis immediately adopted him.

As a child, Kenneth Bianchi was a liar. He attended Catholic school and had extremely disturbed virgin/whore issues with women even at an early age.

Bianchi married immediately after graduating high school in 1971 but his wife made the right decision when she left him after eight months and filed for an annulment.

He then attended community college where he studied police science and psychology but dropped out. He was turned down when he applied for a sheriff's department job so he became a security guard instead—but Bianchi was a security guard who stole from the places he guarded.

Angelo Buono called himself "The Italian Stallion," began raping girls when he was fourteen, and eventually had several wives and several children. He physically and sexually abused everyone in his family, and the serial rapist Caryl Chessman was his role model, idol, and hero.

Buono once beat and raped his wife so violently that she thought he was going to kill her. He also made his children watch when he had sex with their mother. At one point, Buono began living with a woman and, shortly after moving in, started raping her fourteen-year-old daughter. When confronted, Buono admitted it and said the girl needed "breaking in." He also admitted allowing his sons to have sex with the fourteen-year-old as "a gift."

Buono also once tried to abduct Peter Lorre's daughter, but stopped when he learned who her father was.

Bianchi and Buono were finally caught and brought to trial.

After Bianchi was arrested and charged, he crafted a completely ficti-tious scenario in which he was an amnesiac and had multiple personalities. His lawyers claimed that he should be found not guilty by reasons of insanity because his alternate personality named Steve committed the murders. This did not sway a jury and Bianchi is now serving a life sentence in Folsom Prison in California.

Buono was likewise convicted and is serving his life sentence in Walla Walla State Prison in Washington State.

75

Bobby Joe Long

(1951–)

*I knew all I had to do was throw my stuff in a car and move to
Lakeland or Miami or Daytona or out of state and they'd never
track me down. . . . You know there's no way.*

—Bobby Joe Long, in 1992

Bobby Joe Long raped and robbed between 25 and 150 women from 1974
until 1984—*before* becoming one of America's worst serial killers. And
yet, after he was caught, he asked the police to apologize to Lisa McVey, a
seventeen-year-old girl he had kept as a sex slave for twenty-eight hours before letting her go.

Long abducted McVey as she was riding her bike home from work at
2:30 in the morning. He brought her to his apartment, repeatedly raped her
(sodomizing her once), forced her to perform oral sex several times, and kept
her naked in his bed. He did, however, let her get dressed occasionally; and
he took a shower with her, brushed her hair, fed her, and did whatever he
wanted with her body. Long treated McVey like she was his girlfriend and apparently believed that if he was affectionate with her, then she would not
mind him doing whatever he wanted to do sexually with her.

When he was through with McVey, Long drove her out of town and re-leased her, telling her "Take care." It took McVey two hours to walk home. McVey later identified Long in court.

McVey was not the only Long victim who managed to survive. Once, he picked up a young prostitute, forced her to strip, tied her up, and took her to a deserted area. He then beat her and raped her and performed all manner of sexual assaults on her, but this time he took pictures of everything he did to her, and then left her naked, battered, and raped in a desolate area and drove off.

During his six-month murder rampage in 1984, Long was completely impervious to his victims' pleas for mercy, and he took delight in sadistically beating them before raping them and committing anal sodomy on them. Long would then kill them and discard their bodies like unwanted trash, often hurling their clothes out of the car, leaving underwear and other garments scattered around the crime scene. He seemed not to care if evidence was left behind. After a couple of bodies were discovered, police had samples of his head hair, his pubic hair, red fibers from the carpet in his apartment, and semen samples.

Long's stalking and killing routine was to pick up girls on the road, usu-ally hookers, hitchhikers, walkers, or what have you, and force them to get completely undressed and lie facedown in the front seat of his car. He would tie their hands behind their back, immobilizing them (a tactic he said he learned how to do while watching his parents get robbed when he was a child), and sometimes he would rape them in the car. He would then drive his captives to a deserted area where he would remove them from the car, rape them again (sometimes anally the second time), and then kill them by stran-gulation, although if they fought, he would slash their throats repeatedly until he hit an artery large enough to make them bleed out. Sometimes he would save time by simply shooting them in the back of the head.

Long killed on less than a whim. He gave his decision to take a life al-most no thought at all. He admitted in court that he once put a TV dinner in the oven, went to the store for some milk, murdered a woman while he was out, and then returned to his apartment. "My apartment almost burned down by the time I got back," he laughed.

Due to a hormonal disorder, Bobby Joe Long developed gynecomastia and grew full-sized breasts when he was a young boy. This was bad enough for his developing personality, but he also slept in his mother's bed until he was twelve or thirteen.

Long told the police that as an adult, he required up to seven or eight ejaculations a day, and that he would masturbate a half dozen times a day, in addition to having oral sex or intercourse with his wife twice or more. There is speculation that a 1974 motorcycle accident during which Long almost lost a leg had something to do with his voracious libido and anger toward women. It is documented that after Long recovered from the accident, he had a newly insatiable sex drive, as well as uncontrollable rage toward women. Shortly thereafter, the raping began.

Long first married at the age of nineteen and began raping women he would meet through the classified ads. He would scan the ads for those that looked promising (such as, a woman home alone during the day); then go to the address and pretend he was interested in whatever was being offered in the ad. Once he was in the house he would tie the woman up, rape her, and then rob her before he left.

Long's final victim was Kim Swann. When he saw her driving drunk and weaving all over the road, he stopped her car and she got in his vehicle on the pretense of going for a drink. When he tried to tie her up and rape her, she fought back viciously. Long also told police that Swann had diarrhea in his car and that he finally decided that she was so much trouble, and was making such a mess, that he would just kill her and dump her body without raping her.

Long was arrested in November 1984 after police spotted a car resembling the vehicle Lisa McVey had described as being driven by her abductor. Long believed he had finally been caught and he cooperated fully with the police. As soon as police started talking about hair and fiber evidence, he confessed to everything. He admitted killing Lana Long, Michelle Simms, Elizabeth Loudenback, Chanel Williams, Karen Dinsfriend, Kimberly Hoops, Virginia Johnson, Vicky Marie Elliott, and Kim Swann; he was convicted of the murders of Johnson and Simms and given three death sentences.

Bobby Joe Long currently is on Death Row in Florida awaiting rulings on a number of appeals of his sentences.

76

Peter Kürten

"The Vampire of Düsseldorf"
"The Monster of Düsseldorf"

(1883–1931)

*I have [no conscience]. Never have I felt any misgiving in my
soul; never did I think to myself that what I did was bad . . .*
— Peter Kürten, at his trial

*He unites nearly all perversions in one person . . . he killed men,
women, children, and animals . . . killed anything he found.*
— Peter Kürten's defense lawyer

*After my head has been chopped off, will I still be able to hear,
at least for a moment, the sound of my own blood gushing from
the stump of my neck? That would be the pleasure to end all
pleasures.*
— Peter Kürten, at his trial

When Peter Kürten was in his early teens, he began having sex with pigs,
sheep, and goats, and that was when he discovered that his most powerful or-

gasms were achieved by stabbing the animal repeatedly at the moment of climax.

Kürten was a product of a sick and twisted family dynamic, due, in large part, to his alcoholic, abusive, pedophile father, a man who served time in prison for raping his thirteen-year-old daughter and who regularly beat his wife and thirteen children. Kürten's father would also have sex with their mother in front of them, and one expert noted that Kürten's father was so violent during sex that, if he had not been married to Peter's mother, it would have been considered rape.

Peter Kürten began showing signs of what his defense lawyer would later call his "perversions" at a very young age. When Kürten was nine, he drowned one of his playmates by holding his head under water. Around the same time, he got a job with the dog warden, a perverted sadist who taught the young Kürten how to masturbate and torture dogs. Kürten particularly enjoyed the "killing stray dogs" part of this job and found that being cruel to animals sexually aroused him. He told police that he would cut off the heads of swans so he could drink their blood, and he would ejaculate during the act.

Kürten first had sex when he was fourteen, but it was not consensual; he raped a girl when she refused to give in to him.

Kürten's first murder was a sleeping ten-year-old girl, the daughter of the owner of a pub he frequented. He broke into their home, strangled her in her bed, molested her sexually with his fingers, and then cut her throat. He later described how the blood from her neck gushed in an arc over his hand. The girl's uncle (the pub owner's brother) was charged and tried for the crime but acquitted.

Kürten's first victim as the Vampire of Düsseldorf was nine-year-old Rosa Ohliger. On February 8, 1929, he stabbed her to death thirteen times with a pair of scissors. He went back later that evening, soaked her body in kerosene, and set it on fire. He admitted having had an orgasm as the fire blazed and police later determined that he had also stabbed her in the vagina. In his police statement, Kürten said, "In the case of Ohliger, I also sucked blood from the wound on her temple . . ."

Four days later, Kürten stabbed a drunk to death, again with scissors, and drank his blood as it spurted from his wounds.

Kürten committed several other crimes during this period. In August 1929, he had sex with, and then killed a servant girl and drank her blood. That same month he stabbed and strangled a fourteen-year-old girl and her five-year-old sister, and then decapitated the older girl. The following month, he beat a girl to death with a hammer, followed by a similar killing the next month. His final "Vampire" killing was in November 1929. He strangled a five-year-old girl and stabbed her thirty-six times with a scissors.

After a year of horror and fear in Düsseldorf, Kürten was finally arrested in May 1930, through a very strange set of circumstances.

One night, Kürten came upon a girl being assaulted near his residence. Kürten rescued her, but then he himself started to strangle her. After a bit, he suddenly stopped and asked her if she remembered where he lived. She swore she did not, and he let her go. The woman did not tell the police, but she did write about what had happened in a letter to a friend. She mistakenly put the wrong address on the envelope and it subsequently went to the "dead letter" office at the post office. There, it was opened and read, and the clerk gave it to the police. (Some sources say the *addressee* opened and read it and then gave it to the police.) The police then tracked down the girl and she gave them Kürten's address. He was eventually arrested and charged with nine murders.

After his arrest, Kürten dictated to a police stenographer the complete details of all his acts, ultimately claiming responsibility for seventy-nine individual crimes.

Later, at trial, Kürten claimed he confessed to everything to ensure a lucrative future for his wife. He believed that she was entitled to the reward for him because he had first confessed to her. With this defense, he denied his confession and pled not guilty. Two months of hard questioning finally broke Kürten, however, and he reverted to admitting everything to which he had originally confessed.

During his trial, Kürten was kept in a cage, much like Andrei Chikatilo (see page 119) would be likewise imprisoned in court a few decades later. The difference was that for Chikatilo, the cage was to protect him from the survivors of his victims; in Kürten's case, it was to prevent him from escaping.

At Kürten's trial, the prosecution displayed skulls and body parts from his victims as well as some of the weapons and tools he had used to kill them. Kürten, who admitted to greatly admiring Jack the Ripper, pled insanity, but the jury was not convinced and he was convicted.

Peter Kürten brutally killed at least twenty-three people, was charged with nine murders, and claimed responsibility for seventy-nine individual crimes. He was sentenced to death by guillotine and he was thrilled with the verdict.

So were the people of Düsseldorf.

77

Nikolai Dzhurmongaliev
"METAL FANG"
(1960?–)

*[Dzhurmongaliev seemed] absolutely normal, but at one point,
he got a taste for female meat. When we arrested him, he hit me
with the force of Jean Claude Van Damme.*

— Interior Ministry Colonel Yuri Dubyagin

Russia's Nikolai Dzhurmongaliev and Milwaukee's Jeffrey Dahmer have a great deal in common, particularly their overwhelming appetite for the taste of human flesh. However, there is one significant difference between the two cannibals: They did not order off the same menu. Dzhurmongaliev ate only women; Dahmer, only men.

Serial killer Nikolai Dzhurmongaliev killed, butchered, cooked, and served forty-seven of his victims to his family and friends at dinner parties at his home in the Russian republic of Kyrgyzstan.

When Dzhurmongaliev got out of prison in 1980 after serving a sentence for manslaughter, he took a job working on a building site in Almaty in what is now Kazakhstan. After he was finished for the day, he would shave, clean himself up, put on nice clothes, and escort young ladies on walks by the river. It is reported that he liked his women tall, well-built, and pretty.

Once he and his date were out of sight of prying eyes, Dzhurmongaliev would brutally rape the woman, then stab and hack her to death with an axe and knife. Once she was dead, he would head home, her body in tow, where he would cut her up into steaks, chops, and roasts. These he would later cook and serve to his friends.

Dzhurmongaliev got away with these horrific murders repeatedly, and we can only imagine the terror in the hearts and minds of his victims when Dzhurmongaliev opened his mouth and they saw his shiny, bright silver, metal teeth. Dzhurmongaliev's nickname was "Metal Fang," and when his face was contorted in his lust for blood and flesh with his shiny silver teeth bared in a grimace of madness, the scene had to have been surreal.

Dzhurmongaliev's feast of perversity came to an end early in 1981 thanks to the efforts of two alcoholics.

Dzhurmongaliev had invited the two men, whom he knew, back to his house for a drink and something to eat. When they arrived at his home, Dzhurmongaliev realized that he had forgotten to tidy up before he left that morning. On the counter in Dzhurmongaliev's kitchen was a woman's head, and nearby was a bowl filled with a complete set of women's intestines. The drunks did not stay for the snack and, shortly thereafter, Dzhurmongaliev was arrested. Dzhurmongaliev told police during his questioning that two women provided him with about two weeks worth of edible meat—depending on his appetite, of course.

Dzhurmongaliev was also interrogated about the reasons for his killing and eating of women.

In many cases, serial killers who include the consumption of their victims as part of their evil-doing do so for sexual gratification and, truth be told, because they like the taste. In *Cannibal Killers: The History of Impossible Murders*, Moira Martingale (1993) writes:

> They brought the severed heads in first. On golden platters. Frozen in death, the faces of the young slave girls were still fresh and beautiful, the almond eyes lifeless. The men's mouths watered to think how sweet and tender their flesh would be when, in just a few minutes, it was served to them, the honored guests. . . . It was, of course, an awesome demonstration of power . . . slaves were the stock of noble families, no more than their cattle. But more importantly, and more simply, they liked the taste. When all specious moral arguments are swept aside, these are the reasons we now eat animals: we have the unchallenged power to do so, and we enjoy the taste.

However, Dzhurmongaliev did not claim lust nor flavor as his reasons for killing and eating women. The deranged Russian, instead, put forth the

dubious argument that he ate women because females, particularly prostitutes, were the root cause of all evil in the world, and by killing and eating
them, he was doing his part to make the world a better place. Peace through
cannibalism. The police were not swayed by his defense.

Dzhurmongaliev's total death count is believed to be close to one hundred women, but the police could connect him incontrovertibly to only seven.
As might be expected, Dzhurmongaliev was determined to be utterly insane
and declared unfit to stand trial. He was institutionalized in a mental asylum
for the criminally insane in Toshkent in Uzbekistan where he still resides
today.

It is believed he makes do with prison food.

78

Frederick Cowan

(1943–1977)

There is nothing lower than black and Jewish people, unless it's
the police who protect them.

—Frederick Cowan

Racial hatred was the sinister engine that motivated Frederick Cowan. Cowan was consumed with hatred of blacks and Jews, and this hate was so powerful, it exploded on Valentine's Day 1977, when Cowan went on a killing rampage because his supervisor, Norman Bing, had suspended him for refusing to move a refrigerator. And Norman Bing happened to be Jewish.

Not surprisingly, Cowan idolized Adolf Hitler. He had five posters of Hitler in his bedroom. He collected books about Nazis, Nazi weapons, Nazi memorabilia, flags, and helmets; and he actually fantasized about being in Hitler's security force, the SS.

At the age of thirty-three, Cowan still lived with his parents, upstairs in an attic bedroom, and he did not have a relationship with a woman. He lived in an angry, self-created world of hostility, and he focused his rage on Jews and blacks.

Cowan had obviously been unhinged for years when he finally "went crazy," as his mother described his actions, and yet, no one in his New

Rochelle, New York, neighborhood or at the Neptune Moving Company where he worked, ever did anything about it.

Cowan was a card-carrying member of the National State's Rights Party. Their principles include a free white America, complete racial separation, the expulsion of all Jews from the United States, and the confiscation of what the group called "ill-gotten Jewish wealth." The group's slogan was "Honor, Pride, Fight—Save the White."

The warning signs that Cowan was hanging by a thread were easy to recognize. Once, he kicked a puppy to death, simply because its fur was black. Another time, Cowan got into a conversation with a woman in a bar and seemed to be getting along just fine. At some point, however, he learned that the woman was Jewish and he snapped. He became furious and smashed the TV in the bar. Yet another time, Cowan actually threatened a female neighbor with a rifle because he had learned that she had been dating a black man.

On Monday, February 14, 1977, Cowan pulled up outside the Neptune Moving Company, and he was armed for battle. In his trunk was a fully-loaded Saco .308 HK-41 semi-automatic assault rifle. On his chest were two double shoulder holsters, holding two 45-caliber pistols and two 9-mm automatic pistols. In his belt was a 9-inch hunting knife. He also had bandoleers brimming with hundreds of rounds of ammunition, including 45-caliber, 9-mm, and 7.62-mm cartridges. Frederick Cowan was declaring war when he arrived at Neptune that morning.

Cowan got out of the car, entered the building, and immediately shot and killed three African American employees. He then killed a man who had just come to America from India one year earlier. Cowan began rampaging through the building, shouting for Norman Bing, and firing rounds indiscriminately. Employees scrambled for safety; some managed to flee the building. Bing hid under a desk in an office adjacent to his own.

The police arrived at 7:55 and Cowan shot and killed the first police officer to approach the building. He holed up in a second floor office that had tinted glass, and fired a nonstop barrage of rounds at police, onlookers, vehicles, and anyone and anything else that entered his line of fire. He ended up wounding three other police officers.

By noon, there were more than three hundred police and FBI officers on the scene, and a military tank was brought in to retrieve the fallen police officer.

Cowan made one phone call during his siege. He called the police at noon and demanded food. Cowan was over six feet tall and weighed 250 pounds and he told police he wanted potato salad and hot chocolate. As an indication of how unhinged Cowan's mind was, he then explained to the cops that he was hungry and that he got mean when he was hungry.

Two hours later, the police and the FBI decided to enter the building. An assault team of five highly skilled officers entered the Neptune Moving Company through a back door. They were all wearing flak jackets, helmets, and other protective gear. Suddenly, they heard a single shot. Then there was silence. The police found terrified employees and shepherded them out safely. They then proceeded cautiously through the building, not knowing if there was more than one shooter, or if there were bombs in the building.

They finally entered an upstairs room where they found the corpse of Frederick Cowan, the side of his head blown away. He was still wearing his weapons and ammo.

Cowan's final death toll was six. He shot and killed four employees (including three blacks) and a police officer. He also wounded two employees and three police officers. One of the wounded employees died six weeks after the shooting.

The police later searched Cowan's attic apartment and found his Nazi museum and his arsenal of death, including eleven cans of gunpowder, shotgun shells, rifles, a machete, almost two dozen knives, bayonets, and equipment to make his own shells.

The Neptune Moving Department was torn down a few years later and today, a Home Depot store stands in its place.

79

Jack the Ripper

"Saucy Jack, you're a naughty one . . ."
        —from David St. Hubbins's (of Spinal Tap) unproduced
        musical about Jack the Ripper

Jack the Ripper is the name used by the vicious and still-unidentified British serial killer who slaughtered five prostitutes in the period from the last day of August through early November 1888 by slicing their throats and then mutilating and dissecting their bodies.

Jack is included in *The Evil 100* because of his sadistic cruelty and murders, but also for the glee with which he carried out his horrible acts, as evidenced by the taunting letter he sent to George Lusk in October 1888 (see below), believed to be the only genuine correspondence from the homicidal maniac.

The Ripper's Letter to George Lusk

From hell
     Mr Lusk

     Sor

     I send you half the Kidne I took from one women prasarved it for
     you tother piece I fried and ate it was very nise I may send you the
     bloody knif that took it out if you only wate a whil longer

     Signed
     Catch me when
     You can
     Mishter Lusk

Jack the Ripper's body count is minuscule compared with some of the other deviants in this ranking, and yet the savagery of his murders is evidence of the deeply evil nature of his personality.

Jack the Ripper killed prostitutes. And, except for twenty-three-year-old Mary Jane Kelly, believed to be his final victim, all of Jack's prey were in their forties. They were all also dreadfully poor and alcoholics.

Why did Jack the Ripper do what he did? It is worth noting that he did not rape his victims; he obviously derived sole satisfaction from the killing and mutilation of their bodies.

German physician and neurologist Richard Von Krafft-Ebing, well-known for his studies of sexual deviance, wrote of Jack: "He does not seem to have had sexual intercourse with his victims, but very likely the murderous act and subsequent mutilation of the corpse were the equivalents for the sex act."

Who was Jack the Ripper? The following is what is known about the killer:

- Jack did not dress as a laborer or as one of the indigent poor.
- Jack had to have had some medical expertise and knowledge of the human anatomy since he was able to "operate" to specifically acquire the organs he wanted.
- Jack more than likely lived in London's East End.
- Jack was a white male, or was someone who dressed in disguise as a white male.
- Jack was almost certainly single, since it is likely that if he were married, his wife would get suspicious if he roamed the streets in the middle of the night.

- Jack was average or below average in height.
- Jack was between twenty and forty years of age in 1888 at the time of the murders.
- Jack was either independently wealthy or had a regular job, since the murders all occurred on weekends, suggesting he either worked during the week, or laid low weekdays to try and throw police off the track.
- Jack was left-handed.

Possible Rippers

There are several suspects whose names have become part of the Ripper mythology. Here are the ten people often cited as the likeliest candidates for being Jack the Ripper.

- Dr. Thomas Neill Cream (1850–1892). Cream shouted "I am Jack the . . ." as he was being hung for poisoning five London prostitutes.
- John Druitt Montague (1857–1889). Montague committed suicide by drowning, and police were later tipped off that the real Jack the Ripper had drowned himself.
- General William Booth's secretary. This young man once predicted the murder of a prostitute named Frances Coles, who at one time had been thought to be a Ripper victim, but this was eventually discounted.
- Jill the Ripper. Some guessed that perhaps the Ripper was a woman, and, thus, a hypothetical "mad midwife" was viewed as a suspect.
- James Kenneth Stephen (1859–1892). Stephen was considered a suspect because, to some experts, his poetry matched the writing in the Ripper letter thought to be authentic.
- Kosminski, a.k.a. "Leather Apron." This mentally ill Polish shoemaker seems to have been a suspect mainly because he was, well, crazy.
- Prince Albert Victor, Duke of Clarence (1864–1892). A member of the royal family, Albert was a sexual degenerate and gossip labeled him a suspect.
- Sir William Withey Gull (1816–1890). Gull was a doctor who was named a suspect by a medium who had a dream in which he was told that a "distinguished physician" was really Jack, and the attention turned to Gull, who was prominent at the time for curing the Prince of Wales of typhoid.
- Severin Klosowski, a.k.a. "George Chapman" (1865–1903). Klosowski was a barber who was hanged for the poisoning deaths of three mistresses.
- Alexander Pedachenko. He was believed to have been planted in

England by the Russian secret police to kill women and discredit Russian radicals living in London.

Jack the Ripper's Victims

1. *Mary Ann "Polly" Nicholls*, forty-two, was killed August 31, 1888. Her throat was cut and her abdomen was slashed open.

2. *Annie "Dark Annie" Chapman*, forty-seven, was killed September 8, 1888, and was Jack the Ripper's second confirmed victim. When her body was found on September 8, 1888, just after six in the morning, her small intestines were on the ground next to her body, but still attached to her abdomen, and part of her stomach was lying next to her left shoulder. Her vagina and the posterior two-thirds of her bladder had been removed and were missing. Her throat had been savagely cut, almost to the point of decapitating her, her abdomen was slashed open, and her kidney was also missing. It is believed that Jack ate half of Chapman's kidney, since he included the other half of the organ in an October sixteenth letter to George Lusk of the Mile End Whitechapel Vigilance Committee. In the letter, Jack stated that he cooked half of Chapman's kidney and ate it ("I fried and ate it was very nise"), and tests showed that the person to whom the kidney belonged suffered from Bright's disease. It as known that Annie Chapman had that illness. (According to the writer, the letter was "From Hell.")

3. *Elizabeth "Long Liz" Stride*, forty-five, was killed September 30, 1888. Her throat was cut, but her body was otherwise unmutilated. It is believed that Jack was interrupted shortly after killing Stride and had to flee the scene before he could continue his trademark evisceration. This theory may explain why he is believed to have killed another prostitute, Catherine Eddowes, that same night.

4. *Catherine Eddowes*, forty-three, was killed September 30, 1888, shortly after Elizabeth Stride was slain. Eddowes's throat was cut, her face and body were horribly mutilated, and her kidney was taken.

5. *Mary Jane "Jeannette" Kelly*, twenty-four, was killed November 9, 1888, and was the most horrible of Jack's slayings. Unlike the others, Kelly's naked body was found inside a building, in her room and on her bed, which is probably why Jack was able to take his time with her body. Kelly's head was turned to the left, her throat was cut, and her head was almost severed from her body. Her abdomen was cut open, and both her breasts had been hacked off her chest and placed on a table. Her left arm was left hanging by a thread of skin, and her liver was placed between her feet at the foot of the bed. The skin and muscle of her right leg had been removed down to the bone; her nose was cut off and placed on a table alongside her breasts. Her face was unrecognizable. In addition, one of Kelly's hands had been pushed into her eviscerated abdomen.

Breaking News

Crime writer Patricia Cornwell reported in December 2001 that she had conclusively proven that Jack the Ripper was an obscure painter named Walter Sickert. At this writing, she is planning a book on her endeavors and discovery.

80

Mark Essex

(1949–1973)

I have now decided that the white man is my enemy. I will fight to gain my manhood or die trying.
> —Mark Essex, in a letter to his mother

Free Africa! Come on up, pigs!
> —Mark Essex, on the roof of the Howard Johnson's Motor Lodge

Mark Essex, one of the few African American mass murderers, utterly loathed white people and believed himself to be a grievously violated victim of racism. He is ranked in *The Evil 100* because he killed in the name of hatred. He expressed the belief that his life's mission was to kill white people.

Just before Essex was killed on the roof of a Howard Johnson Motor Lodge on January 7, 1973, he told a terrified black hotel maid not to fear for her safety. "This is a revolution," he told her. "Don't worry. I'm not going to hurt you black people. I want the whites. I'm only shooting whites. No blacks." Before climbing up onto the roof, Essex had set fire to several rooms at the hotel to force people out into the open. A few days earlier, he had killed two cops, one in a police lockup, and one at a warehouse ambush.

Police sharpshooters eventually shot Essex to death from a helicopter. Cops emptied their machine gun clips into Essex's body. His right leg was almost severed from his body, his tongue was found a distance away from him on the roof. Essex's total kill count was nine: seven from the roof, and the two cops; he also seriously wounded nine others, all of whom who ultimately survived.

Mark Essex was born in 1949 in Emporia, Kansas, a small town notable for its civic pride and lack of racism. Essex's father was a meat-packing plant foreman; his mother was a school counselor. Essex's childhood was almost idyllic. He did not experience the racial intolerance and bigotry many African Americans in America were living through in the 1950s and the '60s, and he guilelessly dated both black and white girls while in high school. This atypical upbringing is why Essex was stunned when he was first confronted with racial prejudice.

Essex enlisted in the United States Navy in 1969 at the age of nineteen as an apprentice dental technician. Although things are different now, back then, there was rampant racism in the navy. Essex's fellow sailors, especially his superiors, would torment and harass the young man on a regular basis. Whenever he drove through the camp gate, the white guards would arbitrarily demand his registration, his insurance papers, and his license, deliberately delaying him, while waving white sailors through without even a check of their ID. Sometimes the guards would go so far as to remove the door panels in his car, ostensibly looking for contraband, but really just doing it to hassle Essex.

During his stint, Essex got into a fight with a white petty officer and discovered (to the dire detriment of his later victims) that he found tremendous satisfaction in physically hurting white people.

After going AWOL in 1970, Essex was eventually granted an early discharge, but he was stigmatized with an "unsuitable character" evaluation upon his expulsion from the navy. An untethered Essex then made a decision that would transform him into the mass murderer he was soon to become.

Essex visited Harlem, New York, where he met members of the Black Panthers. These radicals, who endorsed an overthrow of America's white, allegedly racist government, found an eager student in Mark Essex. Essex totally embraced their philosophies and, when he returned to Kansas in 1971, he was a walking tinderbox of racial outrage, and the fuse had been lit.

Essex renounced Christianity (it was the white man's religion), embraced violence as a means for social equality and, most significantly, bought a .44-caliber magnum Ruger Deerslayer carbine rifle and began practicing ceaselessly.

Essex soon moved to New Orleans and began studying African culture. He picked an African name—Mata Swahili for "taut bow"—and lived in the projects, where the poorest people lived in often-deplorable conditions. The fact that almost all of the residents of Essex's complex were black certainly fueled his rage against the machine and, on New Year's Eve, 1972, the tinderbox detonated. Essex began his bloody rampage by shooting a cop at a New Orleans' Police lockup. Ironically, the cop Essex shot was black. After shooting another cop from inside a warehouse, Essex managed to escape to his apartment for a few days, where he planned his next assault.

First, he shot a neighborhood grocer. Then he hijacked a car and headed for the local Howard Johnson's, the scene of his mass slaughter and, ultimately, his own death.

Essex made his way through the hotel, shooting people point-blank and setting fires. It wasn't long before the area was utter chaos. There were dead people, wounded people, fires, gushing water, cops, firefighters, and absolute panic, thanks to Essex's hatred of white people.

Eventually, Essex made it to a concrete bunker on the roof of the hotel where he held off cops for hours, even surviving forty-eight strafing runs by police helicopters.

Essex finally decided to make one last stand and he ran out into the open on top of the roof. He was hit with more than one hundred bullets and his body was left on the roof for more than twenty-four hours. The police were not sure that Essex was a lone shooter and they did not want to move in until they had thoroughly searched and secured the hotel.

The police later discovered that Mark Essex had painted anti-white, black-power graffiti on his apartment walls and had obviously stewed for years in his vile hatred for whites. A widely circulated photo of Essex's body lying on the hotel roof showed his right arm extended above his head, looking like a "Black Power" salute.

Even in death, Essex faced off against whitey.

81

Richard Speck

(1941–1991)

Sleep well tonight, your National Guard is awake.
> —a poster the nurses
> had in their residence

Born to raise hell.
> —a tattoo on Richard Speck's forearm

If they don't burn me, what will they do with me? Put me in some kind of nuthouse?
> —Richard Speck, before hearing that he had been
> sentenced to die by electrocution

Help me! Help me! Help me! Everybody is dead! I am the only one alive on the sampan![1] My friends are all dead, all dead, all dead! I'm the only one alive, oh God, the only one! My friends are all dead!
> —Corazon Amurao, the only survivor of Speck's mass murder

[1] A sampan is a flat-bottomed Asian skiff propelled by two oars.

Richard Speck was arrested ten times before he was twenty, and he had been arrested a total of thirty-seven times by the time he was twenty-five.

Beginning late in the evening of July 13, 1966, and continuing until the early morning hours of July 14, Richard Speck brutally murdered eight student nurses in their residence at South Chicago Community Hospital. He did not sexually assault seven of the girls; he did rape, sodomize, and anally violate the nurse that reminded him of his ex-wife.

Around 11:00 P.M. on July 13, Speck climbed through the kitchen window of the nurses' home and quietly climbed the stairs to the second floor. By this time, Speck had been drinking all day, ingested eight Seconals, and had injected himself with a drug he got from some sailors that was never identified. Speck told the police what he remembered about the injection: "They had this disposable syringe and took this stuff from a bottle and started popping. I tied a handkerchief around my left arm and stuck it in. All the way. Before I had the needle out I could feel, you know, feel—zoooommmmm-mmm!—a buzzing all over me, and I was feeling real, real good." Later, Speck would claim that he remembered nothing about the murders, and he would blame the alcohol and the drugs.

When Speck reached the second floor, he knocked on a bedroom door and Corazon Amurao and two of her roommates answered. Speck showed them a gun and a knife and said, "I'm not going to hurt you. I'm only going to tie you up. I need your money to go to New Orleans."

In 1966, mass murder was not part of the American consciousness. It is now speculated that the tied-up nurses actually believed Speck when he told them that he only wanted their money and that he would not hurt them.

Speck then forced the three women to a back bedroom where three other girls sat around talking. Speck made all six lie on the floor and he tied up their hands and feet with strips of bed sheets. (Speck had been a seaman and the sailor's knots he tied in the strips of sheeting helped convict him.) Over the next couple of hours, three more girls returned home and Speck tied them up as well.

Speck then asked the girls where they kept their money, and he took all their cash. He then sat and stared at the bound nurses until he made a decision to take it to the next level.

Speck took Pamela Wilkening into another bedroom, stabbed her in the left breast, and then strangled her with a strip of bed sheet. One dead.

He then took two more nurses to another bedroom. He stabbed one in the neck, breast, and eye, killing her. The second girl resisted but Speck ferociously stabbed her eighteen times, and then strangled her. Three dead.

Speck was a little messy at this point so he went into the upstairs bathroom and washed some of the blood off his hands. He returned to the bedroom and took away another girl. In another bedroom, he made her lie on the bed and then he stabbed her in the neck and strangled her. Four dead.

Over an hour had passed since Speck had begun killing, and he was taking his time with each girl. It was estimated he took twenty to twenty-five minutes for each murder.

There were four nurses left and they all hid under the beds (except for one girl) in a futile attempt to elude this maniacal monster.

Speck found three of the girls, but did not find Corazon Amurao. He took two girls to the front upstairs bedroom where he stabbed one, killing her instantly, and then strangled the other one. Six dead.

Speck again went into the bathroom and washed his hands. He then took one of the two remaining girls (that he knew of) into the bathroom. Amurao recalled hearing this girl say to Speck, "Will you please untie my ankles first?" Speck ignored her request, kicked her brutally in the stomach, and then strangled her to death.

Speck's final victim was Gloria Davy, the girl who looked like his ex-wife.

Hiding under the bed, Amurao heard Speck remove Davy's pants and then get on top of her on the bed. Amurao heard the bedsprings creaking and she heard Speck say to Davy, "Will you please put your legs around my back?" Speck raped Davy for about twenty minutes and then took her downstairs, still naked, to the living room. There he made her lie face down on the sofa and he sodomized her, and also anally violated her with a hard object. He then strangled her to death with a strip of bed sheet. Eight dead. Speck left the house and began hitting the bars.

Amurao waited hours under the bed, until five o'clock that afternoon, when she was completely sure he was gone. She finally crawled out from under the bed, broke a window, crawled outside onto a ledge, and screamed for help.

After the police arrived, Amurao was taken to a hospital and put under sedation. When she awakened, she gave the police sketch artist a perfect description of the suspect, resulting in a drawing that looked remarkably like Richard Speck.

On July 16, three days after the murders, Richard Speck was taken to a hospital following a failed suicide attempt. He had slashed both his arms and was bleeding profusely. He gave the hospital staff his real name and an alert doctor realized that this was the man they were hunting for in connection with the nurse murders. The doctor called the police and Speck was arrested and charged with eight murders.

Speck was tried the following spring and Amurao testified against him. The jury deliberated forty-nine minutes and Speck was found guilty and sentenced to death in the electric chair. During his appeals, the Supreme Court put a moratorium on executions and Speck was resentenced to 400 to 1,200 years in prison.

In 1978, Speck admitted to writer Bob Greene that he did it. "Yeah, I killed them. I stabbed them and choked them." (In Greene's 1983 book, *American Beat.*)

Speck died in prison of a massive heart attack in 1991 at the age of forty-nine. Four years after his death, a videotape shot in 1988 of Speck in prison surfaced and was aired on some TV stations. The tape showed Speck snorting cocaine and performing oral sex on his black lover. The tape also showed Speck wearing blue panties and exposing a pair of female breasts. It seems that Speck not only got his hands on cocaine while in prison, but also was able to get female hormones.

Charles Manson

(1934–)

*I have done my best to get along in your world and now you
want to kill me. I say to myself, "Ha, I'm already dead, have
been all my life." . . . I don't care anything about any of you.*
— Charles Manson, speaking at his trial

Better lock your doors and watch your own kids . . .
— Manson Family member Susan Atkins, after being
sentenced to death for the Tate/LaBianca murders

Voytek Frykowski: Who are you?
Tex Watson: The devil.

Sharon Tate and Roman Polanski's unborn child was murdered with his
mother. His name was Paul Richard Polanski. Tiny Paul was the most defenseless victim of Charles Manson's Family of psychopathic murderers.

Manson prosecutor Vincent Bugliosi considers Charles Manson a "meta-
phor" for evil and has said, "Today, almost every disaffected and morally twisted

group in America, from Satanists to neo-Nazi skinheads, has embraced Manson and the poisons of his virulent philosophy. He has become their spiritual icon, the high priest of anti-establishment hatred." During Manson's trial, Bugliosi also described Manson as "one of the most evil, Satanic men who ever walked the face of the earth" and as a "megalomaniac who coupled his insatiable thirst for power with an intense obsession for violent death."

What did Charles Manson do to warrant his transmutation into an archetype of evil, a paradigm of iniquity? How did Manson's name and "evil" become synonymous?

On November 11, 2001, Charles Manson turned sixty-seven years old. Thirty years of that time has been spent behind bars in a federal penitentiary for his role in the 1969 Tate/LaBianca murders in Beverly Hills, California. It is important to note that Manson never actually killed any of these people, but powerfully influenced the members of his Family to do his dirty work.

The victims of Manson and the Family were:

- Actress Sharon Tate, the wife of director Roman Polanski (Polanski was working on a movie in Europe at the time)
- their eight-month in utero baby, Paul Richard Polanski
- Sharon's close friend Abigail Folger, twenty-five, the heiress of the Folger coffee empire
- Abigail's boyfriend Voytek Frykowski, thirty-two
- Jay Sebring, thirty-five, a famous hair stylist to the stars
- Steve Parent, eighteen, a young man, who, in a tragic instance of truly being in the wrong place at the wrong time, was on the premises visiting the Polanskis' caretaker

Sharon Tate died from five stab wounds that pierced her heart, lungs, and liver. Manson's disciples also stabbed Tate eleven additional times for fun.

Folger was stabbed twenty-eight times.

Frykowski was killed by two gunshot wounds, thirteen savage blows to the head, and fifty-one stab wounds.

Sebring was killed with one gunshot wound and seven stab wounds.

Parent was killed with four gunshot wounds.

Susan Atkins, a member of the Family and a participant in the murders, later admitted everything to a woman with whom she shared a room in prison for another crime. She described the murders in detail and also revealed that they had wanted to cut out Tate's baby, gouge out all their victims' eyes, squash the eyes against the walls, and cut off their victims' fingers, but they did not have time. They did have time, however, to write "Death to Pigs" and "Rise" on the living room walls, and "Helter Skelter" (misspelled) on the refrigerator—all written in the victims' blood.

The following night, August 10, 1969, Manson's family visited the home of Leno and Rosemary LaBianca and killed them both. Leno LaBianca died from twenty-six stab wounds. His wife Rosemary was killed by six fatal stab wounds, but she was also stabbed thirty-five more times by the Manson Family for fun.

Nine days prior to the Tate murders, the Family had murdered music teacher Gary Hinman. They had stabbed him to death, then written "Political Piggy" on his wall. It took quite some time for the Los Angeles Police Department and the Los Angeles Sheriff's Department to connect the Hinman murder with the Tate/LaBianca slaying, but eventually they made the link and the Family was arrested and charged with the crimes.

Before the murders, Manson and his crew were living on the nearby Spahn Ranch. Manson had one of his girls provide George Spahn with as much sex as he wanted in exchange for free rent.

Around this time, Manson came up with his race war philosophy. He believed that blacks would eventually rise up and take over American cities in a bloody revolution. He said this war was called Helter Skelter, a name he got from a song on The Beatles' *White Album*. Manson also believed that he himself was an angel and that after he had taken back Los Angeles with his (by that point) 144,000-member Family (or so he believed), he would be granted entry to the hidden city under Death Valley were there was gold and riches.

Through a combination of charisma, drugs, financial control, brutality, hypnosis, and sex, Charles Manson convinced all his followers that he was a divine creature with godlike powers and that they had to obey his commands. One of his girls once described his miraculous healing abilities. She recounted an episode in which she was performing oral sex on Manson and she accidentally bit off his penis. She said he then grew the organ back almost instantly. In this case, an LSD hallucination was looked to as evidence of Manson's "powers."

After a lengthy investigation, all roads led to the Spahn Ranch and, in December 1969, to the arrest of Manson and his followers.

Charles Manson, Charles "Tex" Watson, Patricia Krenwinkel, Susan Atkins, and Linda Kasabian were each charged with seven counts of murder and one count of conspiracy to commit murder. Leslie van Houten was charged with two counts of murder and one count of conspiracy to commit murder.

Manson appeared in court with an X carved into his forehead (this would be replaced by a swastika for his future parole hearings) and created a great many disturbances, including screaming at the judge and prompting his female followers to chant in Latin.

Everyone was found guilty of all charges and everyone was sentenced to death. However, society would not be rid of Manson and his Family that easily: In 1972, California abolished the death penalty and all of their sentences were commuted to life.

The Manson trial was, to that time, the longest trial in American history. (O.J.'s now claims that ignoble honor.) It lasted nine and a half months, kept the jury sequestered for 225 days, cost the taxpayers $1 million, and produced eight million words of transcripts.

Today, Manson supposedly receives the most mail of any U.S. prisoner and there have been movies, documentaries, and books written about him and what he ordered his Family to do. Guns 'N Roses have recorded one of Manson's songs.

According to Manson follower Susan Atkins, the Tate/LaBianca murders were supposed to be the beginning of a rampage against celebrities. Richard Burton, Elizabeth Taylor, Frank Sinatra, Steve McQueen, and Tom Jones were also targeted. The Family had elaborate plans for these world-famous stars. The plan was to skin Frank Sinatra alive (while he listened to his own music) and make purses out of his skin and sell them; carve the words "Helter Skelter" on Elizabeth Taylor's face and then gouge out her eyes; cut off Richard Burton's penis and put it in a jar with Elizabeth Taylor's eyes and send the jar to Eddie Fisher; and cut Tom Jones throat, but only after Susan Atkins had sex with him.

Neither Manson nor any of his followers have ever been granted parole.

83

Joel Rifkin

(1959–)

There were nights I'd be with more than one girl. One girl would walk away fine, the other would end up dead.

—Joel Rifkin

The defendant acted with unparalleled evil and depravity.
      —District Attorney Fred Klein in his opening statement
      at Rifkin's trial

Joel Rifkin bears the notoriety of being the worst serial killer in New York's history, and he is currently serving a two-hundred-year prison sentence for his crimes.

Rifkin killed seventeen women in a four-year period. Some he dismembered and dumped at various spots in upstate New York and along the Harlem and Hudson Rivers. Some he simply dragged into the woods after he murdered them and left them for the animals and insects. Some he kept around for days in the basement of the house he lived in with his mother. Some he kept in the trunk of his mother's car and drove around town for a day or so until he could dispose of them. Once, his mother actually went shopping with the corpse of one of her son's victims in the trunk of her car.

Rifkin was eventually caught because he had no license plate on his truck. The body of his final victim, Tiffany Bresciani, was wrapped in a tarp in the bed of his truck, and it rolled around as Rifkin led police on a high-speed chase. When Rifkin was finally arrested, he had Noxzema cream smeared under his nose to help him cope with the smell of Bresciani's four-days'-dead rotting corpse.

Joel Rifkin was an adopted child and was considered a nerd in school. He was repeatedly bullied and had trouble connecting with girls. Not surprisingly, he began turning to prostitutes for his sexual needs. It wasn't long before he began killing them.

Rifkin's first victim was an AIDS-infected, drug addict/prostitute who called herself Susie. Rifkin beat her almost to the point of death with a 12-pound howitzer shell and then finished the job by strangling her. "[I was hitting her] two-handed, like a baseball bat," Rifkin told his biographer Robert Mladinich. "Sideways, up from the top, all different ways. I just lost control. Stopped when I got tired."

Rifkin put Susie's corpse in a large trash bag and then dragged it down to the basement. He then took a nap. Upon waking, he decided to dismember her corpse. He used an X-Acto knife. He then cut her head off and put it in a paint can, after, for some reason, first pulling out her teeth with pliers. Rifkin put Susie's different body parts in trash bags and then drove out to a wooded area. He threw the paint can into the woods; he threw the bags with Susie's legs into another part of the woods; he threw the bags with her arms and her torso into the East River. He then went home and cleaned the house. Golfers found Susie's head a week later.

Rifkin's sixteen other victims are a roster of society's most desperate, most troubled, and most vulnerable.

Julie Blackbird was a prostitute Rifkin killed eighteen months after he killed Susie. He used a table leg or a sawed-off bat to bludgeon her to death and he then dismembered her in the basement. This time, he put the body parts in cement and let them dry. Rifkin admitted that he considered having sex with her corpse but rejected the idea. When asked how he could cut off a head with a utility knife, he explained that if you use a new blade and keep the blade extended a short length, it cut just like a scalpel. He explained how he cut through tendons and muscle a little at a time, and eventually he was able to separate her head from her torso by cutting through the gristle at the top of the spinal cord. After hearing this story, Mladinich (2001) wrote, "For the first time I suspected I had come face to face with pure evil, which was something I had always argued did not exist." Blackbird's torso went into a milk crate and into the Hudson River; her arms and legs went into a barge canal in Brooklyn. Rifkin later said that he looked upon the unpleasant task of body disposal as a job that simply needed to be done.

Between his killings, Rifkin kept seeing prostitutes, but did not kill all of the women with whom he had sex. Those he did kill and dismember, he would do at home, but only when his mother was away for several days.

Victim number three was Barbara Jacobs, thirty-one, a prostitute and drug addict. He killed her, stuffed her body into a plastic bag, put the bag in a cardboard box, and threw the box into the Hudson River. Jacobs's body was discovered within hours because the Fire Department was conducting an exercise in the river and the current brought her body to them.

Numbers 4 through 16 were Mary Ellen DeLuca, 22; Yun Lee, 31, a drug addict/prostitute; "Jane Doe," whom he strangled during sex in his truck, put her body into a stolen 55-gallon drum, and threw the drum in the Hudson River; Lorraine Orvieto, 28, a manic-depressive former cheerleader, crack addict/prostitute; Mary Ann Holloman, 39, a crack addict/prostitute; a still-unidentified woman who Rifkin says he also put into an oil drum; Iris Sanchez, 25, a crack addict whose body he left under a mattress in a vacant lot; Anna Lopez, 33, a crack addict Rifkin strangled during oral sex; Violet O'Neill, 21, whose body parts he put in a suitcase and threw into the Hudson River; Mary Catherine Williams, 31, a former cheerleader; Jenny Soto, 23, a drug addict/prostitute; Lauren Marquez, a drug addict/prostitute; and Leah Evans, 28, a judge's daughter.

Rifkin's final victim was the aforementioned Tiffany Bresciani, a 22-year-old prostitute who was found in the back of his truck.

Rifkin claimed he was relieved he had been arrested because he did not have to live with the secrets anymore, but he pled not guilty to the Bresciani murder.

According to his biographer, during the months leading up to his trial, Rifkin loved being in the spotlight, and had it all figured out: he would serve twenty-five years on the Bresciani murder and then live out his life as a celebrity writer. But then the Colin Ferguson subway shootings eclipsed his notoriety and Rifkin got beat up in jail by Ferguson.

Rifkin received a two-hundred-year prison sentence, which he is currently serving.

84

The Son of Sam

(1953–)

*I feel like an outsider. I am on a different wavelength than
everybody else—programmed too [sic] kill. However, to stop
me you must kill me. Attention all police: Shoot me first—shoot
to kill or else keep out of my way or you will die!*
>   —From a letter from David Berkowitz to Captain Joseph
>   Borreli of the NYPD

I've done all the evil a guy could do.
>   —From an August 1999 letter from David Berkowitz to a
>   young Satanist named Craig

There is a reason this chapter is titled "The Son of Sam" and not "David
Berkowitz." This is because Berkowitz now sincerely and wholeheartedly believes that he is a different person than who he was when he committed the
murders that earned him the "Son of Sam" sobriquet. He is now filled with
remorse for Sam's deeds, while he serves out his 365 consecutive years in the
Sullivan Correctional Facility in New York.

Berkowitz now has his own Web site, www.sonofhope.com, on which he
discusses his personal salvation and offers his spiritual testimony to warn peo-

ple against getting involved in the occult. In the past two decades, there has been growing acceptance of the possibility that one or more of the Son of Sam murders could have been the work of a Satanic cult.

Much the way Berkowitz once used a .44-caliber Bulldog revolver to spread terror throughout New York in the late 1970s, he now uses the power of the Internet to spread his gospel of redemption around the world and to preach to people that Jesus saves. Berkowitz now attributes his heinous actions to an "evil force" (his words) that came upon him and guided him in the carrying out of his terrible deeds. He writes "I am utterly convinced that something Satanic had entered into my mind . . ." and he describes himself as a former "devil worshipper."

Berkowitz now preaches the Bible and tries to bring people to Jesus. He has worked as a Chaplain's clerk, has appeared on Christian TV programs, and has a letter-writing outreach ministry from prison. He also believes that Jesus Christ has completely forgiven him for his deeds.

The Son of Sam's body count is low compared with some of the miscreants that make up *The Evil 100:* six people dead; seven people seriously injured for life. Yet, his rampage in New York City from 1976 through 1977 is remembered for its random "murder for the sake of murder" pointlessness; as well as his apparent glee in killing at will. "I didn't want to hurt them," he is quoted as saying after his capture. "I only wanted to kill them."

The Son of Sam's modus operandi was brutal and heartless. He would walk up to his selected victims, whether they were parked in a car, walking along the street, or seated on a stoop, pull out his .44-caliber Bulldog (often from a brown paper bag), and fire at point blank range, usually aiming for their head or chest. Sometimes he would shoot until he emptied his gun. One of his victims, Virginia Voskerichian, tried to protect herself by holding a book up in front of her face. Berkowitz fired right through the book, killing her instantly.

The Son of Sam's first murder—Donna Lauria—occurred on July 29, 1976; his final murder—Stacy Moskowitz—on July 31, 1977.

The following chart details the Son of Sam's murderous spree during the thirteen months from July 1976 through July 1977, a time when disco ruled the dance scene and a psychopath initially dubbed the "44-Caliber Killer" terrorized Queens.

1976

7/29/76:   Donna Lauria—KILLED
7/29/76:   Jody Valenti—WOUNDED

10/23/76: Carl Denaro—WOUNDED
11/27/76: Donna DeMasi—WOUNDED
11/27/76: Joanne Lomino—WOUNDED

1977

1/30/77:   Christine Freund—KILLED
3/8/77:   Virginia Voskerichian—KILLED
4/14/77:   Alexander Esau—KILLED
4/14/77:   Valentina Suriani—KILLED
6/26/77:   Salvatore Lupe—WOUNDED
6/26/77:   Judy Placido—WOUNDED
7/31/77:   Robert Violante—WOUNDED
7/31/77:   Stacy Moskowitz—KILLED

Berkowitz became known as the "Son of Sam" from something he wrote in a June 1, 1977, letter to *New York Daily News* columnist Jimmy Breslin:

> ". . . Not knowing what the future holds I shall say farewell and I will see you at the next job? Or should I say you will see my handiwork at the next job? Remember Ms. Lauria. In their blood and from the gutter, 'Sam's Creation' .44."

The "Sam" referred to in Berkowitz's letter was his neighbor, Sam Carr, who had a Labrador retriever who barked constantly and in whose yelps, Berkowitz heard the voices of demons telling him to kill.

After the explosive impact the Son of Sam murders had on New York City, the arrest of David Berkowitz was as prosaic as the arrest of Al Capone for tax evasion. Berkowitz was arrested for throwing away a parking ticket, which allowed the police to track him down. When they confronted him, Berkowitz assumed he had been caught, and told them, "I'm Sam."

Berkowitz was found sane enough to stand trial but he pled guilty and accepted responsibility for the Son of Sam murders.

Following is an August 4, 2001, letter to the author that is representative of Berkowitz's feelings about his crimes and his redemption. Readers can make up their own minds as to what to think about David Berkowitz.

(Special thanks to Mr. Berkowitz for permission to include this piece in *The Evil 100.*)

A Letter From David Berkowitz

August 4, 2001

Dear Mr. Wolcott:

I have your letter of July 17, and I very much appreciate the fact that you told me about your project. I must admit that it has been hard for me to answer your letter. I've been holding on to it wondering how to answer.

I have to say that, of course any kind of book that deals with the past, I am certainly not happy about this. However I do thank you for the kind words you've said concerning my life today. I do not know if you believe in God or not, but he has certainly been very merciful to me; I do not deserve it!

It has been twenty-four years since the tragedies of 1976–77. So much has changed in my life in the past quarter of a century. I am so very sorry for what had happened, and at times I am haunted by it. But I know that Christ has forgiven me. Little by little I have been able to come to grips with the past. I have learned and I am still learning to accept God's forgiveness. Society will never forgive me, of course. But this is understandable.

I know, too, that I have peace in my heart today. I pray daily for those who were hurt by my actions and for those who've lost loved ones. Their pain and grief are beyond comprehension.

In addition, as much as is in me, I am always trying to make amends when I can. For I owe society a big debt. And over time many opportunities have come about allowing me to share my story of from darkness to light, from despair to hope with many troubled teenagers.

A number of youth ministers all across the nation are frequently sharing my testimony. I am so thankful for this. I've received so many wonderful letters over the years from young people. I wish I could share them for others to enjoy and be encouraged by.

Mr. Wolcott, I know with absolute certainty that God has given me a whole new life. I realize that I will be in prison until the day I leave this world. I have peace about this, however. My days are full and busy and I have nothing to complain about.

Furthermore, please fell free to check the Web sites for updates. Pastor Konitshek and a friend from New York have recently added many photos and other things. I myself have never seen the sites because Internet material is not allowed in here. But God is using these things to reach many people with a message of hope and forgiveness.

God bless you, and I wish you the best with your project.

Sincerely,
/s/ David Berkowitz

P.S. While I did not make a specific "statement," feel free to quote from this letter or from any other statement which is online at one of the sites.

cc/db
www.sonofhope.com
www.inetworld.net/hutrcc/david.htm

85

The Zodiac Killer

I like killing people because it is so much fun. It is more fun than killing wild game in the forest because Man is the most dangerous animal of all. To kill something gives me the most thrilling experience. It is even better than getting your rocks off with a girl. The best part [will be] when I die. I will be reborn in Paradise and all that I have killed will become my slaves. I will not give you my name because you will try to slow down or stop my collecting of slaves for my afterlife.

> —The Zodiac Killer, from a letter confirmed to have come from the killer

I have headaches.

> —The Zodiac Killer, to Attorney Melvin Belli on a TV talk show

Is the Zodiac Killer still alive? Perhaps. It certainly is not an impossibility.

The last time Zodiac was heard from, however, was in 1974—six years after the last of the murders attributed to him were committed. (The *San Francisco Chronicle* did receive a letter in 1978 claiming to be from Zodiac, but that letter has since been confirmed a fraud.)

In 1974, Zodiac sent four letters to the newspaper over a six-month period in which he mentioned popular movies of the time, specifically *The Exorcist* (he called it the best satirical comedy he had ever seen), and *Badlands;* the musical, *The Mikado;* the Symbionese Liberation Army (they had just made headlines for kidnapping Patty Hearst); and the *Chronicle's* "Count Marco" editorial column. Almost all of Zodiac's letters began with "This is the Zodiac speaking" and experts were certain that the media attention, the public publication of his letters, and the anticipation for more letters fueled his ego and were an important part of the satisfaction he received from the perpetuation of his alter ego, the Zodiac Killer. Zodiac's obvious delight at not only killing, but in duping the police, made murder a game to him, making his evil acts that much more depraved.

What were the Zodiac Killer's crimes? Five deaths and two people injured in an eleven-month period, from December 1968 through October 1969. Two teenaged couples and a cab driver were the fatalities; two teenaged boys were seriously injured.

Zodiac was a heartless killer and would target young people parked in cars in "Lover's Lane"-type settings. Zodiac killed one teenaged girl by shooting her nine times with a 9-mm Luger. His final victim, the cab driver, was dispatched with a bullet in the back of the head. Zodiac also tied up two of his victims and stabbed them to death, and he shot a teenaged girl five times in the back as she ran away from him.

Moreover, Zodiac endeavored to strike terror in his victims before he killed them. Coming out of the darkness like a Satanic ghoul from hell, the Zodiac Killer would sometimes dress in a black robe and black hood, with his cross-inside-a-circle symbol in white on his chest. He was also known to paint his symbol on the car doors of those he killed.

In October 1969, Zodiac, a man with a voice described as "soft" and "boyish," called in to a morning TV talk show to speak to famous attorney Melvin Belli, who was on the air at the time. They spoke live and talked about the Zodiac murders. This was also the incident during which Zodiac told Belli, "I have headaches." This was perceived as Zodiac offering an explanation for his acts. Belli later received a letter with a piece of the shirt of the Zodiac's fifth victim, the cab driver, in it.

In 1971, the Zodiac Killer wrote to the *Los Angeles Times* specifically mentioning the "Blue Meanies" from the Beatles' film *Yellow Submarine.* In 1974, prior to his final letters to the *San Francisco Chronicle,* Zodiac wrote again to the *Los Angeles Times,* threatening to start killing again and claiming responsibility for thirty-seven deaths. Police still believe that this number is an exaggeration, but there is no way to be certain.

Over the years, there have been men who were suspected of being the Zodiac Killer. The prime suspect was a convicted child molester named Arthur Leigh Allen. An acquaintance of Allen's told the police that Allen had said things to him that hinted at Allen being the Zodiac. Plus he wore a Sea

Wolf wristwatch, which was manufactured by the Zodiac Watch Company, whose logo was identical to the cross-in-a-circle sign the Zodiac Killer left at his crimes scenes and wore on his robe.

The police did investigate Allen, but to no avail. Allen did seem to have specific details about some of the Zodiac crimes, but they were facts he could have come across in some way other then being the killer himself. In addition, Allen passed a ten-hour polygraph test, and there was never any physical evidence at any of the crime scenes that linked Arthur Allen and the Zodiac Killer.

While researching his book about the killings, *Zodiac* author Robert Graysmith (1986) apparently became convinced that Allen was Zodiac and he created a suspect in his book that was modeled on Allen. This re-ignited interest in Allen as a suspect and once again subjected him to questioning, searches, and condemnation.

Allen was never charged with the Zodiac crimes, and he died in 1992, still believed by many to have been the Zodiac Killer.

Could the Zodiac Killer still be alive? The year 2002 marks twenty-eight years since Zodiac was last heard from. Even assuming Zodiac was in his thirties when he committed his terrible murders, he could easily still be alive today, in his late fifties or early sixties, still gloating over never having been caught.

86

Ian Brady and Myra Hindley

"THE MOORS MURDERERS"

(1938–) (1942–)

It's done. It's the messiest yet. It normally only takes one blow.
—Ian Brady, talking about the bloody mess resulting from
his axe-murder of seventeen-year-old Edward Evans

In the *Encyclopedia of Serial Killers* by Brian Lane and Wilfred Gregg (1995), Brady and Hindley are described as "synonymous with the concept of 'evil.'" This depraved couple preyed upon and abducted young girls and boys, sexually molested and raped them, killed them, and buried their bodies in Saddleworth Moor near Manchester in northern England, over a two-year span, from 1963 to 1964. The Moors Murderers are each currently serving life sentences in England with no chance of parole.

As an adolescent, Ian Brady enjoyed torturing animals. He once put a live cat in a grave and covered the hole with a stone to see how long it would take the cat to starve to death. He eventually graduated to torturing neighborhood children. Brady's mother was single and worked full-time as a waitress. He never really had a home life as a child. During his adolescence, he was shipped to different foster homes and was frequently in trouble for robbery and other petty crimes.

At the age of twenty-one, Brady got a job at Millwards, a chemical plant, and it is at this time that he began to indulge his fetish for Nazi memorabilia, sadomasochism, and pornography. In fact, the first time Myra Hindley saw Brady, he was reading Hitler's *Mein Kampf* in its original German.

Almost two years after Brady started working at Millwards, Myra Hindley was hired as a typist. She was immediately infatuated with Brady and, even though he at first ignored her, eventually her signals that she was interested in him registered with Brady, and he asked her to be his date for New Year's Eve, 1962. That night, she gave him her virginity.

They became inseparable after that and Brady soon began dominating Hindley and persuading her to do whatever he demanded, including posing and taking pornographic snapshots. He would eventually lead her into abducting and killing children.

The Moors Murders became known in October 1965 when the police were told an incredible story by a stunned and terrified, seventeen-year-old David Smith. Smith told the police that he had witnessed a murder and that he had helped carry the body up a flight of stairs to an upstairs bedroom. The murderer was his sister-in-law's boyfriend, Ian Brady, and Smith had seen Brady kill a young man with an axe in the living room of Brady's home.

The previous night, Smith's sister-in-law, Myra Hindley, had asked David to walk her home and, when they arrived at 16 Wardle Brook Avenue, Manchester, Hindley invited Smith in on the pretext that her live-in boyfriend Ian Brady had some miniature bottles of wine for him.

Smith went in, and as he stood around in the kitchen, he heard a scream from the living room. He ran in and saw Ian Brady and Edward Evans, a seventeen-year-old homosexual Brady had picked up at a local bar. As Smith watched in horror, Brady struck Evans in the head with an axe and, when it was obvious that the boy was not dead, whacked him with the axe again. Brady then strangled the boy with an electrical wire until he stopped making any sounds at all, and then callously tossed the body onto the living room sofa.

Shortly after this grisly scene and the violent death of a young man, Myra Hindley made everyone a cup of tea.

David Smith told police that he was in immediate and constant fear for his life, and so decided to act unaffected and calm with Brady and Hindley, until he could get away safely.

Brady made Smith help him carry the body upstairs and then Smith left. Upon his return home, he vomited and told his wife everything. A few hours later, in the early morning of the next day, Smith called the police, went in to the station, and told them everything that had occurred.

More than two dozen police officers descended on Wardle Brook Avenue and once they gained access to the house, they found Evans' body and the murder weapon in the upstairs bedroom, just as David Smith had said they would.

Brady and Hindley were arrested and Smith then told the police that Brady had told him about bodies he had buried on nearby Saddleworth Moor. The police began investigating Smith's allegations and they found the bodies of four children, all of whom had been kidnapped and killed by Brady and Hindley—now known as The Moor Murderers—in 1963 and 1964. All of the children had been sexually molested before being killed.

Tape recordings were later discovered. On the tapes were the sounds of ten-year-old Lesley Ann Downey being tortured, raped, and killed. Hindley can be heard shouting, "Put it in" to the terrified adolescent.

Hindley and Brady were both sentenced to life imprisonment in 1965.

At their trial, Hindley claimed she was forced to participate in Brady's perversity and murder. Brady denied these charges and, in a March 2000 letter to a Liverpool News agency (quoted in "Murder on the Moors" on crimelibrary.com), wrote:

> She has stooped to new depths, alleging I coerced her to serially murder by use of drugs, rape, blackmail, physical violence, and practically every other crime in the book. All the concrete evidence against her has been jettisoned in favour of transparent mendacity and evidential amnesia.

Brady claims that Hindley willing engaged in their crimes out of love for him, and that now she is lying in an attempt to get out of prison. Hindley says she deeply regrets her crimes and ever getting involved with Brady. She is currently in prison in fragile health and her attorneys continue to maneuver for her release. Upon hearing of Hindley's ordeal with angina and a cerebral embolism, the mother of one of her victims expressed the public wish that Hindley would suffer before she died.

Brady recently went on a three-month hunger strike with the intention of killing himself instead of living out his life in prison. On a court order, prison officials force-fed him. He is currently alive. That is more than can be said for his victims.

87

John George Haigh
"The Acid Bath Murderer"
"The Vampire Killer"
"The Acid Bath Vampire"

(1909–1949)

I saw before me a forest of crucifixes which gradually turned into trees. At first there appeared to be dew or rain dripping from the branches, but as I approached I realized it was blood . . . A man went to each tree catching the blood. When the cup was full he approached me. "Drink," he said, but I was unable to move.

> —John George Haigh, recounting a frequent nightmare

Mrs. Durand-Deacon no longer exists! I've destroyed her with acid . . . How can you prove murder without a body?

> —Haigh, speaking in his own defense

The evil of John George Haigh was in his cold, arrogant disregard for the realities of his actions: he would kill people for their money, and then dispose of their bodies by dissolving them in a 40-gallon drum filled with sulfuric acid. Human life was immaterial; cynical opportunism actualized by heartless murder was his life's work. When he was caught, he feigned insanity and said he killed to drink his victims' blood, calculatingly planning on a ten-year sentence spent in the relative comfort of a mental institution. It didn't work.

As has frequently been the case with amoral mass murderers and serial killers, Haigh was raised by religiously fanatical parents. Haigh's mother and father belonged to a sect called the "Plymouth Brethren," biblical fundamentalists also known as (honestly) the "Peculiar People." Entertainment was forbidden and, as a child, Haigh was read Bible stories on a regular basis.

Haigh's father had a blue mark on his forehead that was nothing more than a birthmark or some kind of odd pigmentation, but he told his son that the mark was the devil's mark, and that he had received it because he had sinned. The younger Haigh believed that anyone who sinned would be likewise marked, and immediately became terrified of breaking any of God's rules. As to why Haigh's mother did not have the mark, Haigh's father told his son that his mother was an angel, and that she had never sinned, and thus, would go through life unsullied.

In addition to being frightened of waking up one morning with the Mark of Satan on his forehead, Haigh also began marveling at the fact that he was the result of the union of a corrupt sinner and a pure being of light. This was probably not the healthiest mind-set for an adolescent boy, and his developing personality also had to deal with the paradox of his pure, unsullied angel of light mother beating him when he misbehaved. Later in life, Haigh claimed to recall many incidents when his mother beat him until he bled, and then him licking the blood. He told his psychiatrists that these incidents gave birth to his taste for human blood.

Before Haigh's arrest and trial for his murders, he had repeatedly served time in prison for fraud and forgery. While incarcerated, Haigh began planning the perfect crime: a murder, followed by a plundering of the victim's valuables and estate, capped off with the baffling disappearance (the *complete* disappearance) of the victim's body.

Haigh's strategy involved his own interpretation of what was known as the *corpus delicti* law. This law concerned using a corpse as evidence in a trial. Haigh firmly (yet incorrectly) believed that this law meant that if there were no *corpus delicti*—if the body of the victim could not be produced by the prosecution—then the police would not be able to prove a murder had been committed, and the accused could not be convicted of the crime. Haigh talked about this legal point so often that his prison nickname was "Ol' Corpus Delicti." Haigh ignored the taunts, however, and began experimenting by putting mice in acid and seeing how long it took their bodies to dissolve.

Haigh carried out eight combination murder/robbery/acid baths after he was initially released from prison. Three of his victims could not be verified and some believe Haigh made them up to bolster his insanity defense.

The victim that put an end to Haigh's acid bath rampage was Mrs. Olive Durand-Deacon, a wealthy widow who lived at the Onslow Court Hotel in London at the same time as Haigh. Olive had come up with an idea to sell false fingernails to fashion-conscious women of the times, and she described her idea to Haigh. Haigh told her he loved the idea and invited her out to his "workshop" to look at possible materials that could be used to make the fingernails. Once he got her there, he shot her in the back of the head, stripped her of her valuables, and put her two-hundred-pound body in a 40-gallon drum filled with sulfuric acid.

When Olive's friends became worried about her absence, they began an investigation. Haigh was questioned, and his workshop explored. Police found a .38-caliber revolver that had been recently fired, and Haigh was arrested. In short, he confessed. He told police, "Having taken her into the storeroom, I shot her in the back of the head while she was examining some materials. Then I went out to the car and fetched a drinking glass and made an incision—I think with a penknife—in the side of her throat. I collected a glass of blood, which I drank."

After Haigh confessed, the police took away from his workshop yard 475 pounds of sludge and dirt. After sifting through it carefully, they recovered 28 pounds of human body fat; three human gallstones; part of a left foot, not completely dissolved; eighteen pieces of human bone; an undamaged set of upper and lower dentures; the handle of a red plastic purse; and a lipstick container.

Everything belonged to Mrs. Olive Durand-Deacon.

Haigh then told the police of his other murders and acid disposal jobs and signed a lengthy statement describing how he let the acid dissolve the bodies and then disposed of the sludge down a manhole in his workshop.

Haigh then began strategizing his insanity defense and told the police that he stabbed each of his victims in the neck after killing them, and held a glass beneath the flowing blood and drank it. To embellish and hopefully strengthen his insanity plea, he also drank his own urine in his cell while in custody and then told his psychiatrists about it. He also claimed that he had been forced to kill by "wild blood demons" and that he did not kill for sex, only for blood. No one believed him and everyone knew that he killed not for blood, but for money.

Haigh showed no remorse for his abominable crimes and he was convicted, sentenced to death, and hung in August 1949.

Haigh bequeathed his clothes to Madame Tussaud's Chamber of Horrors and they dutifully put up a wax figure of the Acid Bath Murderer, making sure that his clothing was always pressed and neat, and that his hair was always parted the way he liked it.

Haigh had left instructions.

88

Paul Bernardo and Karla Homolka

(1964–) (1970–)

[Your] acts [were] monstrous and depraved. . . . All these crimes are extremely grave . . . the fact that you continued your crimes after the death of your sister, which occurred during your sexual abuse of her, demonstrates clearly your difficulty in controlling your violent sexual impulses to the point of putting in danger the safety of others. Your modus operandi demonstrates a high degree of indifference to the consequences of your acts.

> —from a March 2001 National Parole Board report on Karla Homolka

There is significant relief on behalf of the families.

> —Tim Danson, attorney for the families of Paul Bernardo's victims, upon hearing that Bernardo will never get out of prison

Paul Bernardo and Karla Homolka met in October 1987 at a veterinary convention in Toronto, and within hours after their first "Hello, how are you?" they were in Karla's hotel room, naked, and having frenzied, animalistic sex— as Paul's friend Van Smirnis and Karla's coworker, Debby Purdis, watched.

This was the beginning of the relationship that would allow Paul Bernardo to satisfy his sickest urges, and that would result in three deaths, countless rapes, and untold violence and pain.

The perverse relationship and deeds of Canada's Paul Bernardo and his wife Karla Homolka starkly illustrate the meaning of the word *gestalt*, which is defined as a total that is greater than, and different from, the nature of its individual elements. One writer who reported on the Bernardo/Homolka rape/murders described the two as "gasoline and fertilizer," referring to the devastating bomb that can be created when these two disparate ingredients are combined. The couples' families, the criminal psychologists, the jury, and the public have all wondered what would have happened if the repulsive Bernardo and the conscienceless Homolka had never met. Would they each have individually committed the kinds of heinous crimes they did as a couple? Would they each have exhibited a similar cruel, sadistic heartlessness they brandished as a couple? Would Karla's sister Tammy be alive today? Would Leslie Mahaffy be alive? What about Kristen French?

Who was the villain in the Bernardo/Homolka dyad?

The amoral Paul Bernardo, intent on indulging his sickest fantasies no matter what the human toll, has been looked to as the Svengali who malevolently manipulated Karla into first endorsing and encouraging his crimes, and then, willingly participating in them.

But then there is Karla, the eager, compliant blonde with supermodel looks who readily betrayed her younger sister to please her husband, although her sister Tammy's death was not planned as part of the fun. Does the fact that Tammy's death was accidental (unintended—the actions causing her death were clearly planned out in detail) mitigate Karla's culpability? Tammy was her *sister*, and yet she excitedly gave Tammy's virginity to her husband in a macabre payback for Karla having not been a virgin when she and Paul first met.

In December 1990, Karla stole some of the anesthetic halothane from the veterinary clinic where she worked and used it soaked into a cloth to keep her sister Tammy unconscious while her husband Paul raped her vaginally and anally. Paul then made Karla perform cunnilingus on Tammy (who had her period at the time), while he videotaped her doing it. During the festivities, Tammy began to throw up from the halothane. Karla thought she knew what to do because she had seen this happen with animals, and so she turned Tammy over. It did not work. Tammy died from suffocation after she swallowed her own vomit.

Tammy's death did not spook Paul and Karla. On the contrary. Soon after Tammy's murder, Bernardo abducted two young local girls, Leslie Mahaffy and Kristen French, and subjected them both to sexual torture, rape, and disgusting abuses, including being urinated on, before killing and dismembering them both. Bernardo and Homolka videotaped everything they did to Mahaffy and French.

Paul's mother was promiscuous (when Paul was sixteen, she revealed to him that he was a "bastard") and his father was a child molester (he was charged in court with fondling a young girl and allegedly sexually molested his young daughter). These revelations provoked a bitter hatred for his parents in Paul and some experts look to his less-than-idyllic childhood as the fertile ground in which the seeds of his later sadistic, perverted behavior took root.

Paul was in his early twenties when his "interests" took a dark turn. He began to force violent anal sex on his dates, whom he also physically battered. He also became a serial rapist, dubbed the "Scarborough Rapist" by the media.

Paul Bernardo was tried and found guilty on all charges, which included two counts of first-degree murder, two counts of aggravated sexual assault, two counts of forcible confinement, two counts of kidnapping, and one count of performing an indignity on a human body. He was sentenced to the maximum penalty allowable in Canada, which is life with the possibility of parole in twenty-five years. (Canada does not have the death penalty.) A court later removed the parole possibility from Bernardo's sentence. Karla Homolka cut a deal with the prosecutor and testified against her husband in exchange for a much briefer sentence with the possibility of parole in 2005.

89

Westley Allan Dodd

(1961–1993)

*Incident 3 will die maybe this way: He'll be tied down as Lee
was in Incident 2. Instead of placing a bag over his head as had
previously planned, I'll tape his mouth shut with duct tape.
Then, when ready, I'll use a clothespin or something to plug his
nose. That way I can sit back, take pictures, and watch him die
instead of concentrating on my hands or the rope tight around
his neck—that would also eliminate the rope burns on the neck.
. . . I can clearly see his face and eyes now. Electrocution also a
good means for quick death.*

—Westley Allan Dodd

*The more I thought about it, the more exciting the idea of mur-
der sounded. I planned many ways to kill a boy. Then I started
thinking of torture, castration, and even cannibalism.*

—Westley Allan Dodd

After Westley Allan Dodd was arrested in 1989, the police searched his
apartment and, in addition to discovering Dodd's own homemade torture
rack, they also found his Bible. Inside the book, Dodd had written, "Satan
lives."

✧   ✧   ✧

Westley Allan Dodd was a predator pedophile, a cannibal, and a murderer. He was one of the last capital punishment inmates to request, and be granted, death by hanging. Before he died, he claimed to have committed 250 crimes against children, and said that he killed the children he molested so he wouldn't get in trouble for the molestation.

When Dodd was eleven, he discovered the thrill of looking at pictures of naked (and often dead) Nazi concentration camp victims. It wasn't long after that, at the age of thirteen, that Dodd began sexually molesting children. His first victims were his own six- and eight-year-old cousins.

At fourteen, Dodd discovered masochism. For fun, he inserted pins into his penis. He also rammed a stick up his rectum and then rode his bicycle naked so that the stick hit the rear wheel and repeatedly stabbed and gouged his rectum.

Around that age, Dodd was also exposing himself to younger children. At first he stood behind a curtain in his bedroom window and hid his face, and when little kids walked by his house, he would show them his genitals. It wasn't long before the kids he flashed told their parents about him, and he was forced to change his MO. He started riding his bike around town and, when he found a group of kids around ten years old, he would get their attention and then pull down his pants. Dodd discovered that it was wiser to do this to boys because they did not tell on him as much as did the girls.

When Dodd turned sixteen, he started baby-sitting and molesting the children in his charge. He later took a job as a camp counselor and convinced the camp kids to play strip poker, spin-the-bottle, truth or dare, and to run around naked. Most of the kids obliged.

An eventual indecent exposure arrest did nothing to keep Dodd away from kids. All the authorities did was recommend counseling.

Dodd began targeting children he did not know when he was eighteen. Shortly thereafter, he joined the navy, and was stationed in Bangor, Washington. While there, he preyed on kids on the navy base and would also travel into town to look for kids at arcades and movie theaters. His strategy was to offer kids money, and then try and lure them away. He was eventually arrested on attempted indecent liberties charges and discharged from the navy after serving nineteen days in jail.

Over the next year or so, Dodd took jobs allowing him access to children. He worked delivery jobs, baby-sitting jobs, and at fast-food restaurants. He drew detailed maps pinpointing locations where he had seen kids so he could go back and try to abduct one.

Dodd was arrested in 1984 for molesting a ten-year-old boy and received a one-year suspended sentence.

In 1986, at the age of twenty-five, Dodd moved to Seattle. By now, he had molested more than thirty children, but he had reached a point where he had decided not to take no for an answer. He was becoming more perverted and more violent as time passed. He began stalking, targeting, and abducting kids. One of his victims was a partially deaf two-year-old boy whom he tied up and molested.

In September 1989 Dodd abducted, molested, and killed the Neer brothers, one of whom was ten, and the other eleven. He stabbed them both repeatedly and later said he found the incident exciting but knew that there was more he wanted to do.

Dodd decided that he enjoyed killing more than child sexual molestation and he determined that he needed to abduct a kid and take him somewhere where he could have all the time he wanted to indulge his perverted torture fantasies. He actually made lists of the ways to kill a child. Dodd also decided that he wanted to try cannibalism and experimental surgeries on his captives. Dodd's writing was so disturbing that one juror almost fainted while listening to an attorney read from Dodd's diary.

A month after the Neer murders, Dodd abducted four-year-old Lee Iseli in Portland, Oregon. He undressed him, tied him to a bed, and took Polaroids of him. He then molested him, after which he let the child watch cartoons. Dodd eventually strangled the Iseli boy and hung his corpse in a closet. He then took more pictures of him.

Dodd was arrested for the final time in November 1989 as he tried to abduct a young boy from a movie theater bathroom. He eventually admitted everything and the detectives who questioned Dodd made a point in their report of noting that Dodd clearly enjoyed recounting his deeds, and that he had experienced great pleasure in both the molestations and the murders.

Dodd was charged with three counts of first-degree murder. He was convicted in January 1990 and was sentenced to death.

Dodd insisted on being put to death by hanging and indicated that he did not want to delay his demise through the appeal process. In addition, he told the court, "If I do escape, I promise you I will kill and rape and enjoy every minute of it." After that statement, Dodd actually expected to be believed when he later expressed remorse. He even said that he knew he was going to heaven, and, unbelievably, that he hoped he would be able to give his victims a hug and an apology.

The American Civil Liberties Union took steps to stop Dodd's execution on the grounds that because hanging was one of the most painful methods of execution, it was "cruel and unusual punishment," but on January 5, 1993, in Washington State, Dodd hanged. He was the first inmate to be executed by hanging since 1965.

90

Gary Heidnik

(1943–1999)

Any person who puts dog food and human remains in a food processor and calls it a gourmet meal and feeds it to others is out to lunch.

—Chuck Peruto Jr., Gary Heidnik's attorney

There was a faction of anticapital punishment activists who pilloried the American justice system for executing Gary Heidnik, a man who was found guilty of being a rapist, a sexual deviate, a torturer, a kidnapper, and a murderer; a man who kidnapped and imprisoned black women, some of whom were retarded, and kept them shackled in a pit in his basement in order to impregnate them and grow his own large family; a man who killed one of his victims by starving her to death, cutting her up, dismembering her, grinding up her flesh in a food processor, mixing it with dog food, and making his other prisoners eat it. Also, a charred (as in *cooked*) human rib was just one piece of the twenty-four pounds of human body parts found in Heidnik's refrigerator and house.

Yet, there were people who believed Heidnik should not have been put to death. Why? Because they believed that anyone who would do what

Heidnik did had to have been crazy, and they felt that crazy people should not be executed for things they do when they are insane.

Psychiatrist Clancy McKenzie, in an essay titled "Not Guilty: The Execution of Gary Heidnik" wrote "Shame on America, Shame on Our Justice System" and asserted that Heidnik's seventeenth-month-old brain, not his adult brain, was in charge when he was committing his heinous crimes. "While the adult portion of his mind coexisted with the reawakened infant part," McKenzie wrote, "it was the infant part of the mind/brain/reality that was in charge."

Opinions differ as to the validity of Dr. McKenzie's argument, but Heidnik's jury obviously was not looking for explanations, nor were they favorably disposed to the consideration of an insanity plea. There was just too much evil and too much *horror* in Heidnik's story and his actions even to put "Not Guilty By Reason of Insanity" on the table. Justice, vengeance, punishment, and the "vaccination" of society against monsters like Heidnik ruled the day, and it ruled their final verdict.

The jury found Heidnik guilty of two counts of murder. Shortly after 10:00 P.M. on July 6, 1999, after a last meal of pizza and black coffee, Gary Heidnik was put to death by lethal injection. At the time of his execution, no one had arranged to claim his body.

Many of the darkest elements of evil—particularly sadism, torture, sexual abuse, rape, and brutality—are part of the Gary Heidnik story.

On Thanksgiving Eve, 1986, Gary Heidnik picked up a prostitute, Josefina Rivera, brought her to his home, had sex with her, and then began choking her almost to the point of unconsciousness. He then took the woman down into his basement and shackled her to a mattress. Rivera noticed that there was a pit dug in the floor of the basement. After forcing her to perform oral sex on him, Heidnik put the half-naked Rivera in the pit, covered the hole with a sheet of plywood, and put heavy weights on top of the wood so she could not escape. Heidnik left Rivera alone in the pit on Thanksgiving Day and returned with a retarded black woman named Sandy. Heidnik immediately chained Sandy to a pipe.

Between Thanksgiving and Christmas, Heidnik held both women captive in his basement, and he used both of them for sex whenever he felt like it. He also put some time into enlarging the hole in his basement floor. Heidnik did not hesitate to beat the women mercilessly if they committed the slightest infraction, and he fed them sparingly.

Over the next several months, Heidnik persuaded three more women—all black and all young—to get into his car. Once they were in the car, he had them. He would bring them home, have sex with them, and bring them downstairs to meet the other imprisoned women he referred to as his "friends."

Heidnik kept his women in the pit or chained to a pipe and he beat them and raped them at will.

Things changed, however, in February 1987, when one of the women, Sandra Lindsay, died. Heidnik used a chain saw to cut her body up and one of the grisliest moments during Heidnik's trial came when one of his victims described seeing Heidnik's dog carry one of Sandra Lindsay's dismembered limbs down to the basement and eat it as they watched.

After Lindsay's death, Heidnik began torturing the women by touching a bare electrical wire to their chains. He also became more inventive. He filled his pit with water, put all the women except Rivera into the water, and covered the hole with the plywood. He had drilled holes in the plywood, though, and he poked the bare wire through the holes to send electric shocks into the women as they sat in the water. One of the women, Deborah Dudley, was electrocuted and died. Heidnik wrapped up her body and placed it in his freezer.

On March 24, 1987, Josefina Rivera convinced Heidnik to let her see her family. How did she pull off such an amazing feat? By promising Heidnik that she would return with a replacement woman to take Debrah Dudley's place. Once free, she convinced her boyfriend to call the police and Heidnik was ultimately taken into custody.

Twelve years later, Gary Heidnik was executed.

91

Theodore Kaczynski
"THE UNABOMBER"

(1942–)

Lock him so far down that when he does die, he'll be closer to hell. That is where the devil belongs.
> —Susan Mosser, wife of Thomas Mosser, who was killed with one of Kaczynski's bombs

Theodore Kaczynski's terrorist deeds were pure evil because he had a willingness and a passion to kill and maim innocent people *to make a point*. And what was that point? Technology is bad.

Kaczynski states his case in the opening paragraph of his bloated and rambling *Unabomber Manifesto:*

> The Industrial Revolution and its consequences have been a disaster for the human race. They have greatly increased the life-expectancy of those of us who live in "advanced" countries, but they have destabilized society, have made life unfulfilling, have subjected human beings to indignities, have led to widespread psy-

chological suffering (in the Third World to physical suffering as well), and have inflicted severe damage on the natural world. The continued development of technology will worsen the situation. It will certainly subject human beings to greater indignities and inflict greater damage on the natural world, it will probably lead to greater social disruption and psychological suffering, and it may lead to increased physical suffering even in "advanced" countries.

After stating his case in the *Manifesto,* and writing in a detached "we" point of view, Kaczynski then advocates a revolution, that, chillingly, he says may or may not make use of violence:

> We therefore advocate a revolution against the industrial system. This revolution may or may not make use of violence: it may be sudden or it may be a relatively gradual process spanning a few decades. We can't predict any of that. But we do outline in a very general way the measures that those who hate the industrial system should take in order to prepare the way for a revolution against that form of society. This is not to be a POLITICAL revolution. Its object will be to overthrow not governments but the economic and technological basis of the present society.

Kaczynski began making homemade bombs when he was sixteen. Upon his arrest, his bombing "career" comprised sixteen explosions, resulting in three deaths and twenty-three injuries. After pleading guilty, he was sentenced (in a plea deal that saved his life) to four life sentences plus thirty years, with no possibility of parole. Federal Judge Garland Burrell, during Kaczynski's sentencing, described the Unabomber's acts as "unspeakable and monstrous."

Kaczynski's reign of domestic terrorism lasted seventeen years, from 1978 through 1995. His targets included airline execs, computer experts, medical scientists, and advertising executives. In his journals, Kaczynski wrote that these people were targeted because they worked in industries that contributed to isolating people from each other and from nature, and that these people were guilty of trying to "manipulate" people's minds, attitudes, and beliefs.

Until the World Trade Center attacks on September 11, 2001, the Unabomber's attacks comprised the deadliest terrorist campaign in American history.

On September 19, 1995, the *New York Times* and the *Washington Post* published Kaczynski's 35,000-word *Manifesto.* Kaczynski's brother David saw great similarities in the published *Manifesto* and his brother Ted's letters, such as comparable phraseology and certain idiosyncratic spellings. Kaczynski's brother investigated on his own, then with the help of a friend, after which he went to the FBI. They found David Kaczynski's evidence compelling and Theodore Kaczynski was arrested in 1996 and charged with the Unabomber bombings.

During the subsequent investigation, police and FBI combed through his Montana cabin, where they had to defuse a live bomb. There was no indication for whom that one was intended.

Chronology of the Unabomber

1978

May 25, 1978:   A bomb explodes on campus at Northwestern University. One person is injured.

1979

May 9, 1979:   A bomb explodes on campus at Northwestern University. One person is injured.

November 15, 1979:   A bomb explodes in the cargo hold of an American Airlines plane in flight. Twelve people are injured, mostly from smoke inhalation.

1980

June 10, 1980:   The president of United Airlines is injured at his home in Chicago.

1981

October 8, 1981:   A bomb is found in a business classroom at the University of Utah. It is successfully removed and defused and no one is injured.

1982

May 5, 1982:   A bomb explodes on campus at Vanderbilt University. No one is injured.

July 2, 1982:   A professor of electrical engineering and computer science is injured when a bomb explodes in the faculty lounge at the University of California, Berkeley.

1983

No attacks.

1984

No attacks.

1985

May 15, 1985:   One person is injured when a bomb explodes in a computer room University of California, Berkeley.

June 13, 1985:   A bomb sent to the Boeing Corporation is successfully defused. There are no injuries.

November 15, 1985: Two people are injured at the University of Michigan, Ann Arbor, when a bomb addressed to a professor at the school detonates.

1986

No attacks.

1987

The Unabomber is spotted in a Salt Lake City computer store.

1987–1992

No attacks.

1993

June: The Unabomber writes to the *New York Times* and explains his ideology.

June 22,1993:   University of California, San Francisco, geneticist Dr. Charles Epstein is injured when a bomb explodes at his home.

June 24, 1993:   Yale University professor David Gelertner is injured when a bomb explodes in his office on campus in New Haven, Connecticut.

1994

December 10, 1994: Advertising executive Thomas Mosser is killed when a bomb explodes at his New Jersey home.

1995

April 24, 1995:   Timber industry lobbyist Gilbert Murray is killed when a bomb explodes in his Sacramento office.

September 19, 1995: The *Washington Post* and the *New York Times* jointly publish the Unabomber's 34,497-word *Manifesto*.

1996

February: David Kaczynski tells the FBI that he thinks his brother Theodore is the Unabomber.

April 3, 1996: Theodore Kaczynski is arrested in his Montana cabin.

1998

January 22, 1998: Theodore Kaczynski accepts a plea bargain which sentences him to four life sentences plus thirty years in a federal penitentiary with no chance of parole. With this plea, Kaczynski avoids the death penalty. The Unabomber's rampage of terrorism is over.

92

Eddie Gein

"THE BUTCHER OF PLAINFIELD"
"THE PLAINFIELD GHOUL"

(1906–1984)

*I'm no robber. I took the money and the cash register because I
wanted to see how it worked.*
> —Eddie Gein, taking offense at being labeled a thief

Writer Robert Bloch based the Norman Bates character in his novel
Psycho on the story of Eddie Gein.

Director Tobe Hooper based the character of Leatherface in his movie
The Texas Chainsaw Massacre on Eddie Gein.

Writer Thomas Harris based the character of serial killer Jamie "Buffalo
Bill" Gumb in his novel *The Silence of the Lambs* on Eddie Gein, and there
are even elements of Gein in Harris's prototypical serial killer, Hannibal
Lecter—specifically the cannibalism and skinning of which Dr. Lecter was so
fond.

Eddie Gein of Plainfield, Wisconsin, was a "helpful" and "reliable"
neighbor who was seen as "odd and shy but harmless" by the Plainfield towns-

folk. What Gein's neighbors did not know until it was too late was that Gein was also a necrophiliac, a grave robber, a transvestite, a cannibal, and a murderer, who (prepare yourself):

- ate soup out of a woman's skull
- had a human lips' mobile hanging in his kitchen
- carried a knife with a human bone handle
- had a shoebox filled with human vulvas (eight dried and one fresh)
- had an armchair in his living room with *real arms* for arms
- kept a collection of amputated female breasts
- kept a container filled with human noses
- kept a selection of human organs in his refrigerator, including livers, intestines, and hearts
- made a belt out of dried female nipples
- made a coat out of a female upper front torso
- wore a human vagina as underwear (but only around the house)
- made a wastebasket out of women's skin
- made lampshades out of women's skin
- propped up a table with human shin-bones
- sautéed human hearts and ate them (Bernice Worden's heart was found on a plate in the dining room after Eddie was arrested)
- topped two posts of his bed with human skulls
- upholstered a chair with women's skin
- used the skin from women's faces as wall hangings
- wore human scalps as wigs

With such heinous behavior to his credit, it should be noted that Eddie Gein is believed to have only been responsible for two deaths, those of Mary Hogan and Bernice Worden (even though some criminologists, to this day, believe Gein killed others. Gein admitted to killing Hogan and Worden, but said he did not kill anyone else).

Gein was found guilty, but insane at his trial, and it seemed that Gein did not consider the totality of his actions as horrible as did the public at large. Of the fifteen bodies found in his house, it's likely that Gein would consider what he did to only two—Hogan and Worden—to be serious crimes. The others, after all, were already dead.

Eddie Gein was born on August 27, 1906, to Augusta and George Gein, a couple which could never have been mistaken for Parents of the Year. George was an abusive, weak-willed alcoholic who was completely dominated by his wife, a harridan with very strong views and a tyrannical personality. Augusta was a religious fanatic who instilled horrible ideas about sex and women in the minds of her two sons—Eddie and his seven-year-older brother Henry. In addition, Augusta so hated her husband that she would force her sons to kneel and pray with her that George would die soon.

Obviously, Eddie Gein did not grow up in a healthy family environment—and there is still debate over how much of a contribution his rigid, obsessive, domineering, demented mother and her twisted worldview made towards creating the monster that would become known as the "Butcher of Plainfield" and the "Plainfield Ghoul."

It can be stated with a fair amount of certainty that Augusta's incessant preaching to Eddie and his brother about the evils of sex and the toxic nature of women in general was the reason neither boy ever married, and is probably why Eddie became morbidly obsessed with female genitalia. Eddie would study female anatomy in medical books, and once he started robbing graves to get female bodies to "play with," he would always pay special attention to the vulvas and vaginas.

Augusta and her boys bought a 195-acre farm in Plainfield in 1914, thanks to the income from a grocery business Augusta started the year Eddie was born. Eddie and Henry were not allowed to make friends in school and, of the two, Eddie was the most worshipful of their mother. After Henry died in a 1944 forest fire, Eddie was alone with Mama. (Dad George had died in 1940.) A few years later, his mother died following a series of strokes, and now Eddie was alone, with the isolation and freedom to indulge the sickest interests inculcated in him by his upbringing and subsequent pursuits, which included Nazi atrocities, head-shrinking, grave robbing, and more.

Eddie began robbing graves shortly after his mother's death. He tried to stick with newly buried corpses because bodies in an advanced state of decay and decomposition did not lend themselves to his need for their skin and other intact body parts. This went on for several years and Eddie built up quite a macabre collection of body parts.

In the winter of 1954, a Plainfield bar owner named Mary Hogan disappeared. Mary is believed to have been Eddie's first murder victim (although there were several unresolved missing person cases during the period prior to Hogan's murder that some have tried to pin on Eddie, but to no avail). Three years later, Eddie shot Bernice Worden and, through a lead provided by her son, Eddie was arrested for the murder. That was when the horrors in Eddie farmhouse were discovered, including Worden's trussed-up, decapitated, disemboweled body in Eddie's deer-dressing shed.

Eddie died of cancer in 1984 and was buried next to his mother.

Lee Harvey Oswald

(1939–1963)

Chasing shadows on the grassy knoll will never substitute for real history. Lee Harvey Oswald, driven by his own twisted and impenetrable furies, was the only assassin at Dealey Plaza on November 22, 1963. To say otherwise, in light of the overwhelming evidence, is to absolve a man with blood on his hands, and to mock the President he killed.

—Gerald Posner, *Case Closed*

Still, in the twenty-first century, there is controversy over whether or not Lee Harvey Oswald was the lone gunman who assassinated President John F. Kennedy on November 22, 1963, in Dallas, Texas. When writing about the assassination, historians still turn to phrases like "supposed assassin" and "apparently assassinated" when referring to Oswald and the assassination. Conspiracy theorists have been convinced since 1963 that Oswald was part of a complex plot to shoot Kennedy, possibly involving Fidel Castro, organized crime, domestic radicals, or all of the above.

Whether or not more were involved, the evidence is unassailable that Lee Harvey Oswald did, in fact, fire three shots from a rifle at President

Kennedy's motorcade, two of which struck the president and resulted in his death. For the purposes of this book, then, Oswald is guilty of the assassination of a United States president and, is thus, de facto evil. If there were others involved, they would, of course, share in this judgment of evil, but their possible participation is essentially irrelevant in mitigating the acts of Oswald, whom history will always regard as the man who shot President Kennedy.

Lee Harvey Oswald was born in 1939 in New Orleans, Louisiana, but spent much of his early childhood years, even attending elementary school, in Fort Worth, Texas. It was in Fort Worth that Oswald enlisted in the marines in 1956 at the age of seventeen, and ultimately was stationed in Japan as a radar operator. Even though Oswald was promoted to private first class, he left the marines with a hardship discharge in 1959 and, a month later, he was in Moscow, requesting permission to become a Soviet citizen.

Oswald was devastated when the Soviets refused his request for citizenship, and he attempted suicide. Following his failed suicide attempt, Oswald was allowed to remain in the Soviet Union, but even though he was still an American citizen, the Marine Corps heard of his attempt to be granted Russian citizenship, branded him a defector, and officially changed his hardship discharge from Honorable to Dishonorable.

Oswald spoke fluent Russian and fell in love with a Russian native named Marina, whom he would eventually marry. The couple had two children and, in 1962, the Oswald family moved back to the United States and set up residence in Dallas, Texas.

In January of 1963 Oswald bought a handgun, followed by the purchase of a rifle in March. He bought both guns through the mail, and he used the phony name of Alek Hidell to make the purchases.

The handgun was a .38-caliber Smith & Wesson revolver for which he paid $29.95. Oswald bought it from Seaport Traders in Los Angeles and had it shipped to his post office box. Oswald would use this revolver to shoot and kill officer J.D. Tippit shortly after leaving the Texas Book Depository following his attack on the president.

In March, Oswald sent a $21.45 money order to Klein's Sporting Goods in Chicago for the purchase of a rifle. He bought a 6.5-millimeter, bolt-action Mannlicher-Carcano carbine, an Italian military rifle, which cost $12.78. He also ordered a four-power telescopic sight for $7.17, which greatly magnified the target and made it quite simple for even the untrained to shoot like a marksman.

Oswald would use this rifle to assassinate President Kennedy.

Ensconced in a sniper's nest of cardboard cartons of books on the sixth floor of the Texas Book Depository in Dealey Plaza in Dallas, Oswald fired three shots at President Kennedy as the president's motorcade wound its way from Houston Street to Elm, past the grassy knoll, where Abraham Zapruder stood shooting footage of what would become the most famous home movie in all of history. The president was in a convertible (the last time that would ever be allowed) and his wife Jackie, Texas Governor Connally, and Mrs. Connally were also in the car.

Oswald's first shot, at 12:30 P.M., missed. Within three seconds, he reloaded and fired again, and this second bullet hit the president and Governor Connally. Within the next five seconds, he reloaded again and fired, and this third bullet blew off the top of President Kennedy's head. Mrs. Kennedy climbed out onto the trunk of the limousine in an attempt to retrieve part of his brain.

Within three minutes, Oswald had fled the Book Depository and was on Elm Street. He took a bus and a cab home to retrieve his Smith & Wesson revolver. When he left his house, he was confronted by Dallas police officer Jefferson D. Tippit. Whether or nor there was a conspiracy, and whether or not Tippit was in on it, Oswald shot three times and killed the young cop in the street.

A little later, at 1:35 P.M., Oswald was in the Texas Theater where he was confronted by several police officers (who were there on a frantic search for a cop-killer) and he was taken into custody. That afternoon and evening Oswald was questioned (without a lawyer), and the police proclaimed that they had caught the killer of President Kennedy.

The following morning, while being transferred to another facility, and while handcuffed to a detective, Jack Ruby shot Oswald once in the stomach. Oswald died before he could officially be charged with the assassination of the president.

John Wilkes Booth

(1838–1865)

This country was formed for the white, *not for the black man.
And looking upon* African slavery *from the standpoint held by
the noble framers of our Constitution, I, for one, have ever considered it one of the greatest blessings (both for themselves and
us) that God ever bestowed upon a favored nation.*
                    —John Wilkes Booth, in a letter to his sister Asia

*Evergreen carpeted the stone floor of the vault. On the coffin
set in a receptacle of black walnut they arranged flowers carefully and precisely, they poured flowers as symbols, they
lavished heaps of fresh flowers as though there could never be
enough to tell either their hearts or his.
And the night came with great quiet.
And there was rest.
The prairie years, the war years, were over.*
                    —Carl Sandburg, *Abraham Lincoln*

A black-and-white print was published in Philadelphia in 1865 shortly after
Lincoln's assassination, showing John Wilkes Booth standing outside Lincoln's
booth at the Ford Theater prior to the shooting. Booth is holding his pistol

and a grotesque, horned demon, clearly Satan himself, stands behind Booth, and points to President Lincoln. The common belief of the time was that anyone who would commit such an abominable act had to have been working in the service of the devil.

At the time of his assassination, Lincoln had an envelope on his desk that contained eighty death threats. None were from John Wilkes Booth. Of this envelope, Lincoln told his Secretary of State William Henry Seward, "I know I am in danger; but I am not going to worry over threats like these."

At the beginning of April 1865, Lincoln had a dream in which he walked into his own wake and saw his own corpse lying in state in the East Room of the White House. In the dream, he demanded a guard tell him what had happened, and he was told that an assassin had shot the president. At that point, a loud cry of grief arose from the crowd and Lincoln woke up, quite shaken from what he had dreamt. This prescient dream would come true two short weeks later.

John Wilkes Booth is the racist assassin who shot and killed Abraham Lincoln, the U.S. president many consider America's greatest leader, perhaps surpassed only by George Washington. Booth killed President Lincoln because he did not want to see slavery abolished, and he blamed Lincoln for betraying his "white" country.

Booth's original plan was to kidnap Lincoln and trade him for Confederate prisoners. Logistics prevented the execution of that plan, so Booth planned an execution instead.

The day was Good Friday, April 14, 1865. John Wilkes Booth had earlier entered the Ford Theater and cut a mortise into the doorframe of the presidential box. When the theater owner heard that the president would be attending that evening's performance, he had taken down a partition separating two boxes, making one large box for the presidential party. Booth cut the mortise so that he could insert a long board after he entered, preventing anyone from opening the door from the outside. Booth had other plans for escape after committing his heinous crime.

The president and his party arrived at the theater around 8:25 P.M. The president's guard, John Parker, had arrived earlier and stationed himself outside the president's box. However, Parker quickly learned that he would not be able to see the play, so he abandoned his post and moved to an area where he would have a clearer view. Parker was not at his post when the president arrived, nor was he at his post when John Wilkes Booth entered the box and locked the door behind him at approximately 10:13 that evening.

Upon entering the box, Booth saw that Lincoln was seated in a rocking chair that the theater owner had brought up from his own residence specifically for the president. Booth walked up behind the president, placed the muzzle of his .44-caliber derringer against Lincoln's head above his left ear, and fired once. The bullet entered Lincoln's skull and lodged behind his right eye. Lincoln was rendered immediately unconscious and slumped forward.

Booth then pulled out a dagger and began stabbing at Major Rathbone, a member of the president and Mrs. Lincoln's party that evening. Booth inflicted a serious wound on the major's left upper arm, and then leaped out of the box, shouting, *"Sic semper tyrannis!"* ("Thus be it ever to tyrants!"), which is what Brutus said to Julius Caesar after the Roman emperor was fatally stabbed.

Booth's foot caught in the flag draped across the front of the box and he landed on his knees on the stage, fracturing his left leg. He nonetheless managed to flee the theater, mount his horse, and ride away.

The president would linger in a coma until the following morning. Abraham Lincoln, the sixteenth president of the United States, died at 7:22 A.M. on Saturday, April 15, 1865.

Dr. Samuel Mudd, who was later indicted as a co-conspirator, even though he claimed ignorance of who Booth was or what he had done, treated Booth's injury. (Mudd's descendants continue to try to exonerate the doctor's name.)

Booth was eventually trapped in a barn, which the authorities set on fire. Booth was shot and forced out of the barn. He died shortly thereafter.

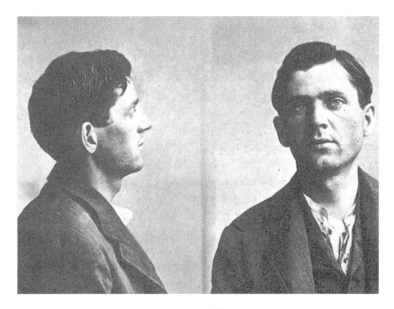

95

Leon F. Czolgosz

(1873–1901)

I killed the President because he was the enemy of the good people! I did it for the help of the good people, the working men of all countries! . . . I am not sorry.
> —the last words of presidential assassin Leon Czolgosz, uttered moments before he was electrocuted

Give him another poke.
> —a prison official ordering another one-minute jolt of electricity for Czolgosz

When Leon Czolgosz pulled the trigger of his revolver and fired two shots point-blank into President William McKinley, he joined the ranks of the other cowardly miscreants who have killed (or attempted to kill) U.S. presidents.

Presidential assassins have always failed. Granted, they may have taken a life, but none of them has ever achieved their misguided and pathetic goals, whatever they might have been at the time that they committed their heinous crimes.

Czolgosz was an anarchist. Anarchists believe that *all* forms of government are oppressive, unwanted, and should, unequivocally, and by any means, be abolished. He believed that he could bring about the demise of the American republic by killing its leader.

September 6, 1901. The line seemed to stretch on forever. The president was in the Temple of Music at the Pan American Exposition in Buffalo, New York, and he was discharging one of his most enjoyable presidential duties: he was shaking hands with some of the American people he had the honor to serve in America's highest office.

McKinley was at his finest when meeting ordinary Americans. He was gregarious and engaging and each person felt like they had actually connected with the president, such was his ability to focus in on each person, even if only for just under one and a half seconds. McKinley was known for his hand-shaking rate: forty-five people per minute.

Usually, McKinley's Secret Service guard stood behind and to the left of the president at public handshaking functions. This allowed the agent to see everyone who approached the president. On this day, however, the Secret Service agent was asked to stand *opposite* the president so that John Milburn, the president of the Pan American Exposition, could stand next to the president.

Around four o'clock, Leon Czolgosz waited his turn to shake the president's hand. When the man in front of him released McKinley's hand, Czolgosz stepped in front of the president. Czolgosz had wrapped a handkerchief around his right hand so that it looked like a bandage. Beneath the handkerchief was his .32-caliber Iver Johnson revolver. President McKinley, seeing the bandaged hand, moved to grasp Czolgosz's extended left hand, and that was when the assassin fired.

Czolgosz hit McKinley with two bullets. The first hit the president in the chest but was deflected by a button; the second ripped through his abdomen, one and a half inches from the midline and about five inches below his left nipple. The bullet tore through his stomach—front and back, hit the top of his left kidney, and buried itself in his pancreas. McKinley remained conscious, but did double over and collapse. It is said that after realizing he had been shot, he gave Czolgosz a look that was filled with scorn and contempt, but he also made a point of instructing his Secret Service contingent not to hurt his assailant.

The president was rushed to a hospital on the grounds of the Exposition and two operations were performed. In the first one, doctors repaired the holes in his stomach and sewed up the wound. They could not find the bullet, however, and it remained in the president's pancreas. The second operation, four days later, was performed to remove a small piece of clothing that had been left in his abdomen.

Five days after the shooting, the president felt well enough to eat, but the following day, the gangrene that had been growing in his gut from the lack of sterile conditions during the surgeries caused a very rapid decline in his overall condition. He died early the following morning, 2:15 A.M.

As for Czolgosz, he was immediately arrested and beaten almost to the point of death by the police and the Secret Service. He survived to stand trial, though, and on September 23, 1901, he was found guilty of killing the president and sentenced to death by electrocution.

To the end, Czolgosz was unrepentant and insisted that he had done a good deed.

During the investigation of the assassination, it was learned that Czolgosz was a supporter of the views of the Russian-born anarchist Emma Goldman. Goldman was brought in for questioning and was in police custody when it was learned that McKinley had died. Goldman did not care about McKinley's death and made her feelings known to the police guarding her. Thanks to the intercession of some cooler-headed officers, Goldman did not suffer the same treatment as did Czolgosz. No connection between Goldman and Czolgosz (except ideologically) was ever established. It was learned that Czolgosz had attended one of Goldman's lectures and actually made contact with her in Chicago, but Goldman had rebuffed him. Goldman was eventually released with no charges against her.

Two years after McKinley's death, the U.S. Congress enacted laws forbidding anarchists from residing in the United States. This law was utilized in 1919 to send Goldman back to Russia.

Czolgosz was electrocuted on October 29, 1901. In order to prevent grave robbers from stealing his corpse or desecrating his remains, sulfuric acid was poured all over his body in his coffin.

96

Charles J. Guiteau

(1841–1882)

*Washington June 16, 1881. To the American People: I conceived
the idea of removing the President four weeks ago. Not a soul
knew of my purpose. I conceived the idea myself and kept it to
myself. I read the newspapers carefully for and against the
Administration, and gradually the conviction settled on me that
the President's removal was a political necessity, because he
proved a traitor to the men that made him, and thereby imper-
iled the life of the Republic. . . . This is not murder. It is a political necessity . . .*

—Charles J. Guiteau

Historians are mostly in agreement that Charles J. Guiteau was insane. He
very well might have been, but there is no doubt that he was also a notoriously
unpleasant man, prone to Brobdingnagian episodes of annoyance. He was
also a liar, a swindler, an embezzler, a lecher, a wife abuser, and an obnoxious
egomaniac.

These "qualities" alone would not warrant Guiteau a spot on this list, but
he was also a presidential assassin, the man who shot President James A.
Garfield for political gain. Guiteau's narcissism was so extreme that, after
being arrested for shooting the president, he wrote a letter to a General

Sherman, requesting that Sherman order his troops to take possession of the jail in which he was being held:

> To General Sherman: I have just shot the President. I shot him several times as I wished him to go as easily as possible. His death was a political necessity. I am a lawyer, theologian, and politician. I am a stalwart of the Stalwarts. I was with Gen. Grant, and the rest of our men in New York during the canvass. I am going to the Jail. Please order out your troops and take possession of the Jail at once. Very respectfully, Charles Guiteau.

Upon receiving Guiteau's letter, General Sherman wrote, "I don't know the writer. Never heard of or saw him to my knowledge. . . ."

On July 2, 1881, Charles J. Guiteau shot President Garfield at a train depot. Guiteau fired twice, and his first shot merely grazed the president's arm. The second shot, however, entered Garfield's back and lodged very close to his pancreas. Even though this shot was not initially fatal, this bullet would cause the president's death.

In 1881, many doctors did not believe that sterile, antiseptic conditions were necessary for surgeries, wound explorations, or many other medical procedures. No one believed the notion that the air was filled with germs that were waiting to attack an open wound. Medical equipment was not sterilized; doctors' hands were not washed. Unfortunately for President Garfield, his chief physician, Dr. D.W. Bliss, was of the school that believed that sanitary conditions were not needed for medical procedures. For several weeks, President Garfield's doctors tried to locate and remove Guiteau's second bullet. They used their bare, unwashed hands, and dirty, nonsterilized medical equipment. President Garfield eventually developed septic blood poisoning and died on September 19 at his home in New Jersey. His final days were spent in great suffering and his last words were, "Can't you stop this pain?"

Garfield's medical care following the shooting is what clinically killed him, although the sole responsibility for his death lies with Guiteau. The president's doctors fed the president steak, eggs, and brandy every day. He soon began vomiting and lost eighty pounds in six weeks. His doctors also gave him enemas consisting of eggs, bouillon, milk, whiskey, and opium. Soon, the president began excreting voluminous amounts of pus, experienced facial swelling, and had to endure his doctors' slicing open his face to drain it.

Following Garfield's death, a homeopathic journal described the care the president received as "the most grossly mismanaged case in modern history."

And all of this was caused by Charles J. Guiteau; the man who had specifically purchased an expensive .44 British Bulldog pistol for the assassination because he knew how nice the gun would look in a museum.

Susan Smith

(1971–)

They didn't get to learn to pass a ball. They didn't get to learn to ride a bike. They didn't get their first day at school. Susan knew she was murdering those children. She knew, puttin' them in the water, what the outcome was gonna be. And how do you accept an apology from someone who is that . . . evil?
>—David Smith, Susan Smith's ex-husband and the father of Michael and Alex Smith

No man would make me hurt my children. They were my life.
>—Susan Smith, speaking to the police before she confessed, unconsciously using the past tense to describe her sons

The police re-creation of Susan Smith's horrible crime revealed one unbearable fact: Smith's burgundy Mazda was so air-tight, it took a full six minutes for the interior of the car to completely fill with water. Try to imagine what Smith's boys—Michael, three, and Alex, fourteen months—experienced strapped into car seats in the back seat of the frigid cold, pitch-dark car, *hanging upside down,* as the water began rising inside the car.

Dr. Roy Baumeister, in his book, *Evil: Inside Human Violence and Cruelty* (1999), tells us that the two main components of evil are "the infliction of harm and the unleashing of chaos." Using these criteria, child killer Susan Smith is a dual offender: She performed an evil act when she murdered her two sons; and she compounded the evil when she lied about being carjacked, thereby inflicting harm on her family and the black community of Union, South Carolina, as well as causing overwhelming chaos on a national level by perpetuating her story before confessing.

Around nine o'clock on the evening of October 25, 1994, an hysterical Susan Smith ran crying to the home of Shirley McCloud, screaming that a black man had just carjacked her Mazda and driven off with her two infant sons in the back seat.

Nine days later, after a staggeringly deceptive performance before the media, her family, and many law enforcement officials, Smith finally confessed to the police that she herself had rolled her car into John D. Long Lake with her two sons strapped into their car seats, deliberately drowning them.

It was later learned that Smith had recently received a "Dear Jill" letter from a former boyfriend (the letter was found in the recovered car), who had told her that he was ending their relationship because she had children, and he did not want the responsibility of raising another man's kids on the chance that the relationship progressed to the point of marriage. Many now believe that Susan Smith, using her own perverted logic, was trying to remove this obstacle from her love life by eliminating her children from the picture, thereby assuring her child-averse boyfriend that he had nothing to worry about, and that they could continue to see each other and allow the relationship to go where it may.

Admittedly, Smith had led a troubled life and this was used as part of her defense. She had attempted suicide on several occasions, she had been sexually molested by her stepfather, she had had to live through her father's suicide, and she was having troubles in her marriage to David Smith. Marital woes led to Susan Smith's being sexually promiscuous and to searching for the attention and love she so desperately needed, which, when not available to her, threw her into the deepest throes of depression. During her trial, one doctor remarked that if Smith had been on Prozac, the murders would have never happened.

But they did happen and, after a brief trial, Smith was convicted of two counts of murder but spared the death penalty. She was given a thirty-years-to-life sentence and will be eligible for parole in 2025, at the age of fifty-three. David Smith, Michael and Alex's father, has stated that he will never forgive Susan for what she did, he will attend every one of her parole hearings, and he will do everything he can to guarantee that her sentence will, in the end, be a life sentence.

Other Mothers Who Have Killed Their Children

Andrea Yates.

In 2001, Yates drowned her five children in a bathtub and then called the police and her husband and confessed. Her defense attorneys blamed post-partum psychosis and pleaded her not guilty by reason of insanity. At this writing, prosecutors are seeking the death penalty.

Melissa Drexler.

The "Prom Mom." In 1997, Drexler gave birth to a son at her prom and threw him in the trash where he later died.

Shawn Heard.

Heard is the borderline retarded (I.Q. of 68) twenty-four-year-old mother who, in 1997, strangled, shook, and beat her nineteen-day-old son to death.

Amy Grossberg.

Grossberg gave birth to a boy at a motel in 1996, then she and her boyfriend suffocated and beat the newborn to death, and threw his body in a dumpster.

Darlie Routier.

In 1996, Routier cold-bloodedly stabbed her two sons to death.

Debora Green.

Green is the doctor who, in 1994, deliberately set fire to her own house, killing her two children. Ann Rule's best-selling book *Bitter Harvest* was based on Green's story.

98

Father James Porter

(1935–)

*It is fair to say . . . that society has been on a learning curve
with regard to the sexual abuse of minors. The Church, too, has
been on a learning curve. We have learned, and we will
continue to learn. Never was there an effort on my part to shift
a problem from one place to the next. It has always been my
contention that it is better to know a problem and deal with it
than to be kept in ignorance of it. . . . In the final analysis, after
we have done all that we humanly can do to ensure that
persons who are a threat to children are isolated from them,
and after we have done all that we can do to bring some measure of healing psychologically and emotionally to all who have
been traumatized by the sexual abuse of minors, it is only the
peace which is the gift of the Risen Lord that can quiet our
minds and hearts. His is a message of reconciling love, and to
the extent that we can accept that message, to that extent we
can all find healing*

> —Cardinal Bernard Law, writing on July 27, 2001 about
> pedophile Roman Catholic priests

Roman Catholic parishioners have, for the most part, always held their parish priests in very high regard—these men wear the same plain black suit and white priest's collar almost all the time; say Mass every day; willingly deny themselves of the joy of romantic love, the carnal pleasures of sex, and the fulfillment of raising a family. Priests usher Catholics from birth to death, beginning with baptism and ending with the Last Rites, which are given during their final moments of life on earth. The priest also presides at their funeral and blesses them as they are buried. Priests marry Catholics; priests hear their sins, and wash them away. To a Catholic, a priest is an avatar of spirituality, a direct conduit to God.

In the past decade or so, that level of respect has been severely tested for many Catholics after the many reports of Catholic priests being charged with, and convicted of, pedophilia—the sexual abuse of children.

To some hard-line Catholics, these revelations are doubly shocking: not only have the guilty priests violated their vow of celibacy, they compounded their sin immeasurably by forcibly having sex with the most innocent of all—children.

James Porter is one of those guilty priests, and he is currently serving time for his crimes. The American judicial system punishes crimes; it does not forgive sins. For that, Porter, who sexually molested at least 125 children of both sexes in five states, will have to look elsewhere.

James Porter was eighteen years old when he molested a twelve-year-old boy. Experts believe he may have begun molesting children well before he turned eighteen, but this twelve-year-old was his first documented victim.

Following his ordination as a Catholic priest in 1959, Father Porter was assigned to St. Mary's Church in North Attleboro, Massachusetts. As in many Catholic parishes, St. Mary's had a grammar school.

Father Porter's crimes at St. Mary's are a history of pedophile perversion. He began by forcing fifth- and sixth-grade boys and girls to fondle his genitals, as he freely used his hands on their private parts. It wasn't long before he moved on to oral sodomy and anal rape of his ten- and eleven-year-old students, often holding his hand over their mouth to silence their screams. He molested both boys and girls and was so cavalier about his actions that it wasn't long before all the St. Mary's grammar school students knew to steer clear of the lecherous priest. Victims recall clearing the halls of the school when someone shouted "Father Porter's coming!"

Father Porter was bold. He would sometimes slide his hands up under young female students' skirts and sexually molest them while seated at his desk as others spoke to him from in front of the desk.

As more and more parents learned of the pedophile priest's crimes, the archdiocese was forced to respond. Father Porter was not arrested, though. He was sent to a hospital and given electroshock treatments, which did absolutely nothing to curb his twisted desires. He was reassigned to a different parish and began molesting children almost immediately after his arrival.

In April 1967, the archdiocese was again forced to act and, again, Porter was removed from a parish, but not arrested. This time he was sent to a retreat for troubled priests in New Mexico where he was supposed to be cured of his deviant urges. Following his release from the retreat, Porter was assigned to parish after parish, but each time was forced to leave after he began molesting local children.

Porter continued to molest children wherever he was assigned until, finally in 1974, he wrote to the pope asking to be released from his priestly vows. The pope granted his request, and, a short while later, Porter married and subsequently fathered four children.

Not being a priest and being a husband and father did not "cure" James Porter. Quite the contrary. He continued his pursuit of children and even went so far as to molest a young girl who baby-sat for his children—as well as her sister.

One of Porter's child victims, Frank Fitzpatrick, came to a realization one day that he had been sexually molested by Father Porter when he was a young boy, and he committed himself to exacting justice from Porter for the former priest's crimes. He contacted other victims, notified the authorities, and even called Porter himself and taped their conversations.

His efforts resulted in Porter's ultimately pleading guilty to forty-one counts of child molestation and being sentenced in 1993 to eighteen to twenty years in prison, with the possibility of parole after serving six years. His first parole request was denied and he is currently incarcerated for his crimes.

The Marquis de Sade
(COMTE DONATIEN ALPHONSE FRANÇOIS DE SADE)

(1740–1814)

Realize that all decent bodily indulgence . . . in any of its form,
is to be expressly excluded from this collection . . .
> —Marquis de Sade, from the Introduction to his
> *120 Days of Sodom*

At the time of his death, the Marquis de Sade was working on an ambitious ten-volume novel called *The Days of Florbelle or Nature Unveiled*, which would likely have been the ultimate catalogue of every deviant perversion known to man—and woman.

De Sade was writing this epic while locked up in an insane asylum in Charenton, France. After his death, the manuscript to *The Days of Florbelle* was turned over to de Sade's eldest son, who promptly burned it. This drastic action on the part of de Sade's heir may have been a commentary on the quality of the writing, or it simply could have been that de Sade's son had read his father's earlier works, especially *The 120 Days of Sodom*, and decided that he would not be responsible for disseminating to the world any more of the

Marquis de Sade's writings. In all likelihood, this was not a decision based on the son's devotion to his father's literary reputation. If anything, the son probably felt he was doing mankind a service.

If you have not read any of the Marquis's work, or have not seen the film *Quills* (which was rather loosely based on the Marquis's life, but which did include excerpts of his writing), then you can experience the imagination of the Marquis de Sade firsthand by visiting the Web site (www.angelfire.com/oh/SIEMENS/) on which the complete text of de Sade's *120 Days of Sodom* can be found. (Reader discretion is advised.)

We admit some hesitation at including the Marquis de Sade on a ranking of the most evil people in world history. De Sade was a writer who delighted in the perverse and who led a somewhat less-than-virtuous life, but who is remembered more for his scandalous behavior and his books than for genocide or horrible terrorist acts (behaviors evident and abundant by many of the other people on this list). Yet, the term *sadism*, which is defined as taking pleasure from inflicting pain on others, was named for the Marquis. De Sade's personal worldview was so influential that the discipline of psychology responded by defining as a sadist anyone who took sexual gratification or other extreme delight in deliberate cruelty on others.

That was convincing enough to include him in this ranking (influence, after all, can often be profound); but what tipped the scales were selections from the Marquis's aforementioned book, *The 120 Days of Sodom*. *120 Days* is truly vile and depicts some of the most heinous and horrific acts of sexual torture of which man is capable.

The 120 Days acts as a primer for performing some of the filthiest and cruelest abominations imaginable.

De Sade often wrote intentionally to offend. Some of his favorite targets were the clergy and the religiously minded. There are scenes in his work in which lust-crazed orgy-goers insert consecrated hosts into bodily cavities prior to intercourse. Imagine how those scenes were received during a time when the Church was the de facto government and monarchies often deferred to the rulings and wishes of the pope.

De Sade was a misogynist, a bisexual, a sadist, and an abuser. He delighted in writing about coprophilia, pedophilia, torture, homosexuality, mutilation, and rape, and was obsessed with concocting elaborate variations on every perversion he could think of. He wrote *The 120 Days of Sodom* in an astonishing thirty-seven days.

Following is a selection of excerpts from *The 120 Days of Sodom, Part the Fourth.* Note: These are some of the *tamest* passages in the book and yet, they may shock and upset certain readers. Here is how de Sade warned *his* readers about what they were about to read:

Now at once, dear reader, you should dispose your heart and soul to the most impure story told ever since the world began . . .

His first passion is for bestiality, his second is to sew the girl into an untanned donkey's skin, her head protruding; he feeds and cares for her until the animal's skin shrinks and crushes her to death.

Once he was wont to mistreat nipples, but has progressed since then and now buckles a sort of small iron pot over each breast and lowers her over a stove; the iron heats, and she is allowed to perish thus in frightful pain.

That evening, the Bishop, his spirits in a great ferment, wishes to have Aline tormented, his rage against her has reached its fever pitch. She makes her appearance naked, he has her shit and embuggers her, then, without discharging, he withdraws in a towering fury from that enchanting ass and injects a rinse of boiling water into it, obliging her to squirt it out at once, while it is still boiling hot, upon Thérèse's face. After that, Messieurs hack off all the fingers and toes Aline has left, break both her arms and burn them with red-hot pokers. She is next flogged, beaten, and slapped, then the Bishop, still further aroused, cuts off one of her nipples, and discharges.

Wherewith they transfer their attentions to Thérèse, the interior of her vagina is seared, her nostrils, tongue, feet, and hands are all burned too; then she is given six hundred lashes with a bull's pizzle. Out come the rest of her teeth, fire is introduced into her throat. A witness to these harsh proceedings, Augustine falls to weeping; the Duc lashes her belly and cunt until he has drawn a suitable amount of blood therefrom.

Upon that day and at the same hour, another kitchen servant is found being embuggered, this time by the Duc; he pays the fine, the servant is summoned to the orgies, where everyone cavorts with her, Durcet making good use of her mouth, the others of her bum, and even of her cunt, for she is a virgin, and she is condemned to receive two hundred lashes from each of her employers. She is a girl of eighteen, tall and well made, her hair is auburn in color, and she owns a very fair ass.

That same evening, Curval utters the opinion that it is a matter of extreme urgency that Constance be bled again on account of her pregnancy; the Duc embuggers her, and Curval bleeds her while Augustine frigs his prick against Zelmire's buttocks and while someone else fucks Zelmire. Upon discharging, he executes the puncture; his aim is true.

✢ ✢ ✢

As a young man he used to kick a woman in the ass, tumbling her into a brazier, whence she would emerge before suffering excessively. He has lately refined this stunt, now obliges a girl to stand upright between two blazing fires: one cooks her in front, the other behind; and there she remains until the fat on her body melts.

The Marquis de Sade was born in June 1740 at the Condé Mansion in Paris. He attended a Jesuit college until he was fourteen and then entered cavalry training school. When he was nineteen he was promoted to captain in the Burgundy Horse. De Sade fought in the Seven Years War, and then left the army and entered into an arranged marriage to please his father. Marriage did not tame the Marquis, however, and four months after he wed, he was in prison for committing several offenses while in a brothel.

After getting out of prison, the Marquis embarked on a five-year orgy of, well, orgies. He indulged in every perversion he could think of, regularly seducing and ravishing ballet dancers, prostitutes, actresses, society women, and anyone else he could persuade to join in.

On Easter Sunday, 1768, De Sade picked up a prostitute, imprisoned her in his hideaway apartment, and whipped her mercilessly with a whip and a cat-o'-nine tails. She managed to escape, went to the police, and de Sade was arrested and again imprisoned. Upon his release, he went right back to his deviant ways, beginning with an affair with his sister-in-law.

In 1772, the Marquis commissioned four young girls for an orgy and beat them, sodomized them, and even poisoned one girl with deliberately tainted candies. De Sade then fled to Italy but he was arrested nonetheless, and, once again, ended up in prison. He escaped twice, was caught both times, and ended up serving almost six years. During this period, he wrote *The 120 Days of Sodom.*

In 1789, during the French Revolution, De Sade incited the crowds below his cell and was transferred to an insane asylum at Charenton for his actions. He wrote extensively while in prison, including *Aline and Valcour, Justine, Stories Long and Short*, and *The Portfolio of a Man of Letters.*

De Sade was eventually freed by the Revolutionary Tribunal but was arrested in 1801 yet again for his writings. He did not get out again; he died in prison in December 1814.

The Marquis de Sade was perceived in his time as a monster. Yes, his writings were part of the reason he was persecuted and hated, but his *actions* were despicable and loathsome as well.

Virus Writers

(1981–)

The gods are just, and of our pleasant vices
Make instruments to plague us.
                —William Shakespeare, *King Lear,* Act 5, Scene 3

Are computer hackers and computer programmers who conceive and write computer viruses truly *evil,* and do they *really* warrant inclusion on this ranking? In the opinion of many who have been injured by their efforts, the answer to both questions is a categorical "yes."

Computers run the world. Anyone who has had a problem with an invoice due to computer troubles knows just how dependent the worlds of business, communication services, and public utilities are on electronic communication and commerce.

Computer viruses serve no purpose but *to do damage* to computers, businesses, and to impede and, in some cases, stop the smooth flow of electronic information of all kinds. Granted, there are benign viruses that simply present an innocuous message on the screen when activated, but these are a tiny percentage of the truly destructive viruses (self-replicating programs that attach themselves to other programs), worms (a virus that spreads by e-mailing itself), and Trojan horses (viruses disguised as games or other programs) cre-

317

ated by malevolent programmers and then sent out into the electronic world to wreak havoc and disrupt lives.

Originally, computer viruses were spread by floppy disk. In the early years of computers, many machines did not have a hard drive and used floppies to run programs and store data. The sharing of floppy disks among users was commonplace and, in most cases, the virus was disabled once the infected disk was removed from the floppy drive and the computer turned off.

Nowadays, incalculable connections to the Internet, vast, multinational computer networks, and enormous computer hard drives have changed all that.

Almost all computer virus infections these days are spread by e-mail or from downloaded programs from newsgroups and Web sites.

What, specifically, can an effective, that is, "deadly," computer virus do? It can erase hard drives; it can reformat hard drives; it can destroy files; it can vandalize and render unusable computer programs; it can send random files from one person's hard drive to everyone in their address book without the sender knowing about it; it can hide itself and then spring to life on a certain date and wipe out files and system software, rendering a computer useless.

It can disrupt *lives* and cost millions if not detected and inactivated.

The creation and dissemination of a computer virus is a malicious, cowardly act. It is electronic terrorism in its purest form. Moreover, like terrorism using physical violence, this cyber-terrorism comes out of nowhere, it targets the innocent and unsuspecting, and it leaves untold damage in its wake. The only thing electronic terrorism does not do is physically injure or kill people. But it injures and, in some instances, kills businesses and corporations who lose millions or billions in revenue due to virus attacks and spend enormous sums of money to rebuild computer systems and restore and re-create destroyed or corrupted documents, files, and data.

The first non-research virus was the "Elk Cloner" in 1981. The first IBM MS-DOS virus was the "Brain" in 1986. The most successful virus (it has infected the most computers) is the essentially harmless 1987 "Stoned" virus from New Zealand. The first virus created for the Windows 95 operating platform was 1996's "Boza" virus. The 1999 "Love Bug" virus, disseminated by e-mail all over the world, caused *more than $10 billion* in damage to computer systems and in lost business.

Viruses are a plague upon computer users and their authors can do as much damage via electronic terrorism as human terrorists can do with biological and chemical terrorism.

The Evil 100 *by Location*

Afghanistan

bin Laden, Osama
The Taliban

Armenia

Pasha, Talat, and Enver Pasha

Asia

Basil II, the Bulgar Slayer
Khan, Genghis
Tamerlane

Cambodia

Pot, Pol

Canada

Bernardo, Paul, and Karla Homolka
Lépine, Marc

Chile

Pinochet, Augusto

China

Zedong, Mao

England

Brady, Ian, and Myra Hindley
Haigh, John George
Jack the Ripper
Nilsen, Dennis
Ryan, Michael
Sutcliffe, Peter
West, Fred and Rosemary West

Europe

Attila the Hun

France

Landru, Henri Desiré
Medici, Catherine de
Petiot, Dr. Marcel
Rais, Gilles de
Sade, Marquis de

Germany

Eichmann, Adolf
Haarmann, Fritz
Himmler, Heinrich
Hitler, Adolf
Kroll, Joachim
Kürten, Peter
Ludke, Bruno

Mengele, Dr. Josef
The Nazi Doctors

Guyana

Jones, Jim

Iraq

Hussein, Saddam

Italy

Mussolini, Benito

Japan

Hideki, Tojo

Romania

Bathory, Erzsebet
Vlad III, the Impaler

Rome

Caligula
Nero

Russia

Chikatilo, Andrei
Dzhurmongaliev, Nikolai
Ivan the Terrible
Lenin, Vladimir Ilich
Onoprienko, Anatoly
Stalin, Joseph

Scotland

Hamilton, Thomas

South Africa

Sithole, Moses

South America

Lopez, Pedro

Spain

de Torquemada, Tomás

Tasmania, Australia

Bryant, Martin

Uganda

Dada, Idi Amin

United States

Bianchi, Kenneth, and Angelo Buono Jr.
Bird, Jake
Booth, John Wilkes
The Boston Strangler
Buchalter, Louis "Lepke"
Bundy, Ted
Corll, Dean Allen
Cowan, Frederick
Czolgosz, Leon F.
Dahmer, Jeffrey
Dodd, Westley Allan
Essex, Mark
Fish, Albert

Gacy, John Wayne
Gaskins, Donald "Pee Wee"
Gein, Eddie
The Green River Killer
Guiteau, Charles J.
Harris, Eric, and Dylan Klebold
Heidnik, Gary
Hennard, George
Huberty, James Oliver
Kaczynski, Theodore
Kemper III, Edmund
Kuklinski, Richard
Long, Bobby Joe
Lucas, Henry Lee
Manson, Charles
McVeigh, Timothy
Mudgett, Herman Webster, a.k.a. H.H. Holmes
Nelson, Earle Leonard
Ng, Charles, and Leonard Lake
Oswald, Lee Harvey
Panzram, Carl
Porter, Father James
Ramirez, Richard
Rifkin, Joel
Smith, Susan
The Son of Sam
Speck, Richard
Stano, Gerald
Starkweather, Charles and Caril Ann Fugate
Toppan, Jane
Unruh, Howard
Whitman, Charles
The Zodiac Killer

Worldwide

Virus Writers

BIBLIOGRAPHY AND SUGGESTED READING

Books

Abrahamsen, David. *Confessions of Son of Sam.* New York: Columbia University Press, 1999.

Abukhalil, Asad. *Osama Bin Laden and the Taliban: Consequences of U.S. Foreign Policy.* New York: Seven Stories Press, 2001.

Aburish, Said K. K., and Said, Aburish. *Saddam Hussein: The Politics of Revenge.* London: Bloomsbury, 2001.

Acton, Harold. *The Last Medici.* London: Methuen and Co., 1973.

Alexander, Yonah, and Michael S. Swetnam. *Usama bin Laden's al-Qaida: Profile of a Terrorist Network.* Ardlsey, N.Y.: Transnational Publishers, 2001.

Allen, William. *Starkweather: The Story of a Mass Murderer.* New York: Houghton Mifflin, 1976.

Altman, Jack, and Marvin Ziporyn. *Born to Raise Hell: The Untold Story of Richard Speck—The Man, the Crime, the Trial.* New York: Grove Press, 1967.

Amin, Idi; Benoni, Turyahikayo-Rugyema, editor. *Idi Amin Speaks: An Annotated Selection of His Speeches.* Madison: University of Wisconsin-Madison, 1998.

Arnold, Ron. *EcoTerror: The Violent Agenda to Save Nature: The World of the Unabomber.* Bellevue, Wash.: The Free Enterprise Press, 1997.

Arriagada, Genara. *Pinochet: The Politics of Power.* Boston: Unwin Hyman, 1988.

Avirgan, Tony, and Martha Honey. *War in Uganda: The Legacy of Idi Amin.* Chicago: Chicago Review Press, 1982.

Banks, Harold K. *The Strangler!* London: Mayflower-Dell, 1967.

Baram, Amatzia. *Building toward Crisis: Saddam Hussein's Strategy for Survival.* Washington, D.C.: Washington Institute for Near East Policy, 1998.

Bardens, Dennis, and Peter Davies. *The Ladykiller.* London: Senate Books, 1998.

Baumeister, Roy F., Ph.D. *Evil: Inside Human Violence and Cruelty.* New York: W.H. Freeman and Company, 1999.

Becker, Jasper. *Hungry Ghosts: Mao's Secret Famine.* New York: Free Press, 1996.

Begg, Paul. *Jack the Ripper: The Uncensored Facts.* London: Robson Books, 1992.

Begg, Paul. *The Jack the Ripper A to Z.* London: Headline Book Publishing, 1996.

Belin, Jean. *My Work at the Sûreté.* London: Harrap, 1950.

Benedetti, Jean. *Gilles de Rais—The Authentic Bluebeard.* London: Peter Davies Books, 1971.

Bergen, Peter L., and Rachel, Klayman. *Holy War, Inc.: Inside the Secret War of Osama Bin Laden.* New York: Free Press, 2001.

Berry, Jason. *Lead Us Not Into Temptation: Catholic Priests and the Sexual Abuse of Children.* New York: Doubleday, 1992.

Bhatia, Shyam, and Dan McGrory. *Brighter than the Baghdad Sun: Saddam Hussein's Nuclear Threat to the United States.* Washington, D.C.: Regnery, 2000.

Bingham, Mike. *Suddenly One Sunday.* New York: HarperCollins, 1996.

Bishop, Jim. *The Day Kennedy Was Shot.* New York: Gramercy, 1984.

Bloom, Howard. *The Lucifer Principle: A Scientific Expedition into the Forces of History.* New York: Atlantic Monthly Press, 1995.

Boar, Roger, and Blundell, Nigel. *The World's Most Infamous Murders.* London: Octopus, 1983.

Bobrice, Benson. *Fearful Majesty: The Life and Reign of Ivan the Terrible.* New York: Putnam, 1987.

Bodansky, Yossef. *Bin Laden: The Man Who Declared War on America.* New York: Random House, 2001.

Bolitho, William. *Murder for Profit.* New York: Harper & Brothers, 1926.

Boswell, Charles, and Lewis Thompson. *The Girls in Nightmare House.* New York: Gold Medal Books, n.d.

Brady, Ian; Wilson, Colin, Foreword. *The Gates of Janus: Serial Killing and Its Analysis by the Moors Murderer, Ian Brady.* Portland, Ore.: Feral House, 2001.

Brailey, Jeffrey. *The Ghosts of November: Memoirs of an Outsider Who Witnessed the Carnage at Jonestown, Guyana.* San Antonio, Tex.: J & J Publishers, 1998.

Breitman, Richard. *The Architect of Genocide: Himmler and the Final Solution,* Vol. 14. Hanover, N.H.: University Press of New England, 1992.

Breo, Dennis L., and William J. Martin. *Crime of the Century: Richard Speck and the Murder of Eight Student Nurses.* New York: Bantam, 1993.

Briffett, David. *The Acid Bath Murders.* West Sussex, England: Field Place Press, 1988.

Brody, Reed, and Michael Ratner. *The Pinochet Papers: The Case of Augusto Pinochet in Spain and Britain.* London: Kluwer Law International, 2000.

Browne, Courtney. *Tojo: The Last Banzai.* New York: Da Capo Press, 1998.

Bruno, Anthony. *The Iceman: The True Story of a Cold-Blooded Killer.* New York: Delacorte, 1993.

Buchanan, Carl Jay; Howard, Richard, editor. *Ripper!* Columbia: University of South Carolina Press, 1998.

Bugliosi, Vincent, and Curt Gentry. *Helter Skelter.* New York: Bantam, 1975.

Bugliosi, Vincent, and Curt Gentry. *The Manson Murders.* London: Bodley Head, 1975.

Bullock, Alan. *Adolf Hitler: A Study in Tyranny.* New York: HarperCollins, 1962.

Burkett, Elinor, and Frank Bruni. *A Gospel of Shame: Children, Sexual Abuse, and the Catholic Church.* New York: Viking, 1993.

Burnside, Scott, and Alan Cairns. *Deadly Innocence.* New York: Warner, 1995.

Cadzow, John F., Andrew Ludyani, and Louis J. Eleto. *Transylvania—The Roots of Ethnic Conflict.* Kent, Ohio: Kent State University Press, 1983.

Cahill, Tim. *Buried Dreams: Inside the Mind of a Serial Killer.* New York: Bantam, 1986.

Call, Max. *Hand of Death: The Henry Lee Lucas Story.* Lafayette, La.: Prescott Press, 1985.

Calohan, George H. *My Search for "The Son of Sam."* New York: iUniverse, 2001.

Carcopino, Jerome. *Daily Life in Ancient Rome: The People and City at the Height of the Empire.* New Haven: Yale University Press, 1976.

Carlo, Philip. *The Night Stalker: The True Story of America's Most Feared Serial Killer.* New York: Kensington, 2000.

Carpozi, George, Jr., and William Balsamo. *Crime, Inc.: The Inside Story of the Mafia's First 100 Years.* Far Hills, N.J.: New Horizon Press, 1990.

Carr, Franci. *Ivan the Terrible.* New York: Barnes & Noble, 1981.

Cender, Stephen, and Kenneth Cender. *A Serial Killer: David Berkowitz: Son of Sam/Son of Hope.* [e-book] Bloomington, Ind.: 1stBooks Library, 2001.

Chandler, David. *Brother Number One: A Political Biography of Pol Pot.* Boulder, Colo.: Westview Press, 1999.

Charyn, Jerome. *Back to Bataan.* New York: Farrar, Straus & Giroux, 1993.

Cheney, Margaret. *The Co-Ed Killer.* New York: Walker & Co., 1976.

Chester, Andrew, and H. Amanda Robb, editors. *Criminal Quotes: The 1,001 Most Bizarre Things Ever Said by History's Outlaws, Gangsters, Despots, and Other Evil-Doers.* Detroit, Mich.: Visible Ink, 1997.

Chidester, David. *Salvation and Suicide: An Interpretation of Jim Jones, the People's Temple, and Jonestown.* Bloomington: Indiana University Press, 1991.

Clark, James C. *The Murder of James A. Garfield: The President's Last Days and the Trial and Execution of His Assassin.* Jefferson, N.C.: McFarland, 1993.

Clark, Ronald C. *Lenin: A Biography.* New York: Harper & Row, 1988.

Coleman, John S. *Bataan and Beyond: Memories of an American POW.* College Station, Tex.: Texas A&M University, 1993.

Conquest, Robert. *Harvest of Sorrow: Soviet Collectivization and the Terror-Famine.* New York: Oxford University Press, 1986.

Cooley, John K. *Unholy Wars: Afghanistan, America, and International Terrorism.* London: Pluto Press, 2000.

Cooper, Marc. *Pinochet and Me: A Chilean Anti-Memoir.* New York: Verso Books, 2001.

Courtois, Stéphanie, Nicolas Werth, Jean-Louis Panné, Andrzej Paczkowski, Karel Bartosek, and Jean-Louis Margolin. *The Black Book of Communism: Crimes, Terror, Repression.* Boston, Mass.: Harvard University Press, 1999.

Cox, Mike. *The Confession of Henry Lee Lucas.* New York: Pocket Books, 1991.

Cross, Roger. *The Yorkshire Ripper: The In-Depth Study of a Mass Killer and His Methods.* New York: HarperCollins, 1995.

Crowley, Kieran. *Sleep My Little Dead: The True Story of the Zodiac Killer,* Vol. 1. New York: St. Martin's, 1997.

Cullen, Robert. *Citizen X.* New York: Ballantine, 1993.

Dadrian, Vahakn N. *The History of the Armenian Genocide: Ethnic Conflict from the Balkans to Anatolia to the Caucasus.* New Providence, N.J.: Berghahn Books, 1995.

Dadrian, Vahakn N. *The Key Elements in the Turkish Denial of the Armenian Genocide: A Case Study of Distortion and Falsification.* New Providence, N.J.: Zoryan Institute Canada Staff BPR Publishers, 1999.

Davey, Frank. *Karla's Web: A Cultural Investigation of the Mahaffy-French Murders.* New York: Viking, 1994.

Davis, Don. *The Milwaukee Murders.* New York: St. Martin's, 1991.

Davis, Scott C. *The Road from Damascus: A Journey through Syria—with Reflections on Terrorism, Radical Islam, the Hezbollah, Osama Bin Laden, Shiites, & Sunnis.* Seattle, Wash.: Cune, 2000.

Davison, Jean. *Oswald's Game.* New York: W.W. Norton, 1983.

Dawidowitz, Lucy. *The War Against the Jews, 1933–1945.* New York: Holt Rinehart Winston, 1975.

Deac, Wilfred, and Harry Summers. *Road to the Killing Field: The Cambodian War of 1970–1975.* College Station, Tex.: Texas A&M University Press, 1997.

Djilas, Milovan. *Conversations with Stalin.* New York: Harvest Books, 1963.

Doob, Leonard E. *Panorama of Evil.* Westport, Conn.: Greenwood Press, 1978.

Douglas, John. *Unabomber: On Trail of America's Most Wanted Serial Killer.* New York: Pocket Books, 1996.

Douglas, John E., Ann W. Burgess, Allen G. Burgess, and Robert K. Ressler. *Crime Classification Manual.* New York: Lexington Books, 1992.

Dunboyne, Lord, editor. *The Trial of John George Haigh.* London: William Hodge & Company, 1953.

Dwyer, Jim, Peg Tyre, and Deidre Murphy. *Two Seconds Under the World: Terror Comes to America—the Conspiracy Behind the World Trade Center Bombing.* Collingdale, Penn.: Diane Publishing, 1997.

Eddleston, John J. *Jack the Ripper: An Encyclopedia.* Santa Barbara, Calif.: ABC-CLIO, 2001.

Eddowes, Michael. *The Oswald File.* New York: Clarkson N. Potter, 1977.

Ellis, Deborah. *Women of the Afghan War.* Westport, Conn.: Greenwood Publishing Group, 2000.

Englade, Ken. *Cellar of Horror: The True Story.* New York: St. Martin's, 1989.

Ensalaco, Mark. *Chile under Pinochet: Recovering the Truth.* Philadelphia: University of Pennsylvania Press, 1999.

Epstein, Edward Jay. *Inquest: The Warren Commission and the Establishment of the Truth.* New York: Bantam, 1966.

Evans, Stewart P., and Keith Skinner, editors. *The Ultimate Jack the Ripper Companion.* New York: Carroll & Graf, 2000.

Faith, Karlene. *The Long Prison Journey of Leslie Van Houten.* Boston: Northeastern University Press, 2001.

Feinsod, Ethan, and Odell Rhodes. *Awake in Nightmare—Jonestown: The Only Eyewitness Account.* New York: W.W. Norton & Company, 1981.

Fes, Joachim C. *The Face of the Third Reich.* New York: Pantheon Books, 1970.

Fido, Martin. *The Chronicle of Crime: The Most Infamous Criminals of Modern Times and Their Heinous Crimes.* London: Carlton Books, 1999.

Fleischer, Richard, director. *The Boston Strangler.* Feature Film, 1968.

Fleming, Gerald. *Hitler and the Final Solution.* Berkeley: University· of California Press, 1984.

Florescu, Radu R., and Raymond T. McNally. *Dracula: Prince of Many Faces.* New York: Little, Brown, 1989.

Florescu, Radu R., and Raymond T. McNally. *In Search of Dracula.* New York: Houghton Mifflin, 1994.

Flowers, Anna. *Blind Fury.* New York: Pinnacle, 1993.

Flowers, Anna. *Bound To Die.* New York: Pinnacle, 1995.

Fox, James Alan, and Jack Levin. *Overkill, Mass Murder and Serial Killing Exposed.* London: Plenum, 1994.

Frank, Gerold. *The Boston Strangler.* London: Jonathan Cape, 1967.

Franke, David. *The Torture Doctor.* New York: Hawthorn Books, 1975.

Gaddis, Thomas E., and James O. Long. *Killer: A Journal of Murder.* New York: Macmillan, 1970.

Garrison, Jim. *On the Trail of the Assassins.* New York: Warner Books, 1991.

Gaskins, Donald, and Wilton Earle. *Final Truth: The Autobiography of a Serial Killer.* Atlanta, Ga.: Adept, 1992.

Gekos, Anna. *Murder by the Numbers: British Serial Sex Killers Since 1950.* London: Andre Deutsch, 1998.

Gelertner, David. *Drawing Life: Surviving the Unabomber.* New York: Simon & Schuster, 1997.

George, Edward; with Dary Matera. *Taming the Beast: Charles Manson's Life Behind Bars.* New York: St. Martin's Press, 1999.

Gernet, Jacques. *Daily Life in China on the Eve of the Mongol Invasion, 1250–1276.* Stanford, Calif.: Stanford University Press, 1977.

Gerolmo, Chris, director. *Citizen X.* HBO Made-for-Cable movie, 1995.

Glut, Donald F. *The Truth About Dracula.* Metuchen, N.J.: Scarecrow Press, 1975.

Godin, Seth. *Technophobe: The Unabomber Years.* Los Angeles: NewStar Media, 1997.

Godwin, George, and Karl Berg. *Monsters of Weimar,* comprising *The Sadist* (1945), and *Peter Kürten: A Study in Sadism* (1938). Del Mar, Calif.: Nemesis Books, 1993.

Gohari, M. J. *The Taliban: Ascent to Power.* New York: Oxford University Press, 2001.

Gollmar, Judge Robert H., and Charles Hallberg. *Edward Gein.* New York: Pinnacle, 1990.

Goodman, Jonathan, editor. *Celebrated Trials: The Moors Murderers.* London: Newton Abbot, 1973.

Goodson, Larry P. *Afghanistan's Endless War: State Failure, Regional Politics, and the Rise of the Taliban.* Seattle, Wash.: University of Washington Press, 2001.

Gordon, R. Michael. *Alias Jack the Ripper: Beyond the Usual Whitechapel Suspects.* Jefferson, N.C.: McFarland & Company, 2000.

Gould, Lewis L. *The Presidency of William McKinley.* Lawrence, Kans.: Regents Press of Kansas, 1980.

Graber, G. S. *The Caravans to Oblivion: The Armenian Genocide 1915: A Portrait of Genocide.* New York: John Wiley & Sons, 1996.

Grant, Michael. *Emperor in Revolt: Nero.* New York: American Heritage Press, 1970.

Grant, Michael. *Nero.* New York: Dorset Press, 1970.

Gray, Francine Du Plessix. *At Home with the Marquis de Sade: A Life.* New York: Simon and Schuster, 1998.

Graysmith, Robert. *Unabomber: A Desire to Kill.* Washington, D.C.: Regnery, 1997.

Graysmith, Robert. *Zodiac.* New York: St. Martin's, 1986.

Greenlee, Sam. *Baghdad Blues: The Revolution That Brought Saddam Hussein to Power.* New York: Kayode Publications, 1994.

Griffin, Marcus. *Heroes of Bataan, Corregidor, and Northern Luzon: Corregidor and Northern Luzon.* Las Cruces, N.M.: Yucca Tree Press, 1994.

Griffin, Michael. *Reaping the Whirlwind: The Taliban Movement in Afghanistan.* London: Pluto Press, 2000.

Griffin, Miriam T. *Nero: The End of a Dynasty.* New Haven: Yale University Press, 1984.

Grombach, John V. *The Great Liquidator.* London: Sphere Books, 1982.

Gurwell, John K. *Mass Murder in Houston.* Austin, Tex.: Cordovan Press, 1974.

Hamilton, Sue L. *Death of a Cult Family: Jim Jones.* Edina, Minn.: ABDO Publishing, 1989.

Hamza, Dr. Khidhir. *Saddam's Bombmaker: The Terrifying Inside Story of the Iraqi Nuclear and Biological Weapons Agenda.* New York: Simon & Schuster, 2000.

Hayes, H. G., and C. J. Hayes. *A Complete History of the Trial of Charles Julius Guiteau, Assassin of President Garfield.* Philadelphia, Pa.: National Publishing Company, 1882.

Heimer, Mel. *The Cannibal.* Secaucus, N.J.: Lyle Stuart, 1971.

Henderson, Simon. *Instant Empire: Saddam Hussein's Ambition for Iraq.* San Francisco: Mercury House, 1991.

Hibbert, Christopher. *The House of Medici: Its Rise and Fall.* New York: William Morrow, 1975.

Hilsman, Roger. *George Bush vs. Saddam Hussein: Military Success! Political Failure?* Novato, Calif.: Presidio Press, 1992.

Hingley, Ronald. *Joseph Stalin: Man & Legend.* New York: McGraw-Hill, 1974.

Hitler, Adolf. *Mein Kampf.* New York: Houghton Mifflin, 1971.

Hoffman, Bruce. *Inside Terrorism.* New York: Columbia University Press, 1999.

Hope, Thomas. *Torquemada, Scourge of the Jews: A Biography.* London: Allen & Unwin, 1939.

Hovannisian, Richard G. *Remembrance and Denial: The Case of the Armenian Genocide.* Detroit, Mich.: Wayne State University Press, 1999.

Howarth, Patrick. *Attila King of the Huns: The Man and the Myth.* New York: Carroll and Graf, 2001.

Hoyt, Edwin Palmer. *Warlord: Tojo Against the World.* Lanham, Md.: Madison Books, 1991.

Hussein, Saddam. *Iraq Speaks: Documents of the Gulf Crises.* Collingdale, Pa.: Diane Publishing, 1994.

Jackson, Karl. *Cambodia 1975–1978: Rendezvous with Death.* Princeton, N.J.: Princeton University Press, 1989.

Jaeger, Richard W., and M. William Balousek. *Massacre in Milwaukee: The Macabre Case of Jeffrey Dahmer.* Oregon, Wis.: Waubesa Press, 1991.

Jakubowski, Maxim. *The Mammoth Book of Jack the Ripper.* New York: Carroll & Graf, 1999.

Jamison, Martin, compiler. *Idi Amin and Uganda: An Annotated Bibliography.* Westport, Conn.: Greenwood Publishing, 1992.

Jernazian, Ephraim K.; Alice Haig, translator. *Judgment unto Truth: Witnessing the Armenian Genocide.* Piscataway, N.J.: Transaction Publishers, 1990.

Jones, Jim. Introduction by Eden Karl. *The Jonestown Massacre: Transcript of Jim Jones' Last Speech, Guyana 1978.* San Francisco: AK Press, 1994.

Jones, Stephen, and Peter Israel. *Others Unknown: Timothy McVeigh and the Oklahoma City Bombing Conspiracy.* New York: PublicAffairs, 2001.

Josephs, Jeremy. *Hungerford: One Man's Massacre.* [e-book] www.jeremy josephs.com, 2000.

Jouve, Nicole Ward. *The Street Cleaner: The Yorkshire Ripper Case On Trial.* New York: Marion Boyars, 1986.

Kamen, Henry. *The Spanish Inquisition: A Historical Revision.* New Haven: Yale University Press, 1999.

Kelleher, Michael D., and David Van Nuys. *This Is the Zodiac Speaking: Into the Mind of a Serial Killer.* Westport, Conn.: Greenwood Publishing Group, 2001.

Keppell, Robert D., Ph.D. *The Riverman—Ted Bundy and I Hunt for the Green River Killer.* New York: Pocket Books, 1995.

Kiernan, Ben, editor. *Genocide and Democracy in Cambodia.* New Haven: Yale University Press, 1993.

Kiernan, Ben. *The Pol Pot Regime: Race, Power, and Genocide in Cambodia Under the Khmer Rouge, 1975–79.* New Haven: Yale University Press, 1998.

Kirakossian, John S.; Shushan Sltunian, translator. *The Armenian Genocide: The Young Turks Before the Judgment of History.* New York: Sphinx Press, 1992.

Knox, Donald. *Death March: The Survivors of Bataan.* New York: Harcourt Brace Jovanovich, 1983.

Krivith, Mikhail, and Ol'gert Ol'gin. *Comrade Chikatilo: The Psychopathology of Russia's Notorious Serial Killer.* Fort Lee, N.J.: Barricade Books, 1993.

Kyemba, Henry. *A State of Blood: The Inside Story of Idi Amin.* New York: Grosset & Dunlap, 1977.

Labeviere, Richard. *Dollars for Terror: The U.S. and Islam.* New York: Algora Publishing, 2000.

Lamb, Harold. *Genghis Khan, The Emperor of All Men.* New York: McBride & Company, 1927.

Landau, Elaine. *Osama Bin Laden: A War Against the West.* New York: Twenty First Century Books, 2002.

Lane, Brian, and Wilfred Gregg. *The Encyclopedia of Serial Killers*. New York: Berkley, 1995.

Lane, Mark. *Rush to Judgment*. New York: Fawcett Crest, 1967.

Larsen, Richard W. *Bundy—The Deliberate Stranger*. New York: Prentice-Hall, 1980.

Lasseter, Don. *Die For Me*. New York: Pinnacle Books, 2000.

Lavergne, Gary M. *A Sniper in the Tower; The Charles Whitman Murders*. Denton, Tex.: University of North Texas Press, 1997.

Layton, Deborah. *Seductive Poison: A Jonestown Survivor's Story of Life and Death in the People's Temple*. New York: Doubleday, 1998.

Leech, Margaret. *In the Days of McKinley*. New York: Harper, 1959.

Lifton, David. *Best Evidence: Disguise and Deception in the Assassination of John F. Kennedy*. New York: Carroll & Graf, 1988.

Lifton, Robert Jay. *The Nazi Doctors: Medical Killing and the Psychology of Genocide*. New York: Basic Books, 1986.

Linedecker, Clifford L. *Night Stalker*. New York: St. Martin's, 1991.

Linedecker, Clifford L. *The Man Who Killed Boys*. New York: St. Martin's, 1994.

Maeder, Thomas. *The Unspeakable Crimes of Dr. Petiot*. New York: Little Brown, 1980.

Maenchen-Helfren, J. Otto. *The World of the Huns*. Los Angeles: University of California Press, 1973.

Maley, William editor. *Fundamentalism Reborn?: Afghanistan under the Taliban*. New York: New York University Press, 1998.

Manchester, William. *A World Lit Only by Fire: The Medieval Mind and the Renaissance*. New York: Macmillan, 1993.

Manchester, William. *The Death of a President*. London: Michael Joseph, 1967.

Manson, Charles. *The Manson File: Writings by Charles Manson and His Family*. New York: Amok Press, 1988.

Manson, Charles; as told to Nuel Emmons. *Manson in His Own Words*. New York: Grove/Atlantic, 1988.

Manson, Charles, and Sy Wizinski. *Charles Manson: Love Letters to a Secret Disciple: A Psychoanalytical Search*. Danville, Ill.: Crime & Criminals, 1976.

Mansson, Martin. *Heinrich Himmler: A Photographic Chronicle of Hitler's Reichsfuhrer*. Exton, Pa.: Schiffer Publishing, 2001.

Marriner, Brian. *Cannibalism, the Last Taboo*. London: Arrow Books, 1992.

Marsden, Peter, and Jerrold E. Marsden. *The Taliban*. New York: St. Martin's Press, 1998.

Martingale, Moira. *Cannibal Killers*. New York: Carroll & Graf, 1993.

Masters, Brian. *Killing for Company: The Case of Dennis Nilsen*. London: Jonathan Cape, 1985.

Masters, Brian. *She Must Have Known: The Trial of Rosemary West*. London: David Corgi Books, 1996.

Matinuddin, Kamal. *The Taliban Phenomenon: Afghanistan, 1994–1997.* New York: Oxford University Press, 1999.

McKenzie, F. A. *The Notable Trials Library: Landru.* London: Bles, 1928.

McMillan, Priscilla Johnson. *Marina and Lee.* New York: Harper & Row, 1977.

McNally, Raymond T. *Dracula Was a Woman: In Search of the Blood Countess of Transylvania.* New York: McGraw-Hill, 1983.

McNaughton, John, director. *Henry: Portrait of a Serial Killer.* Feature Film, 1990.

Meaures, B. *Amin's Uganda.* New York: Minerva Press, 1998.

Medvedev, Roy. *Let History Judge: The Origins and Consequence of Stalinism.* New York: Knopf, 1972.

Melady, Thomas, and Margaret Sheed Melady. *Idi Amin Dada: Hitler in Africa.* Kansas City, Mo.: Andrews and McMeel, 1977.

Melanson, Philip H. *Spy Saga: Lee Harvey Oswald and U.S. Intelligence.* New York: Praeger Publishers, 1990.

Mello, Michael. *The United States of America Versus Theodore John Kaczynski: Ethics, Power, and the Invention of the Unabomber.* New York: Context Books, 1999.

Melson, Robert, and Leo Kuper. *Revolution and Genocide: On the Origins of the Armenian Genocide and the Holocaust.* Chicago: University of Chicago Press, 1994.

Mendenhall, Harlan. *Fall of the House of Gacy.* West Franfurt, Ill.: New Authors Publications, 1998.

Meyer, Cheryl L., Priya Batra, Tara C. Proano, Kelly White, Michelle Rone, and Michelle Oberman. *Mothers Who Kill Their Children: Inside the Minds of Moms from Susan Smith to the "Prom Mom."* New York: New York University Press, 2001.

Michaud, Stephen, and Hugh Aynesworth. *The Only Living Witness.* New York: Linden Press, 1980.

Michel, Lou, and Dan Herbeck. *American Terrorist: Timothy McVeigh and the Oklahoma City Bombing.* New York: HarperCollins, 2001.

Mikac, Walter. *To Have and To Hold.* New York: Macmillan, 1997.

Miller, Donald Eugene, and Lorna Touryan Miller. *Survivors: An Oral History of the Armenian Genocide.* Berkeley: California Press, 1999.

Mitscherlich, Alexander, and Fred Miekle. *Doctors of Infamy: The Story of the Nazi Medical Crimes.* New York: Henry Schuman, 1949.

Mladinich, Robert. *From the Mouth of the Monster.* New York: Pocket, 2001.

Moore, Jim. *Conspiracy of One: The Definitive Book on the Kennedy Assassination.* Fort Worth, Tex.: The Summit Group, 1991.

Morgan, H. Wayne. *William McKinley and His America.* Syracuse, N.Y.: Syracuse University Press, 1963.

Murphy, Bob. *Desert Shadows: A True Story of the Charles Manson Family in Death Valley.* Las Vegas, Nev.: Sagebrush Press, 1993.

Murphy, John F. *Day of Reckoning: The Massacre at Columbine High School.* Philadelphia, Pa.: Xlibris Corporation, 2001.

Murray, Wendy. *Day of Reckoning: Columbine and the Search for America's Soul.* Grand Rapids, Mich.: Brazos Press, 2001.

Musallam, Musallam Ali. *Iraqi Invasion of Kuwait: Saddam Hussein, His State and International Power Politics.* New York: St. Martin's Press, 1996.

Mustain, Gene, and Jerry Capeci. *Murder Machine: A True Story of Murder, Madness, and the Mafia.* New York: Onyx, 1993.

Mylroie, Laurie. *Study of Revenge: Saddam Hussein's Unfinished War Against America.* Washington, D.C.: American Enterprise Institute for Public Policy Research, 2000.

Nash, Jay Robert. *Bloodletters and Badmen: A Narrative Encyclopedia of American Criminals from the Pilgrims to the Present.* New York: M. Evans and Company, 1995.

Netanyahu, Benjamin. *Fighting Terrorism.* New York: Farrar, Straus & Giroux, 1997.

Nicolle, David, and Argus McBride. *Attila the Hun.* London: Osprey Publishing, 2000.

Norman, Elizabeth M. *We Band of Angels: The Untold Story of American Nurses Trapped on Bataan.* New York: Pocket, 2000.

Norris, Dr. Joel. *Henry Lee Lucas.* New York: Kensington, 1991.

Nyiszli, Dr. Miklos. *Auschwitz, A Doctor's Eyewitness Account.* London: Granada Books, 1973.

O'Brien, Darcy. *Two of a Kind: The Hillside Stranglers.* New York: New American Library, 1985.

Odell, Robin. *Jack the Ripper in Fact and Fiction.* London: Harrap, 1965.

Olok-Apire, P. A. *Idi Amin's Rise to Power: The Inside Story.* Chicago: Independent Publishing Group, 1983.

Olsen, Jack. *The Man with the Candy.* London: Talmy Franklin, 1975.

Omoike, Isaac I. *The Columbine High School Massacre: An Investigatory Analysis.* Baton Rouge, La.: Isaac Omoike Books, 2000.

Oswald, Robert L.; with Myrick Land, and Barbara Land. *Lee: A Portrait of Lee Harvey Oswald.* New York: Coward-McCann, 1967.

Oyarzun, Maria. *Augusto Pinochet.* Buenos Aires, Argentina: Sudamericana, 2000.

Padfield, Peter. *Himmler Reichsfuhrer-SS: A Biography.* New York: Henry Holt, 1993.

Padfield, Peter. *Himmler.* New York: Cassell Academic, 2001.

Pasha, Talat. *Talat Pasha's Memories.* Istanbul: Librairie de Pera, 1946.

Pender, Patrick, and Brian Innes. *Richard Ramirez: The Night Stalker.* London: Midsummer Books, 1993.

Penrose, Valentine; Alexander Trocchi, translator. *The Bloody Countess.* London: Calder & Boyars, 1970.

Perl, Dr. Gisela. *I Was a Doctor in Auschwitz.* New York: International Universities Press, 1948.

Philbin, Tom. *Murder U.S.A.* New York: Warner Books, 1992.

Physicians for Human Rights. *The Taliban's War on Women.* Boston: Physicians for Human Rights, 1998.

Pillar, Paul R. *Terrorism and U.S. Foreign Policy.* Washington, D.C.: Brookings Institution Press, 2001.

Posner, Gerald. *Case Closed: Lee Harvey Oswald and the Assassination of JFK.* New York: Random House, 1993.

Posner, Gerald, and John Ware. *Mengele: The Complete Story.* New York: Dell, 1986.

Pran, Dith, and Ben Kiernan. *Children of Cambodia's Killing Fields: Memoirs. Survivors.* New Haven: Yale University Press, 1999.

Pron, Nick. *Lethal Marriage: The Unspeakable Crimes of Paul Bernardo and Karla Homolka.* New York: Ballantine Books, 1996.

Pulitzer, Lisa Beth. *Crossing the Line: The True Story of Long Island Serial Killer Joel Rifkin.* New York: Berkley, 1994.

Rashid, Ahmed. *Taliban: Militant Islam, Oil and Fundamentalism in Central Asia.* New Haven: Yale University Press, 2001.

Reader's Digest Press. *Legend: The Secret World of Lee Harvey Oswald.* New York: McGraw-Hill, 1978.

Reeve, Simon. *The New Jackals: Ramzi Yousef, Osama Bin Laden, and the Future of Terrorism.* Boston: Northeastern University Press, 1999.

Reich, Walter. *Origins of Terrorism: Psychologies, Ideologies, Theologies, States of Mind.* Washington, D.C.: Woodrow Wilson Center Press, 1998.

Reinhardt, James Melvin. *The Murderous Trail of Charles Starkweather.* Springfield, Ill.: Public Science Series, 1960.

Rekers, George A. *Susan Smith: Victim or Murderer?* Aurora, Colo.: Glenbridge Publishing, 1995.

Rhodes, Richard. *Why They Kill: The Discoveries of a Maverick Criminologist.* New York: Vintage Books, 2000.

Rosenberg, Charles E. *The Trial of the Assassin Guiteau: Psychiatry and the Law in the Gilded Age.* Chicago: University of Chicago Press, 1995.

Roth, Cecil. *The Spanish Inquisition.* New York: W.W. Norton & Co., 1996.

Rule, Ann. *The Stranger Beside Me.* New York: Norton, 1988.

Rumbelow, Donald. *The Complete Jack the Ripper.* London: W.H. Allen, 1975.

Russell, Linda; with Shirley, Stephens. *My Daughter Susan Smith.* Brentwood, Tenn.: Authors Book Nook, 2000.

Sabatini, Rafael. *Torquemada and the Spanish Inquistion.* London: House of Stratus, 2001.

Sandburg, Carl. *Abraham Lincoln: The Prairie Years and the War Years: One-Volume Edition.* New York: Harcourt, Brace and Company, 1954.

Sanders, Ed. *The Family: The Story of Charles Manson.* New York: Dutton, 1971.

Schaffer, Neil. *The Marquis de Sade: A Life*. New York: Knopf, 1999.

Schechter, Harold. *Deviant*. New York: Pocket Books, 1989.

Schechter, Harold, and David Everitt. *The A to Z Encyclopedia of Serial Killers*. New York: Pocket Books, 1996.

Schwartz, Ted. *The Hillside Strangler: A Murderer's Mind*. New York: Doubleday, 1981.

Scott, Margaret. *Port Arthur: A Story of Strength and Courage*. New York: Random House, 1997.

Serrano, Richard A. *One of Ours: Timothy McVeigh and the Oklahoma City Bombing*. New York: W.W. Norton, 1998.

Seth, Ronald. *Petiot—Victim of Chance*. London: Hutchison, 1963.

Shirer, William L. *The Rise and Fall of the Third Reich*. New York: Simon & Schuster, 1960, 1976.

Short, Philip. *Mao: A Life*. New York: Henry Holt, 2000.

Shotter, David. *Nero*. London: Routledge, 1997.

Sigmund, Paul E. *The Overthrow of Allende and the Politics of Chile, 1964–1976*. Pittsburgh, Pa.: Pittsburgh Publishing, 1977.

Sipe, Richard. *Sex, Priests, and Power: Anatomy of a Crisis*. New York: Brunner/Mazel, 1995.

Smith, Bradley F. *Heinrich Himmler: A Nazi in the Making, 1900–1926*. Stanford, Calif.: Hoover Institution Press, 1971.

Smith, Carlton, and Tomas Guillen. *The Search for the Green River Killer*. New York: Onyx/Penguin Books, 1991.

Sounes, Howard. *Fred & Rose*. New York: Warner Books, 1995.

Spignesi, Stephen J. *The Italian 100: A Ranking of the Most Influential Cultural, Scientific, and Political Figures, Past and Present*. Secaucus, N.J.: Citadel Press, 1997.

Stefoff, Rebecca. *Saddam Hussein: Absolute Ruler of Iraq*. Brookfield, Conn.: Millbrook Press, 1995.

Steinhorst, Lori. *When the Monster Comes Out of the Closet*. Salem, Ore.: Rose Publishing, 1994.

Stern, Jessica. *The Ultimate Terrorists*. Cambridge: Harvard University Pres, 2000.

Stern, Philip Van Doren. *The Man Who Killed Lincoln: The Story of John Wilkes Booth and His Part in the Assassination*. New York: Random House, 1939.

Stewart, Gail B. *Life During the Spanish Inquisition*. Farmington Hills, Mich.: Gale Group, 1997.

Stickney, Brandon M. *All-American Monster: The Unauthorized Biography of Timothy McVeigh*. New York: Prometheus Books, 1996.

Stoker, Bram. *Dracula*. New York: St. Martin's Press. 2001.

Sugden, Philip. *The Complete History of Jack the Ripper*. New York: Carroll & Graf, 2001.

Sullivan, Terry, and Peter T. Maiken. *Killer Clown*. New York: Grosset & Dunlap, 1997.

Tenney, Lester I. *My Hitch in Hell: The Bataan Death March.* London: Brassey's, Inc., 2000.

Terris, Susan. *Angels of Bataan.* Johnstown, Ohio: Pudding House Publications, 1999.

Terry, Maury. *Ultimate Evil: The Truth about the Cult Murders: Son of Sam and Beyond.* New York: Barnes & Noble Books, 1999.

Thebaut, Jim, director. "The Iceman." *HBO America Undercover,* 1992.

Thebaut, Jim, director. "The Iceman Confesses." *HBO America Undercover,* 2001.

Thompson, Josiah. *Six Seconds in Dallas: A Microstudy of the Kennedy Assassination.* New York: Berkley, 1976.

Thorne, Tony. *Countess Dracula: The Life and Times of the Blood Countess, Elisabeth Báthory.* London: Bloomsbury, 1997.

Toland, John. *Hitler.* Garden City, N.J.: Doubleday, 1976.

Troyat, Henri. *Ivan the Terrible.* New York: Dutton, 1984.

Tucker, Robert C., editor. *The Lenin Anthology.* New York: W.W. Norton & Co., 1975.

Turkus, Burton, and Sid Feder. *Murder, Inc.: The Story of the Syndicate.* New York: Farrar Straus Giroux, 1951.

Turner Publishing Company Staff. *American Defenders of Bataan and Corregidor.* Paducah, Ky.: Turner Publishing, 1991.

Ulam, Adam B. *The Bolsheviks.* New York: Macmillan, 1965.

Ulam, Adam B. *Stalin: The Man and His Era.* New York: Viking, 1973.

Wagner, Margaret Seaton. *The Monster of Düsseldorf.* New York: Faber and Faber, 1932.

Waits, Chris, and Dave Shors. *Unabomber: The Secret Life of Ted Kaczynski.* Helena, Mont.: Farcountry Press, 1998.

Wansell, Geoffrey. *The Life of Frederick West.* London: Headline Book Publishing, 1996.

Watkins, Paul, and Guillermo Soledad. *My Life with Charles Manson.* New York: Bantam Books, 1979.

Weissman, Jerry. *The Zodiac Killer.* New York: Kensington, 1979.

Wertham, Fredric. *The Show of Violence.* London: Gollancz, 1949.

Williams, Emlyn. *Beyond Belief: The Moors Murderers.* London: Pan, 1969.

Williams, Stephen. *Invisible Darkness: The Horrifying Case of Paul Bernardo and Karla Homolka.* New York: Bantam, 1996.

Wills, Donald H., and Reyburn W. Myers. *Sea Was My Last Chance: Memoir of an American Captured on Bataan in 1942 Who Escaped in 1944 and Led the Liberation of Western Mindanao.* Jefferson, N.C.: McFarland, 1992.

Wilson, Colin. *The Corpse Garden: The Crimes of Fred and Rose West.* New York: St. Martin's Press True Crime Library, 1998.

Wilson, Colin. *The Mammoth Book of the History of Murder.* New York: Carrol & Graf, 2000.

Wilson, Francis. *John Wilkes Booth: Fact and Fiction of Lincoln's Assassination.* New York: Houghton Mifflin, 1929.

Woodhouse, Diane, editor. *The Pinochet Case: A Legal and Constitutional Analysis.* New York: Hart Publishing, 2000.

Wurmser, David. *Tyranny's Ally: America's Failure to Defeat Saddam Hussein.* Washington, D.C.: American Enterprise Institute for Public Policy, 1999.

Wyndham Lewis, D. B. *The Soul of Marshall Gilles de Raiz.* London: Eyre and Spottiwoode, 1952.

Yallop, David. *Deliver Us From Evil.* London: David Corgi Books, 1993.

Young, Colonel G. F. *The Medici.* New York: The Modern Library, 1930.

Young, Donald J. *The Battle of Bataan: A History of the 90 Day Siege and Eventual Surrender of 75,000 Filipino and United States Troops to the Japanese in World War II.* Jefferson, N.C.: McFarland, 1992.

Periodicals

Bellamy, Patrick. "Murder on the Moors: Update." The Crime Library Web site.

Berkowitz, David. "Letter to Jimmy Breslin." The *New York Daily News.* June 1, 1977. "Letter to Martin G. Wolcott." *The Evil 100,* June, 2002.

Carroll, Rory. "Italy's Bloody Secret." *The Guardian.* June 25, 2001.

Chamber, John Whiteclay II, editor. *The Oxford Companion to American Military History.* New York: Oxford University Press, 1999.

Cullen, The Honorable Lord. *The Public Inquiry into the Shootings at Dunblane Primary School on 13 March 1996.* Edinburgh, Scotland: The Stationery Office, the Government of Scotland, October 16, 1996.

De Sade, Marquis. *120 Days of Sodom.* Web site: *http://www.angelfire.com/oh/SIEMENS/*

Greene, Bob. *American Beat.* New York: Athaneum, 1983.

Guiteau, Charles J. "Letter to General Sherman." 1881.

Hampson, Rick. "Hometown eager to let fame pass." *USA Today.* June 20, 2001.

Hart, Michael H. *The 100: A Ranking of the Most Influential Persons in History.* New York: Citadel Press, 1992.

Hinman, Al. "Mass suicides raise the question: Why?" Web site: *http://www.cnn.com/HEALTH/9703/27/nfm/suicide.psychology,* March 27, 1997

Kaczynski, Theodore. "The Unabomber Manifesto." *The New York Times, The Washington Post.* September 19, 1995.

Lamb, Christina. "Interview with Hafiz Sadiqulla Hassani." *The Telegraph.* September 30, 2001.

Laytner, Ron. "Interview with Pedro Lopez." *National Examiner.* January 12, 1999.

Lohr, David. "The Terminator." Web site: *http://www.angelfire.com/zine2/serialarchive/holmes.html,* undated.

McCallum, John Dennis. *Crime Doctor, Dr. Charles P. Larson.* Mercer Island, Wash.: Writing Works, 1976.

Morgenthau, Henry. *Murder of a Nation.* New York: Doubleday. 1915.

Nekerk, Philip von. "A Time to Kill." *Maxim.* October 2000.

Smith, Dennis Mack. *Mussolini.* New York: Alfred A. Knopf. 1982.

Solzhenitsen, Alexander. *The Gulag Archipelago, 1918–1956.* New York: Harper. 1973.

U. S. Department of State, International Information Programs, Bureau of Near Eastern Affairs, January 21, 2001. Web site: *http://usinfo.state.gov*

Electronic Sources

- http://138.110.28.9/acad/intrel/interwar.htm (Documents Relating to the Interwar Period)
- http://americanhistory.si.edu/presidency/home.html (The American Presidency: A Glorious Burden)
- http://members.aol.com/RVSNorton/Lincoln.html (Abraham Lincoln Assassination)
- http://www.apbnews.com/newscenter/majorcases/index.html (APB Major Cases)
- http://www.cnn.com (CNN)
- http://www.crimelibrary.com (The Crime Library)
- http://www.drudgereport.com (The Drudge Report)
- http://www.fbi.gov (The FBI)
- http://www.law.ou.edu/hist/ (US Historical Documents)
- http://www.lib.msu.edu/harris23/crimjust/serial.htm (Criminal Justice Resources—Serial or Mass Murder)
- http://www.midnightgrafitti. com
- http://www.msnbc.com (MSNBC)
- http://www.nara.gov/ (National Archives and Records Administration)
- http://www.newsmax.com (NewsMax)
- http://www.nytimes.com (The *New York Times*)
- http://www.suntimes.com (The *Chicago Sun Times*)
- http://www.thepresidency.org/pubs/links.htm (Presidency Reference Center)
- http://www.usatoday.com (*USA Today*)
- http://www.usdoj.gov/ag/ (Office of the Attorney General)
- http://www.washingtonpost.com (The *Washington Post*)
- http://www.whitehouse.gov (The White House)

ACKNOWLEDGMENTS

Photo Credits: Associated Press (for Adolf Hitler, Joseph Stalin, Mao Zedong, Pol Pot, Osama bin Laden, Vladimir Lenin, Adolf Eichmann, Josef Mengele, Benito Mussolini, Heinrich Himmler, Sadam Hussein, Idi Amin Dada, Augusto Pinochet, The Taliban, Jim Jones, Hideki Tojo, Albert Fish, Pedro Lopez, Herman Webster Mudgett, Timothy McVeigh [photo by Stephen Jones], Andrei Chikatilo, Anatoly Onoprienko, Jake Bird, Gerald Stano [photo by Department of Corrections, HO], Ted Bundy, Moses Sithole [photo from *The Star*], Martin Bryant [photo from News Ltd.], John Wayne Gacy, Louis "Lepke" Buchalter, Dr. Marcel Petoit, Charles Ng and Leonard Lake, George Hennard [photo by Ron Heflin], James Olive Huberty, Thomas Hamilton [from *The Guardian*], Jeffrey Dahmer, Dennis Nilsen, Richard Ramirez, Charles Whitman, Eric Harris and Dylan Klebold [photos from the Columbine High School Yearbook], Joachim Kroll, Howard Unruh [from the *Courier-Post*], The Boston Strangler, Peter Sutcliffe, Fred West and Rosemary West, Charles Starkweather and Caril Ann Fugate, Kenneth Bianchi and Angelo Buono Jr., Frederick Cowan, Mark Essex, Richard Speck, Charles Manson, Joel Rifkin [photo by Michael Albans], The Son of Sam, John George Haigh, Gary Heidnik, Theodore Kaczynksi [from Department of Motor Vehicles], Lee Harvey Oswald [photo by Jack Beers], John Wilkes Booth [from Sun Classic Pictures, Inc.], Leon F. Czolgosz [from the *South Bend Tribune*], Charles Guiteau [from the New York Public Library], Susan Smith, Virus Writers. CORBIS: Vlad the Impaler [with Reuters NewMedia, Inc.], Tomás de Torquemade [photo by Stephanie Maze], Caligula [with Archivo Iconografico, S.A.], Bail II [by Werner Forman], Nero [the Stapleton Collection], the Marquis de Sade [by Franz-Marc Frei]; Bettman/CORBIS (for Genghis Kahn, Ivan the Terrible, Catherine de Medici, Henri Desiré Landru, Fritz Haarmann, Richard Kuklinski, Dean Allen Corll, Jane Toppan, Henry Lee Lucas, Edmund Kemper, Ian Brady and Myra Hindley, Eddie Gein); Hulton-Deutsch Collection/CORBIS (for Attila the Hun, Jack the Ripper)

INDEX